T0147930

Also by Harvey Arden and Steve Wall

WISDOMKEEPERS

By Harvey Arden

NOBLE RED MAN

DREAMKEEPERS

By Steve Wall

WISDOM'S DAUGHTERS

SHADOWCATCHERS

DANCING WITH GOD

Travels
in a Stone Canoe
The Return to the
Wisdomkeepers
Harvey Arden
and Steve Wall

Simon & Schuster

This book is dedicated to our mentors,
who taught us what it means to be a Wisdomkeeper—
Chief Leon Shenandoah
Tadodaho of the Six Nations Iroquois Confederacy
and
Chief Mathew King, Noble Red Man,
Spokesman of the Lakota/Dakota/Nakota Nation

SIMON & SCHUSTER
Rockefeller Center
1230 Avenue of the Americas
New York, NY 10020

Designed by Karolina Harris
Photographs by Steve Wall
Narrative arrangement by Harvey Arden
Manufactured in the United States of America
10   9   8   7   6   5   4   3   2   1
Library of Congress Cataloging-in-Publication Data
Arden, Harvey
    Travels in a stone canoe: the return to the wisdomkeepers/Harvey Arden and Steve Wall
        p.   cm.
     1. Indians of North America—Religion. 2. Indian philosophy.
I. Wall, Steve. II. Title.
E98.R3A7   1998
299'.7—dc21   *98-19189*
                                        CIP

ISBN 978-1-4767-0265-0

Contents

Preface

Y O U don't take the journey. The journey takes you.

Nearly twenty years ago two unlikely and unknowing white journalists—ourselves, or those we thought ourselves to be—set out on what we've come to see now as a spirit-journey, a simultaneous exploration of outer and inner worlds. We thought at the time that we were going out on a magazine assignment after a good "story"—the supposed demise of the last generation of Native American spiritual elders, or Wisdomkeepers. But something happened to us along the way. We set out on the path of the Wisdomkeepers, and we've never quite gotten back. We find ourselves shuttling between worlds, not quite part of either. We've become unwitting and at times unwilling messengers, or "runners," between those worlds. We crossed an invisible boundary, passed through a kind of mystic membrane between what most people think of as North America and what others—many of whom you'll meet in these pages—think of as Great Turtle Island. This last is as much a spiritual metaphor as it is a physical place, not only the living continent that sustains our earthly existence—the primal Native American vision of the land as it once was and in a visionary sense still is—but also, in an equally visionary sense, the very inward landscape of our being, of our humanness.

We've come to realize that North America and, yes, even the United States of America—like Europe or Germany or Australia— are as much metaphors as Great Turtle Island. They exist in the minds of those who acknowledge them. When they cease to be acknowledged, they cease to exist. Witness the Soviet Union, that fallen metaphor. None of these metaphors, in the ultimate analysis, is any "truer" than the others. A metaphor's power is in its meaning, not its truth. And we ourselves give metaphors their meaning, their power, not some outside agency or external reality. The choice is ours. Great Turtle Island, like America, is as much inside of us as outside of us.

Our years-long journey has taught us more about being white than about being red. That can be a chastening experience, to say the least. Seeing around the edges of yourself is unsettling. But white and red, too, are metaphors, as are all racial stereotypes. Our skin color is within us. The great challenge of our time is to find metaphors that include rather than exclude.

❋

This journey of ours, then, is a journey into metaphor, into meaning, into human subjectivity, into the belief systems of others and of ourselves, into the very meaning of belief itself. And yet, despite its inward aspects, this spirit-journey is and has been absolutely real, filled with rented cars and cheap motels and fast-food restaurants and shopping malls and interstate highways, and—most significant to us—with out-of-the-way dirt roads leading to the always open doors of those we call Wisdomkeepers, the spiritual elders of Native America. These wonderful men and women don't simply preserve the old wisdom. They live it. And, yes, they share it and teach it, too—not only with their words but with their example, their presence, their lives . . . lives always lived for others, never for themselves.

We are not, definitely not, experts on Indians. We aren't scholars or anthropologists or historians; we're not even journalists anymore. Yet our journey, our spirit-journey is inexorably ongoing. Whenever we think it's finally over and done with, we somehow find ourselves swept back into it once again despite ourselves, flung back onto the road, into the current, back on the path of the Wisdomkeepers.

But don't mistake it for an easy path. Life, we've learned from the Wisdomkeepers, is not an entertainment. Life is a task, a holy task. There's a path you follow, and there's a set of Original Instructions for following that path. Our journey, our life's work, has been an unfolding of those Instructions, which—as Wisdomkeeper Uncle Frank

Davis showed us—lie within our souls like shredded, crumpled pieces of paper, hieroglyphed with the meanings of life, our own personal life in particular. When we at last open those crumpled messages, read them, and then translate them into our everyday lives, we will finally be on the path of the Wisdomkeepers. That path, though, is definitely not for the casual tourist or the pleasure-seeker or the merely curious. It can be hard to find and difficult to follow, at times even dangerous to your being, both physical and spiritual. Unless it's *your* path, it's pointless to follow. But if it *is* your path, then, alas, it's pointless to follow any other.

We cannot tell you where this path leads. Perhaps only to itself. It may be simply an endlessly looping circle of meaning that is self-evident only to those who travel along it. Indeed, that could be a definition for any belief system—since all belief systems may be seen as metaphorical constructions devised to explain the inexplicable, to give meaning to the otherwise meaningless, to make humanly accessible the fathomless mystery—or, as our Lakota friends call it, *Wakan Tanka*, the Great Mysterious, the Great Holy—not a thing but a state of being, the very ground of existence and of human meaning.

We have explored, not systematically but intuitively, the metaphorical systems of "natural" earth-based indigenous peoples, in particular that overarching visionary system presented to us by scores of Native American spiritual elders, both men and women, those we call Wisdomkeepers. We have sought them out in their homes in the isolated fastnesses of their reservations across the vast sweep of this stolen continent, and, violating the first law of journalism—yes, we admit it, we confess it shamelessly—we have lost our objectivity. We have been moved to the roots of our souls. We are changed. We have been seized and shaken, given a new meaning for our own lives, an unexpected set of both general and personal instructions for being human, a way both new and ancient of approaching the very act of living.

❀

Take, for instance, the matter of "signs." Every path has its signs, its signposts. If you can't read them or refuse to acknowledge them, they're certainly not going to help you find your way. Those signs are as much within you as they are "out there." Dismiss them with a skeptical sneer and in the end you're left with the ashes of your own disbelief. But open your eyes to their possible meaning, to their soul-charging poetry, and you may suddenly find yourself "on the wind," as we call it. This doesn't mean to believe everything or anything but simply to be open to the meaning, the poetry, of things and events, of your own life.

We've learned to be open, too, to the meanings and beliefs of others, not to copy them or steal them but to learn from them, to be moved within the depths of our being by them. Belief isn't necessary at all. Only respect is necessary. Respect opens you to the meanings of others and to your own meaning as well. Signs—and, yes, even wonders—can occasionally light your path, illuminate those meanings. These signs are both inner and outer. We've learned to be open to them but never expectant or demanding. They come when they come, and when they do, they're always intensely personal and specific, like those you'll read of in these pages—an eagle's feather, an owl's claw, a shaman's walking stick, a wild-visaged False Face mask. Sometimes they're hopeful, sometimes foreboding; sometimes they're harbingers, sometimes confirmations, sometimes warnings, sometimes seemingly cosmic jokes. For any and all such "signs" we make no claims beyond the ordinary. Indeed, we've learned that the ordinary is at times the most visionary state of all. The ordinary, this very passing moment, this holy unstoppable Now, is the entry point, the gateway, to what Wisdomkeeper Mathew King called the Great Reality. Or so goes another metaphor. Metaphors within metaphors. All is metaphor.

The Wisdomkeepers taught us that wisdom isn't something you believe, it's something you do. And they taught us also that the Instructions for doing it may not come to you until the last possible and least expected moment—sometimes just as you've abandoned all hope and stopped trying.

❁

Among the Iroquois, or Haudenosaunee, who have taught us so much, there is a story, a still-living tradition, a sacred memory of a luminous prophet and deliverer called the Peacemaker. Don't, please, think of it as a legend or a myth—those are white man's words, any Indian will tell you, for the "quaint" beliefs of cultures other than his own. His own myths white man calls "history." As a sign that the Creator had sent him on a sacred mission, the Peacemaker traveled in a miraculous stone canoe. Carved from white granite, this magical vessel floated as lightly as a feather, carrying the Peacemaker wherever he was meant to go. He didn't have to paddle. The stone canoe simply took him there. From this story, which you'll hear in detail from the lips of the Peacemaker's descendants in the pages ahead, we have respectfully borrowed another metaphor for our spirit-journey: the Stone Canoe.

We like to think that, in our own small way, we've been privileged to travel these past two decades in a kind of symbolic Stone Canoe, a magical vessel that takes us wherever it is we're supposed to go. We're not supposed to steer it or paddle. We're not supposed to plan a fixed itinerary. We're just supposed to go along, letting the unseen current take us wherever we're meant to go. We continually have to remind ourselves: Don't try to pre-think or pre-envision it all. The best ideas are the ones you find yourself doing without even thinking about them. You can't think your way to the Truth. Truth, like Beauty, isn't something you think, it's something you feel. Just as you can't think the wind, you can only feel it. And the same with the Stone Canoe. You can't think yourself aboard, you can only feel it under you and realize you've been riding in it all along. When that happens, you're on the wind, you're riding in your own personal Stone Canoe, you're following the path of the Wisdomkeepers.

❁

We make no pretense to being wise or in any way holier than thou. Indeed, our very imperfection has saved us time and again. Without it we'd never have discovered that the path of the Wisdomkeepers even existed. From the Wisdomkeepers themselves we've learned that you don't have to be perfect to do holy work. You don't even have to be holy. You can be a couple of contraries, a couple of shapeshifters like ourselves, and still lead a life worthy of being called human. We're not saying we've done it, but we're trying.

Authors' Note

Chapters headed by a claw are in the voice of Harvey Arden.
Chapters headed by a feather are in the voice of Steve Wall.

One
ne *Finding the Path*

Chapter 1

"**H**ARVEY, *I've met this Indian. . . .*"

Nothing has been the same for me since those simple words were spoken. My life's real work had abruptly and inexorably begun, and I was merely annoyed.

Looking back now, nearly two decades later, I try to reconstruct how it all began, how it came about that we—two unlikely white journalists—became runners stumbling between two worlds, spirit-journeyers on the path of the Wisdomkeepers. Events that seemed isolated and utterly unconnected at the time I now see as parts of an emerging whole. What's more, the whole itself keeps changing, as do we. The ever-shifting parts dissolve and reform, metamorphosing in and out of each other as in a dream.

The pieces of memory come floating back at me.

There was Steve Wall, who got me into all of this, and there was Two Trees, who envisioned this spirit-journey in the first place and who remains a dark and unsettling enigma to this day. There was the Maestro's mystic condor in Peru, and there was Frank Fools Crow's miraculous eagle at Wounded Knee. There was Leon Shenandoah, who taught us there *was* a path, and Mathew King, who taught us there was a set of instructions for following that path. "Original

Instructions for being human," he called them. There was the eagle's feather and the owl's claw—the signs that Two Trees predicted we would receive and which assumed a special metaphoric power for us as they propelled us onto the path. And then there was me, yanked out of the ordinary and flung into it all despite myself, protesting and complaining all the way.

I remember that pale gray morning in late November 1981. A light snow was falling at an angle past my seventh-floor window at National Geographic Society headquarters in Washington, D.C. I was at my desk writing an article for the magazine about the return of the Sinai Peninsula from the Israelis to the Egyptians ("Eternal Sinai," April 1982). Just six weeks earlier I had stood some twenty-five yards from Anwar Sadat at the moment of his assassination during a military parade in a sports stadium outside Cairo—not quite the usual stuff for a *National Geographic* staff writer and, since my article wouldn't be published for many months, hardly a major news scoop. But I was properly shaken by the incident, seeing some special if indefinable personal providence at having been present at that vortex of history. I remember, moments after the first shooting began, standing there poised on the stadium tarmac, frozen more in amazement than fear, caught with arms akimbo in the crossfire between Sadat's fleeing assassins and the security police, bodies falling all around me. As I stood there a young dark-skinned Egyptian man in army fatigues, probably no more than seventeen or eighteen, ran wildly past me, his doelike eyes wide with fright; he was followed by half a dozen screaming security police in their blue uniforms and white helmets. Perhaps thirty seconds later they carried him back past me like a sack of potatoes, pummeling his limp form with fists and truncheons. I managed a few frames with my camera before being pushed into a crowd of journalists by police. "No pictures! No pictures!" they screamed. I remember most vividly the tumbled wooden chairs, thousands of them, which had been flung aside by the terrified crowd as it tried to escape the shooting, and the astonishing redness of the blood spreading out from under the bodies strewn around me on the tarmac. I distinctly recall asking myself, "What in God's name am I doing here?" and, all the while, thinking of my wife, Lorraine, and our children back in Washington. Though she hadn't told me for fear of upsetting me, weeks before Lorraine had had a kind of dream or presentiment about my being surrounded by blood. She follows the way of Subud, based on the Latihan, a spiritual exercise of surrender to God, and for weeks before Sadat's assassination she had the inward experience of there being a shooting, with blood everywhere and me in the midst of it. When she'd received that blood vision repeatedly during her Latihan, she feared the worst but knew I couldn't opt out of a major magazine assignment on the basis of a dream or presentiment; nor would I have. She even secretly packed a bag so that she would be ready to fly out to Egypt in an emergency. When she watched TV that day, October 6, 1981, and heard the first news of Sadat's assassination—she knew I'd be seeing him that day—she was actually relieved; she instantly realized it was Sadat's blood she had seen in her Latihan, not mine. I don't know why she didn't think it was my blood, too, which it might well have been, but she simply knew it wasn't, she said—which I confirmed to her by phone from Egypt a few hours later.

Now, months later, back out of the vortex of history and safely ensconced in the secure confines of my office, I was trying to reduce the complex elements of that event to a few paragraphs of crisp, factual, unemotional copy for the magazine when the telephone rang and my new life began.

The voice on the phone was Steve Wall's. He was calling from the Appalachian wilds of northeast Georgia, where he was at work on a freelance contract for the magazine photographing a story ("Wild Water, Proud People," April 1983) on the Chattooga River, the wild-watered river of the movie *Deliverance*. Steve and I had worked together briefly a couple of years earlier on an article about Vietnamese boat people who had migrated to the Gulf Coast. He had a pleasantly blasphemous manner about him and was one hell of a photographer. He also had a way with ideas and a mulishly stubborn habit of seeing them through to the end, come what may. The article on Vietnamese boat people had been his idea; he'd been given a speculative go-ahead or "flyer" by the magazine, then found that the elusive refugees he'd hoped to photograph at Empire, Louisiana, had fled white persecution to Biloxi, Mississippi. For weeks he hung out on the Biloxi fishing docks, where the Vietnamese fishermen congregated, getting to know them, winning their friendship and trust, and sending back to *Geographic* a trove of remarkable photographs—rich, warm, intensely personal, and human—that demanded publication. I was assigned the writing end of the article, which appeared in the September 1981 issue as "Troubled Odyssey of Vietnamese Fishermen." Steve and I had gone our separate ways on different assignments after that but had taken something of a liking to each other and had spoken of getting another magazine assignment together if the opportunity arose.

His voice on the phone was, as usual, excited. Steve doesn't chitchat. He expounds. He discourses. He overflows with passions and wild enthusiasms. In that mellifluous North Carolina accent of his—"*You're* the one with the accent!" he has told me many a time—he announced, "Harvey, I've met this Indian."

I could hardly have been more dismissive. "Really?" I asked him. "You've met an Indian? So . . .?"

Steve continued, unruffled at my tone: "He's a medicine man, a Cherokee named Two Trees. An incredible character. Told me he knew I was coming to see him before I got here. Said he'd been *expecting* me."

"Oh, sure . . ."

"Now listen to this, Harvey. There's something very special about this guy. He has this idea. I think it'd make a terrific story for *Geographic*. He says he's had a vision about a journey to what he calls the Grandfathers—the greatest medicine men and spiritual leaders of the seven great Indian nations. He says it's a kind of mission, a journey of penance. He calls it a 'spirit-journey.' He wants us to go with him—"

"*Us?*"

"Yeah . . . you and me! You didn't think I'd forget you, did you, partner?"

Something within me groaned.

Steve went on: "He wants me to go with him and photograph the whole thing. He says he's no writer any more than he's a photographer. I told him about you, how we worked together on the Vietnamese boat people article. 'That's the one!' he said. 'He'll be the writer, this Harvey guy!' He wants you to go along and handle the word side, write it all up just as it happens and also record the Grandfathers' words. So . . . what do you say? Want to go on a spirit-journey? Think the magazine would be interested?"

"Now, Steve, hold on a minute."

Deaf to my protestations, Steve rolled on with unchecked enthusiasm.

"Now just keep listening, you hear? This is important. He says the Grandfathers are dying out and that the old ways, the old wisdom, is dying out with them. He says someone has to go out to them, take their photographs, record their words. He says you and I are the ones chosen to go out and do it. He says we'll receive signs when it's time to start."

"Signs? What signs?"

"He says we'll know when we get them."

It all seemed a bit too much to swallow as I sat there in the marbled confines of *National Geographic* headquarters with blood visions of Sadat dancing in my head.

Indians? Grandfathers? Spirit-journey?

I wanted none of it.

✿

Over the years, in the course of my travels for the magazine, I'd had a few troubling experiences with Indians. Once, in 1970, I was escorted at shotgun-point off the Crow reservation in Montana. I was working at the time on an article about the Big Horn Mountains and Basin—never published—and had been exploring a beautiful wilderness area called Black Canyon, deep within the reservation, when I stumbled on a summer encampment of Crow Indian teenagers at the canyon's bottom. After parking my shiny rented car and walking up to a group of Indians standing near the rough-timbered camp gate, I smiled, extended my hand, and announced my usual "Hi! I'm Harvey Arden, *National Geographic* . . ." A pretty picture of self-importance I must have made. A young Indian man cradling a shotgun walked toward me, grim-faced. He stopped a foot short of my nose, staring me down hard.

"Ain't suppose t'be here, mister. Better leave."

"Uhhh . . ." I stammered, taken by surprise, "the . . . uh . . . the Tribal Council chairman . . . Edison Real Bird up at Crow Agency? . . . He told me I could drive around the rez— Doing a story for the magazine."

I put on my most authoritative and confident smile.

The young Indian man sniffed at me.

"He ain't got no authority down here, that Edison Real Bird. And neither do you, Mr. National Geographic. You're trespassing on foreign soil, mister. This ain't your U.S.A. down here. This is Crow land. Indian Country. Better leave, you hear?"

"Uh . . ."

"Better leave," he reiterated, suggestively jiggling the cradled shotgun in his arms and toying with the trigger.

There was no room for argument in his voice, and that look in his eye was not brotherly love. I left.

It would be my first—though by no means my last—experience with the almost inescapable schisms between various "progressive" and "traditional" factions on most Indian reservations. I may have had Tribal Chairman Edison Real Bird's permission to explore the rez, but nobody else's. I was learning that when a white person makes a friend on an Indian reservation, he or she is also likely to be making, quite unwittingly, half a dozen enemies. This I could see was no easy world for an outsider to enter. You are seen through by every pair of eyes, friendly or otherwise. You are indeed an intruder. This *is* foreign soil! What other purpose could you possibly have for being here than some kind of exploitation or other? Frankly, I felt no strong personal pull to explore that problematical world despite my alerted journalistic instincts. Indians, after all, do "make a good story." They've always been as much a staple of *National Geographic* as of the silver screen. But the thought of walking up cold to an Indian reservation and finding my way back to the living, beating heart behind it all—although alluring in its way—was, to be blunt, *uninviting*. Hell, I could be going on a magazine assignment anywhere in the world—Bali, Paris, Timbuktu. If I wanted to report on human suffering, why not get an assignment in Calcutta? The Indian reservations I had glimpsed now and again from the road during my travels seemed, well, dismal, unpleasant, distant from my usual world, seemingly in another dimension of time and space altogether. I'd driven past or through some of the Navajo and Pueblo reservations in the Southwest and had seen the slouch-roofed hovels in the distance, the forlorn figures weaving barefooted by the side of the highway, the roadside signs announcing CAUTION—DANGER: ESCAPEES MAY POSE AS HITCHHIKERS. No, not a place a lone white man—or two white men, for that matter—would want to dawdle around, nosing into people's business, looking for a "good story."

❉

I didn't make the connection at the time, but only recently I had had another somewhat unnerving "Indian experience." That had been in Iquitos, in the Amazonian jungle east of the Andes, where, as part of my coverage for a *Geographic* article on Peru just eight months before ("The Two Souls of Peru," March 1982), I had witnessed an all-night curing rite by an Indian *curandero*, or folk healer, using the hallucinogenic native drug *ayahuasca*.

I'd actually been looking for a *brujo*, a sorcerer or witch doctor— standard *Geographic* curiosities—but had been told by the locals that there were no *brujos* around there anymore, only *curanderos*. The *curanderos*, I was told, cured the spells cast by the *brujos*. When I asked how they could cure the *brujos'* spells if there were no *brujos* anymore, I received only a blank stare and a nonresponsive shake of the head from my uneasy informants. It was the kind of dumb question only a gringo journalist could ask. In any case, my guide, fellow gringo Tony Luscombe, finally found the name of a *curandero* who worked at the local slaughterhouse. "Just ask for the Maestro," he was told.

I remember that, just as we walked up to the place, a young bull had broken through the slaughterhouse doorway as if out of a rodeo chute and was racing and bucking madly through the streets, snorting and bellowing, followed closely by a screaming crowd of men, women, and children brandishing sticks and flinging stones. They chased after the terrified beast, striking him repeatedly, until he finally veered wildly back through the doorway into the slaughterhouse, where the infuriated workmen he'd escaped from immediately and unceremoniously bludgeoned him to death with huge clubs to the joyous cheers of the crowd. The women quickly rushed up with their slop buckets to get some of the still-steaming blood and guts from this spirited beast. One old woman dipped her hand in the red gore and put it to her lips. *"Para la fuerza!"* she said with an ecstatic smile and a wild roll of her eyes. "For strength!"

When I asked for the Maestro, I was directed to a small second-floor apartment in a building just down the street. There I met Maestro Cristóbal, a wiry, angular, rheumy-eyed elder of Quechuan, or Inca, ancestry, who sat cross-legged on a low sofa with a tray of stained old colored bottles in his lap. He'd apparently been examining them when I came in. They looked like something Macbeth's witches might have filled from their bubbling broth of evil. The Maestro snorted when I asked if he was a *curandero*. He held up a small grimy corked bottle filled with a nasty-looking reddish brown liquid. "This is my power," he told me, using the same word— *fuerza*—as the old woman in the slaughterhouse had used for "strength." He pointed a finger at his right eye; the pupil seemed misshapen, a discolored yellow, like a broken egg yolk. He explained: "As a young man one day I had a terrible pain in this eye. It went blind. I went to the doctors, but they couldn't help. Then I went to a *curandero*. He told me a *brujo* had cast a spell on me, and at a ceremony he gave me the holy *ayahuasca*. It comes from the bark of a jungle vine. He prayed over me. He massaged my eye. The pain went away, but the eye was still blind. He told me that the *brujo* who had made the spell had too much *fuerza*, too much power. He, that *curandero*, could only cure the pain, not the blindness. For months I studied with him, and I became a *curandero* myself. All my life I have looked for the power to break the spell of that *brujo* and cure the blindness." He shook his head. "I am sorry to say that I have failed. I cannot cure the blindness itself or other maladies. My *fuerza* only makes the pain go away. You come to me because you have a pain, *señor?*" He looked at me hopefully. I explained to him that I'd like to witness one of his curing ceremonies and write about it in the magazine I worked for. He'd never heard of *National Geographic* but nodded at my proposal.

The next night, in an abandoned thatch-roofed tanning factory on the outskirts of Iquitos, I watched for hours as the old *curandero,* amidst great ceremony and communal drinking of the bubbly red *ayahuasca,* sucked the sickness out of his patients' bodies with a "sucking stone." Leaning over their prostrate forms and setting the egg-shaped stone over their stomach or other afflicted body part, he sucked mightily at one end of the stone, every so often jerking his mouth away and, with a look of great distaste, spitting out some dark loathsome-looking liquid. Without exception his patients arose claiming to feel restored and without pain.

I was, frankly, unimpressed. I saw what had happened as a kind of quackery, perhaps benign but quackery nonetheless. The sucking stone and the fluid, I had not the slightest doubt, were phony props. If those patients felt better after this treatment, it was simply the power of suggestion enhanced by the power of the hallucinogenic *ayahuasca.* I wasn't buying their metaphor, and hence it all lacked essential meaning for me except as a quaint ceremony—just as a mass or a bar mitzvah or a sun dance may lack essential meaning and seem quaint to the unknowing and uncaring outsider. To the nonbeliever, which we all are when it comes to systems we don't "believe" in, the belief systems of others tend to be quaint, bizarre, even silly. The more we're stuck on the truth of our own metaphors, the more the metaphors of others seem false.

And yet those patients of the Maestro's that night did go away feeling vastly better, I couldn't deny that. Every one of them insisted that his pain was gone or at least lessened. All would come back for further treatments. If this was quackery, it was apparently successful quackery. Does it matter how we're healed as long as we're healed?

At one point late in the night, having completed the curing ceremony and put away his bottles of *ayahuasca,* the old *curandero* stood up and walked away from his patients, strode to the edge of the jungle clearing outside the factory, lifted his arms to the starless night sky, and started singing in low and guttural but strangely beautiful tones.

"O Condorcito . . . Condorcito . . . " he sang, his eerie voice rising into the darkly overhanging jungle canopy.

He cupped one hand to his ear, listened intently, then sang out again, *"O Condorcito . . . Condorcito . . . "*

Again he cupped his ear, as if straining to hear something out there in the murmuring darkness.

Then suddenly he said, "Listen! Listen! Do you hear?"

And I swear I *did* hear something out there, unmistakable and absolutely real, the loud whir and thunderous beating of huge wings. It was coming out of the impenetrable darkness directly above our heads, seemingly hovering above us.

"There!" the Maestro said triumphantly. "Sometimes when we call him, the condor's spirit comes! And sometimes . . . sometimes when we call him the *real* condor comes! He's a messenger from Pachac Mama—our Mother the Earth. *Listen!*"

Again, as loud as someone beating a rug, came that beating of invisible wings in the darkness just above our heads. A vague chill slithered up and down my spine. Disbeliever though I was, I felt something palpable out there, something *physical.* I had declined to take any of the *ayahuasca*—that at least might have explained such a reaction. My own overwrought imagination was the only explanation, I figured, or perhaps a mild hypnotic episode somehow triggered by the Maestro's power of suggestion. Nonetheless, the sound of those invisible beating wings had been disturbingly real.

I think if that bird had actually materialized there before us at that moment, I might actually have become a believer. But the beating of the wings stopped as suddenly as it had begun, as if a switch had been turned off, and the presence above us—or was it within us?—abruptly disappeared.

The Maestro smiled at me.

"So . . . now you have met her. She smiles on you. She doesn't come for everyone. You can always call on her now when you need her. Pachac Mama . . . just call Pachac Mama, and she'll come to you."

The Maestro went on, casually explaining to me how the condor in Inca lore symbolizes the Indian, just as the bull symbolizes the white man. He spoke of the old ritual, now banned but still secretly practiced in remote Andean villages, of tethering a condor to the back of a bull and letting the two of them fight it out to the death. More often than not the condor—with its ten-foot wingspread and axe-sharp beak—would finally triumph, giving the Indian a much-deserved metaphorical revenge over his white oppressor.

But that sound of wings in the darkness when the Maestro had called out *"O Condorcito . . ."* had definitely not been metaphorical. I somehow sensed, despite myself, at least the *possibility* of something out there beyond the ordinary—yes, even, let me dare say it, the miraculous—but I didn't particularly think of it as an "Indian experience." It was simply a personal experience that happened to take place in an Indian context. No, I didn't *believe* in that mystic condor as the Maestro did. But ever since that incident I have sensed an inner connection in some inexplicable and intensely personal way with that condor and with Pachac Mama, as if something long closed had reopened within me at that unexpected moment. Some inward nonthinking part of myself accepted the condor as *meaningful,* even if it had been wholly imagined, and in accepting the emotional reality of that meaning—indeed, taking what I can only describe as a kind of spiritual comfort in it—I had somehow cracked the eggshell of disbelief that had hitherto safeguarded me, the objective journalist, from those nonobjective experiences that lay at the core, the inner quick, of indigenous thinking and belief. What before would have seemed to me merely quaint folkloric belief suddenly rang with an unnerving inner truth. I could not have defined it; I could only feel it.

Oddly, looking back on it now in light of the way my life was suddenly being propelled despite myself in some new direction, my guide in Peru, Tony Luscombe, had repeatedly mentioned to me his experiences with a great North American medicine man named Frank Fools Crow. "He's much more powerful than the Maestro. You really ought to go out to South Dakota and meet him sometime," Tony told me. "Old Frank Fools Crow can do real miracles. Just go out to Pine Ridge and ask for him." I could not have dreamt that two years later I would be doing just that and that I would witness that same Frank Fools Crow pray an eagle out of the empty South Dakota sky at Wounded Knee—a luminous moment when it finally came home to me that miracles and signs aren't merely possible, they're a natural and essential part of everyday life.

❊

Such experiences not infrequently afflict the traveler to faraway places; you come back to your ordinary world, in my case the offices of *National Geographic,* and what you have experienced in that other world suddenly seems to fade like an old weathered photograph. The most overwhelming experience out in the field, when retold over coffee in the staff cafeteria, somehow becomes no more than an amusing anecdote. We had a periodic in-house staff newsletter back in those days, put out by then Director of Photography Robert Gilka. It consisted almost entirely of reports of the misadventurous episodes of intrepid *Geographic* staffers in the field: falling out of canoes into raging rivers, getting stranded on icebergs in the Arctic, or rescued by cannibals on an island off Madagascar—that sort of thing. Every veteran staffer and contract photographer worth his or her salt and expense account had half a dozen such experiences to their credit. My own chief claim to laurels along this line was the Sadat assassination, but I had also been in an earthquake and a race riot, nearly drowned in the Red Sea, gotten lost in deserts, stranded on mountains in snowstorms, and done all the other standard stuff expected of a magazine staffer. This incident with the condor was hardly worth mentioning and, if at all, only with an embarrassed smile. How could I tell my colleagues that since that incident I "sensed" something I hadn't sensed before—an "inexplicable meaning," or at least the possibility of such a meaning? They'd have scoffed and shaken their heads in amusement, as I suppose I'd have done myself if they'd told *me* of such an incident.

✽

And so when Steve Wall announced to me on the telephone that he'd met this Indian medicine man named Two Trees who had predicted that the two of us would receive signs when we were to begin our spirit-journey, I winced inwardly. This matter of Indians frankly made me uneasy. I had grown up in Chicago. To me, Indians were those costumed figures in warbonnets I saw in dusty glass cases on school trips to the Field Natural History Museum. They came to life, these wondrously befeathered people, only in the movies and seemed somehow always to be futilely riding around the circled wagon trains of the U.S. Cavalry, intent on mayhem. Sometime in the vague past, I knew, they'd actually lived hereabouts and given us all those wonderful multisyllabic place names: *Chi-ca-go* ("place of the wild onions"), *Mis-sis-sip-pi, Mich-i-gan,* even *Indiana!* Then they'd gone off, apparently out West somewhere, to fade conveniently into history after doing in Custer at the Little Big Horn—their final shining moment. To be sure it was an absurdly overdrawn and stereotypical view, but in the popular mind Indians somehow had always seemed to be overdrawn and stereotypical, a caricature of a people. But "real" living Indians like Steve's Cherokee? Well, of course, they were colorful enough in their beads and feathers, stomping out a war dance at summer powwows. But then, everybody knew, they went back to their dreary reservations and drank themselves into an unjust but inevitable oblivion. The reality of who they might actually be, what they were actually like, seemed of little interest. Depressing at best. A matter for sociologists and anthropologists and ethnohistorians.

Such knowledge is worse than mere ignorance. Ignorance at least has a certain purity to it. What you don't know you don't know. You are the proverbial tabula rasa, a blank slate. But the slate of my mind had been scribbled on with a thousand scrawls of misinformation concerning Indians. I had five hundred years of history to unlearn, and, I must admit, I am still unlearning. But of this I had little concept that day in 1981. What's more, I couldn't even imagine how appalling my ignorance was.

❉

I tried to calm Steve down. This Two Trees fellow seemed to have found an easy mark. And yet, as what he was saying slowly began to sink in, I had to admit it *was* a lovely idea. It had a quintessential poetry to it. My editorial mind began to envision the story line: A younger medicine man goes out across America in search of the Old Ones—the Grandfathers and, yes, the Grandmothers—the fragile living repositories of the ancient sacred knowledge and ways. He seeks them out in their own homes, sits at their knees, records their words, and makes a photographic record . . .

"Well, it does have a certain ring to it," I admitted grudgingly to Steve. "But it sounds a little mystical for the magazine. I don't know. Maybe work up a proposal and send it to the planning council next month."

Steve shrugged off my caution.

"I think I'll bring Two Trees up right away to see Garrett!"

Bill Garrett was then the editor of *National Geographic.* Something of a visionary himself, he'd taken the magazine in exciting new directions from its stodgily conservative origins and . . . who knows? I'd heard he occasionally spoke proudly about a Shawnee great-grandmother. He might just take a flyer on such an alluring story. But, still, I was discouraging to Steve. How did he know this Two Trees fellow was for real? I didn't want any embarrassments in our objective magazine. I knew that many a fake and charlatan guard the entrances to the Native American otherworld. Was this guy authentic? A real medicine man?

I could almost hear Steve grimacing over the phone. He heard me out. I'll never forget one thing he said: "Harvey, why is it Indians always have to be real or authentic? I've never heard anyone ask if a white man was real or authentic. Can you answer me that?"

I couldn't.

Needless to say, Steve brought Two Trees up to see Garrett.

Chapter 2

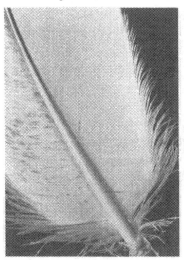

CALL me stubborn. Harvey says I'm too gullible. Maybe so. If living by hunches and intuitions and insights is gullibility, then I guess I'm gullible. But that's just how things come to me. The most important thing, to me, is just being open to possibilities. Don't shut everything out with a knee-jerk skepticism. Harvey grudgingly admitted to me that he half-believes in that condor he heard that night in Peru. He even tells me he talks to Pachac Mama sometimes. Then he just shakes his head, embarrassed, and says it's all a bunch of nonsense. "I just imagined it," he laments. Hell, *I* believe he *did* hear something, and I end up trying to convince *him!*

It burns me how he's always scoffing, always doubting, as if there's some virtue in disbelief. It's been that way ever since the beginning of this crazy journey of ours, right from the start. "Harvey, I've met this Indian," I remember telling him that day, and right off he was discouraging, skeptical, dismissive. A hundred times he's reacted that way to my enthusiasms. Even though I'd received a message that was for him, too! Even though he himself was about to be swept into the strangest and most wonderful experience of his life!

I remember him once telling me, as if it somehow explained his skepticism, "I'm from Chicago! I don't believe in *anything*!" Makes me laugh every time I think of it. I asked him what he meant by that, and he told me, "Missourians say, 'Show me!' Chicagoans say, 'Don't bother me! No way I'll believe it even if I see it!' Hell, if you're from Chicago, you don't fall for anything, not even the truth!"

Yes, he's a funny man as well as a serious man, this Harvey Arden. Outrageous, certainly. As abrasively annoying at times as it's possible to be, no doubt. But not a flake or a shirker. He's reliable, a good partner. He's there when you need him. He's got a big heart and an almost disconcerting generosity. He'd give away the keys to the kingdom if he found them. And he's as good a man as any I've ever known to go through an unfamiliar door with. Since we've gone through many an unfamiliar door together in many an unfamiliar place, this last has been especially important over the years.

❀

Anyway, despite Harvey's objections on the telephone, I drove up from Georgia with Two Trees to see Bill Garrett. The chances of getting a mere written proposal through *Geographic*'s planning council were so remote that I figured, wild idea as it was, it had a chance to make the pages of the magazine only if the editor himself took a personal interest. Harvey had mentioned that he'd heard Garrett had a Shawnee great-grandmother, so I thought maybe I could reach through to his heart. Or maybe Two Trees could.

As for Two Trees himself, well, Harvey was right—I didn't know much about him. This guy was as complex and hard to read an individual as I'd ever met. I didn't really know what to make of him. But he definitely seemed interesting, even compelling, both blustery and otherworldly, friendly enough on the surface yet somehow threatening, dark, mysterious underneath that smiling, enigmatic exterior.

I'd met him while working on the Chattooga River article. It was sort of a river-rat story, and I was just roughing around, looking for local characters and interesting situations. In northeast Georgia I met a mountain man, Frank Rickman—an easy-laughing, backslapping bear of a man who helped me to get the lay of the local landscape, both geographic and human. One day we were standing in his horse pasture, shooting the breeze, when Frank just happened to say, "There's a guy you oughta meet. Calls himself a medicine man.

Says he's Cherokee. Known all over these parts. People come to him for healing—herbs and all that. They say he even does a miracle or two. Calls himself Two Trees. Quite a character!"

I think I just sort of shrugged. I hadn't had any Indians in mind for this story. It hadn't even occurred to me that there were any Indians in Rabun County, Georgia.

But Frank was persistent. Not pushy, just persistent.

"Anyway, maybe you oughta meet him. Might just make a picture for your story!"

Well, no sooner had he uttered those words than this old battered truck came rumbling up in a cloud of red dust and screeched to a halt just on the other side of a sagging barbed-wire fence at the edge of the pasture. It was one of those old double-cab, double-tandem trucks you can pull horse trailers with, and that old sucker was half falling apart, its fenders and body beaten and mangled and seemingly held together by nothing but rust.

Frank laughed real big and said, "Damn! That's Two Trees now! Just like him! Shows up just when you're thinking about him. It's eerie!"

And it was.

For maybe a minute no one got out of the truck. The motor coughed, ending with a loud grind and clank and a final shudder, and the driver just sat there in the shadowed cab and looked out at us through the settling dust. I could hardly make out his face at first, just two eyes like glowing coals casing us. Finally he kicked open the cab door. I half-expected it to fall off. Then this large, big-bellied, yet tall and angular man emerged, unwedging himself from behind the steering wheel with an audible grunt. He plopped a well-worn cowboy hat at a cocky angle on his head and swaggered up to us with a kind of rocking horse gait, pushing down the sagging barbed wire with a scuffed cowboy boot and stepping lightly over it into the pasture with an almost dancelike two-step. Dusting off his clothes—jeans and a Western shirt, tooled silver belt buckle, rough sheepskin vest—he stood there in front of us flashing a wide but mercurial grin. He doffed his hat, ran his fingers through his long and scraggly gray-brown hair, then set the hat jauntily back on his head. I couldn't tell if he looked like an Indian or not. Might be or might be not, as they say. What's an Indian supposed to look like anyway? He gave Frank a smiling wink, then glanced at me—sort of in a hard way, I thought. I don't know what I expected him to say—

something profound or otherworldly, I suppose. Instead, he just said, "Howdy!"

He took my hand in a powerful grasp and pumped it like a pump handle—getting me primed, I suppose.

He was a tall, powerfully proportioned man, fiftyish, radiating some kind of powerful energy. I could feel it. I didn't like it.

He looked at me, right down into me.

Chills went through me. I felt like a squirming bug that somebody has just picked up on a pin. Those red-coal eyes had skewered my soul. Even as he smiled casually, he wouldn't let go of that look. I did my best to keep my eyes on his but found I had to look away. I wanted to run, but my feet wouldn't go. I guess I just froze, smiling at him inanely. There was something enormously unsettling about this guy. Being a photographer, working on a lot of stories, you come in contact with all sorts of people. You kind of pick up a sense, and I had that kind of sense with this guy, sort of like when you take both Ex-Lax and paregoric for a bad belly; one starts it and one stops it, and after a while you don't know whether you're coming or going! It was something like that. Anyway, he pumped my hand until I thought water would squirt out my ears, and then he said with an almost mocking smile, "Well, I couldn't wait till you got here! I knew you were coming. Didn't know when, but I knew you'd finally get here. Been looking for you!"

It was a strange thing to say. I figured it was some kind of a come-on. We started talking a little bit, and I asked him where he lived. He said, "Oh, up on Scaly Mountain." That was just across the border in North Carolina. Turns out he had an old barn up there with a motor home parked beside it. He said, "I have a few racehorses up there. How about coming by sometime?" I said I'd try but didn't figure I really would. I didn't feel that I wanted to be around this guy. Finally, after a few minutes, he said, "I better run. Catch y'all later." I felt relieved when he left. Not much had been said, but I had a heavy feeling that a lot of things had been left *unsaid* and I wasn't sure I wanted to know what those were.

We'd told him that Frank and I would be heading out for some picture-taking near Sandy Creek on the Chattooga River. Frank had gotten me invited to a pig-picking, and Two Trees said, "Well, maybe I'll just come on out there and see y'all!"

I hoped he wouldn't.

Down at Sandy Creek that afternoon and evening I photographed a rowdy bunch of old boys, local river rats, washing down a lot of barbecued pig with a river of moonshine. About eleven o'clock I decided I'd get out of there but realized my car was blocked in. I asked some guys if they could help me find the people who owned those cars and trucks to see if I couldn't get out of there. Well, they went off, and I leaned against the front of the car. I looked around, and by God! there was old Two Trees the medicine man walking right toward me, not five feet away. It was as if he'd dropped out of the sky. He had his cowboy hat set at a cocky angle as usual, and he strode up to me with that same big grin and said, "Well, Steve, I've been looking for you!"

I did a double take.

He pulled out a pack of cigarettes and offered me one. I grabbed it from the pack, lit up, and puffed deep, smiling what must have been a mighty weak smile. I was really uneasy. We made small talk for a few minutes, I can't remember about what, and then the cars that were blocking my way got pulled out so I could leave. I said my good-byes to Two Trees and the others, and happily got out of there. I could feel his eyes on me as I pulled away. Once again I felt that chill race down my spine.

Over the next week it seemed as if wherever I went he'd just be standing there. Was he following me? What was he after? He was always friendly enough, chitchatting about this and that. He kept asking me to come out to his place and see his horses. Finally one day, against my better judgment, I went.

His place was well up the mountain among some steep, rocky pastures. The barn was big, falling apart as you'd expect, with a beat-looking old motor home parked under a shed in back. On the side of the trailer were painted the words *Ramblin' Tepee* in roughly scrawled, faded, rainbow-colored letters. Inside the barn I glimpsed a bunch of used furniture strewn around almost at random, like someone had just moved in or just moved out. Two Trees came out the side door of the motor home when I arrived, and through the open doorway I could see stuff stacked everywhere: piles of clothes, boxes, tools, saddle ropes, long johns, and God knows what else. Just tumbled in there helter-skelter like a tornado had just blown through and dumped it there.

With glowing pride he showed me his small herd of horses out in the pasture.

"I have a way with the horses," Two Trees said, not boastfully but just matter-of-factly. "They come and they talk to me. We tell each other things."

"Things like what?"

"Like . . . who the hell's this white guy with the beard and the cameras coming up here?"

He laughed loud at that one, though, frankly, the humor sort of fell flat on my ears. We seemed out of register with each other somehow. It was as if I were looking at him through a broken viewfinder, and no matter how I focused the lens, his image never quite came clear.

Maybe his name was a kind of reflection of that. I asked him what Two Trees meant.

"One tree in this world, one tree in the other world," he said. "It means I have roots in both places."

He wasn't really out of focus. He was just focused on two worlds. Maybe that was why I kept getting a split image of him.

❉

I'd noticed, of all things, a chiropractor's table back at the barn.

"You do some chiropracting?" I asked him.

"Oh, I'll crack a few folks," Two Trees said. "It's not my specialty. I just use it to supplement the healing process. Mostly herbs. That's what I do. There's an herb or a combination of herbs for every ailment known to man. There's no incurable diseases, you know. There's only incurable people. Sometimes people get bent out of shape, and a little cracking by a chiropractor can help. Really, it's just like natural bone-setting. People come and ask me, and I do it. I'm not really a chiropractor, but I know enough about it to help sometimes. Tend to the outside with some cracking and body massage, while I tend to the inside with herbs and medicines. Getting a harmony between the two, that's what healing's about."

I thought he spoke really well, though with just a vague hint of braggadocio. I couldn't tell if he'd come up with this stuff himself, gotten it from some elder, or read it in a book somewhere. Maybe all three. And then somehow in the contours of his face I began to see a certain *Indianness*—high cheekbones, tomahawk profile, deep-set eyes, gravity of expression. A two-row bear-claw choker around his neck added verisimilitude.

"Frank says you're Cherokee," I remarked.

"Like *you!*" he said.

That hit me like a bolt of lightning. I'd never told anybody around there about that. It might make me sound like a wannabe Indian or, worse, a boaster. I've never played Indian, and I never will. But, yes, I've got a holy drop or two in my veins. It's not spoken of much in my family. We're not proud or unproud. It's just so. I have a Cherokee great-grandfather back somewhere in the 1800s named Tsiladihi or something like that. I'd never said a word about it to Two Trees or anyone else in these parts and rarely to anyone anywhere.

He just nodded.

"But how'd you know?" I asked him.

"I didn't. Just taking a guess, that's all."

He laughed with a knowing look on his face.

"Lots of Black Dutch and Black Irish hereabouts," he went on. "People hide it. Some don't even know they have the blood. Me, my family's in Oklahoma. Mother and father don't mention it. They're ashamed. Want none of it. But my Grandmother now—she was the one who taught me I was Cherokee. She took me when I was three, raised me till I was nine. Said I was 'picked-born'—that's what she called it. 'You been "picked-born" to be a medicine man,' that's what she told me. She taught me the plants, all the herbs, all the old stories about the seven original Indian nations and how the Cherokee was one of them. Then my folks got me back and brainwashed it all back out of me. Went off to a white man's school, and it wasn't until after I got out of the Air Force thirty years later that I knew what my life was really supposed to be about. Something in my blood was calling me. Hell, I just followed the Trail of Tears from Oklahoma back here to Georgia and North Carolina. This is my real home. I had to learn all the plants over again, 'cause they're different here than in Oklahoma. Still have to go back there to get lots of things I need. People started coming to me. I didn't ask them. They had to ask me. Only when they ask can you help them. And I never ask for money. Those who can will usually give me something, maybe just a bucket of potatoes or whatever. It's important you give *something*—that completes the cycle of energy."

He seemed to speak with authority. I started to believe—almost.

❃

One night we squared off knee to knee—and soul to soul, you might say—on two rickety card chairs outside the barn. Two Trees just sat there awhile, staring me down hard. His eyes, when they weren't glowing like coals, were a cool green flecked with brown, but even that green had a molten intensity. And he could smile a smile so friendly it just melted your willpower.

Later, a mutual friend, chiropractor, and spiritual healer, Dr. James Chastain, would explain to me the source of Two Trees' power: "It's the power of suggestion, pure and simple. Two Trees is a master of suggestion. That's his highest art, his greatest power. *Suggestion!*"

Now Two Trees bent his eyes to mine and locked on. I figured it was finally coming, the reason behind all this.

"Coupla years ago," he said almost casually—and I thought, Shucks, he's just going to tell me another funny story.

"Coupla years ago," he went on, "I was up North Carolina way, up in Cherokee country, to see an old man, a famous old guy— Amonyeeta Wolf Sequoiah was his name. He was a high medicine man of the eastern band of Cherokee, one of the great Grand-fathers of this century. I was there to ask him about some herbs I was looking for. Figured he'd know the local varieties. I'd known this old boy for years. They said he could make a feather lift right off the table and fly through the air, then come back and settle back on the table. He was a really great medicine man, and I was, well, in awe of him, I suppose. He was scary but very kind, too. We took a liking to each other, him and me. Like I say, I was looking for herbs, not miracles, so I couldn't have been more surprised when after some talk about wormwood and turkey root, he looked at me and said, 'I want you to learn some *mysteries. . . .* I want you to come study with me.'

"Well, hell . . . I didn't figure myself for more than a middle-level herbalist. Not on Amonyeeta's level at all. I wasn't sure I *wanted* to know these mysteries he was talking about. Everything you learn in this life, every power you receive, means more responsibility, more burden, more sacrifice. True knowledge doesn't come free. You have to pay for it, and you pay for it by using it in a correct and spiritual way."

"So did you accept?" I asked. "You became Amonyeeta's disciple?"

Two Trees sighed, his head down.

"No. No, I didn't. I told Amonyeeta, 'Grandfather, I'm sorry. I just can't do it. Why me? I'm not qualified for that kind of responsibility.' Well, old Amonyeeta didn't get angry or anything. He just shook his head at me, sort of exasperated like, and he told me, 'Either you stay with me and learn it now, the easy way, or you'll have to learn it later under more difficult circumstances, the hard way.'"

Two Trees' sigh rose and fell, almost whistling through his teeth. Finally he raised his eyes and looked up at me. I never saw anyone look sadder.

"Anyway, I came back home, then learned a few months later that Amonyeeta had died. I realized my chance was gone, I'd muffed it, just as I'd done with the old Seminole medicine man, Josie Billie. I'd gotten to know him, too, and he'd made a similar offer just the year before. He wanted me to come down to Big Cypress there in the Everglades and study with him, carry on the old knowledge. Then he'd died, too, just a while before Amonyeeta. Both of them gone, gone on the long hunt, as they say. And all of that knowledge was gone with them! I'd missed both opportunities and only now saw what a fool I'd been."

Two Trees had an almost pleading look in his eyes. He went on:

"It was a false sense of modesty that made me decline. I realize that now. But then I realized, hey, these old boys are passing on, and they're not leaving anybody to carry on. So I've made a kind of pact with myself—and with the Grandfathers, too. Call it a mission, if you like, or a spirit-journey. A kind of penance. I'm going to go out to as many of the Grandfathers around the country as I can find, the Old Ones, the Elders, the Grandfathers, and the Grandmothers, those who'll see me and talk with me. You know, we have this legend, this story, that once there were seven original Indian nations who came to this Great Turtle Island, not across the Bering Strait from the north, like the white historians'll tell you, but across the great water to the south, the Caribbean, probably. It's said they settled at first in this area around the Carolinas and after a time split up and each moved out to its own territory. One of those nations became the Cherokee, who stayed in these parts. Others became the Creek and the Sioux and the Iroquois, and so on.

"Well, I've decided to go out and see if I can't find the seven Grandfathers of the seven original nations. I'll ask them to share whatever they want to share with me, to at least pass on what they

can, what I'm capable of receiving, before they, too, go on the long hunt. Maybe I can find them, maybe not. Maybe they'll talk to me, maybe not. But *I'm sure as hell going to give it a try!*"

"Hey, Two Trees, that sounds like a wonderful idea!" I told him.

He shook his head. Remorse etched his face.

"The Grandfathers are dying out," he said, "and the old ways are going with them. It's more than I can handle alone. The responsibility's too great for one man. I need someone to come with me, take their pictures, record their words. Otherwise, it'll all be lost. I'm no photographer or writer. I need you to go with me, Steve."

"Well, Two Trees," I told him, getting excited myself, "if you go with me, I'll do it!"

"You think *Geographic* might be interested in doing a story on it?"

"Hell, I'll call Harvey Arden! He'll help us!"

I showed Two Trees a copy of our article on the Vietnamese boat people. Harvey's text on that had brought a difficult subject into moving, poignant focus. Even the Vietnamese refugees themselves had praised it for its accuracy and understanding. Two Trees read the article. "This Harvey guy, he writes about the inside of things. He does with words what you do with pictures. I like that," Two Trees

said. "Okay, he'll be the word man. You'll take the pictures. I believe you two guys have been chosen to do it!"

"When do we start?" I asked him.

"You'll get a sign," Two Trees said. "You'll both get signs. You never go on a spirit-journey without a sign that it's time to begin."

"But what'll it be?"

"You'll know when you get it. That's when we'll begin!"

❄

Bringing Two Trees up to see Bill Garrett was a gamble. Maybe, like Harvey, he'd figure Two Trees wasn't real enough. Harvey had cautioned me: "Oh, no, don't bring this Two Trees character up to see Garrett. How do you know this guy's not a phony, some kind of cigar-store Indian?"

But Two Trees must have worked some kind of spell on Garrett. The three of us talked excitedly in his ninth-floor glass-walled office with its panoramic view of the Washington, D.C., skyline. It was so elegant in there that Two Trees confessed to me afterward, "I felt like spitting on the gold carpet just to feel more at home!" And darned if Garrett didn't strike an instant connection with Two Trees. He seemed immediately convinced by this notion of a spirit-journey. He never even questioned if Two Trees was real or authentic. That Shawnee great-grandmother must have been whispering in his inner ear. Two Trees and I walked out of Garrett's office with an assignment. It even had an official tentative title: "Grandfather Medicine Men."

"Go on out to the Grandfathers," Garrett told us. "Work out a timetable and keep in touch. Harvey'll be your editor. We'll take a flyer on it!"

Harvey was amazed. He'd figured Garrett would toss us right out of his office. But then Harvey and Two Trees seemed to hit it off, too. Since I was still working on the Chattooga River story and Harvey was finishing his story on Sinai and was scheduled to go off that summer to do an article on California's central coast, we figured Two Trees and I would start our spirit-journey in the fall sometime.

"I'll be waiting for my sign," Harvey said, amusement in his eyes.

"Me, too!" I enthused.

"It won't be long," Two Trees vowed. "I'll get the *Ramblin' Tepee* ready for the trip!"

Chapter 3

THAT summer of '82, after finishing the text on the Sinai story, I headed out to California to begin my coverage on a story about the state's central coast—"California's Middle Kingdom"—between Santa Barbara and Monterey. Thoughts about Steve Wall and Two Trees and their upcoming spirit-journey quickly receded to the back burner of my mind. I would simply be their editor, in any case, and, frankly, I doubted that there would ever be a story to edit. As a matter of  fact, Steve was at the same time some five hundred miles to the north, photographing the Smith River on the California-Oregon border for a Geographic book on America's wild and scenic rivers. Immersed in our new and separate assignments, we lost touch with each other over the summer months.

While touring the Santa Barbara Mission in mid-July, I chanced to meet an elderly Chumash Indian woman, Juanita Centeno, who was standing out in the flowered courtyard lecturing to a group of schoolchildren about the history of her people. I stopped and listened.

"We Chumash people had no weapons of war," she was saying, smiling benignly at the upturned faces of her young listeners. "There was no reason to fight. We had everything we needed." She held up a long gnarled stick with a sharp point. "This was our only weapon—a digger stick. That's why they call us 'Digger Indians.' With this stick we could tend our crops and find all the clams and mussels and abalone we could ever want in the sands along the seashore. The Creator put us here. We were the happiest people on earth . . . until the white men came."

I was struck by the gentle and poignant sadness of her voice and by the pride shining in her eyes. After her talk I introduced myself and explained that I'd like to interview her for the article on central California's coast, her ancestral homeland. She was plainly delighted at my interest and offered to take me on a tour of nearby Vandenberg Air Force Base, where she worked part-time as an American Indian "specialist observer," monitoring excavations for the runways and launchpads on the base.

"It's a paid position mandated by California state law," she told me. "Almost anywhere they dig on the base they find Chumash remains. If they dig up a skeleton, I call the tribal elders, and we arrange for a proper reburial. If they find only a bone or two, they let me bury it in a special place I have among the dunes. I herded sheep out there as a girl, you know. We had our camps and villages out there. That's where I grew up. That's where my grandfather is buried, and that's where my heart is. Then the government came, and we Indians had to move out. My people can't even visit there anymore without special permission. We're not allowed to hunt or gather or fish."

Tears stood in her eyes as she spoke. Her grief was palpable.

We spent an afternoon wandering the long shoreline of Vandenberg. Here and there Juanita poked her digging stick into a pile of sand as we walked among the dunes. "Look there!" she said. "See all those shells? My ancestors had a feast right here. I can *feel* them even now. I can see them. I can hear their voices. Oh, it was a wonderful life. All gone now. All gone."

I kicked at the sand and unearthed a small arrowhead. I stopped to pick it up.

"You think I could take this as a souvenir?" I asked her.

Juanita's sad-eyed face turned momentarily stern.

"Oh, you white people and your souvenirs!" she said, her voice cracking. "Can't you see that's a holy thing? It belongs to my people. Please, please, put it back!"

Mortified, I dropped it back on the sand, and Juanita reburied it with her digger stick. She sat down in the sand and actually started weeping. I felt an aching guilt.

"You just don't understand," she lamented. "White people will never understand how much they've taken, how much we've lost."

A few days later I attended a birthday party she was having in Lompoc for one of her relatives. It was a typically happy occasion, replete with a sixty-five-candled birthday cake for Juanita's cousin, Anna Parra, from Oxnard. I struck up a conversation with a darkly handsome young man, Joe Parra, Anna's son. He kept looking at me with a special intensity, asking about what I was planning to put in my *Geographic* article and speaking of Chumash history and legends with an easy eloquence. He recited for me the legend of how the Chumash people had come to the mainland from Santa Cruz island, traveling across a Rainbow Bridge.

"There was a great famine on the island," he said, "and the people were starving. The Great Spirit felt pity for them, so he sent a Rainbow Bridge that reached right across from the island to the mainland. He told the people to cross over that Rainbow Bridge to the mainland, and there they would have all their abundance again. He gave them only one warning: 'Don't look down as you cross the Rainbow Bridge! If you do, you'll fall!'

"So the people started across the bridge. Most got across okay, but some of them couldn't resist looking down. And, sure enough, they fell into the ocean. Then the Great Spirit, who still felt sorry for them, transformed them into dolphins. That's why dolphins are sacred to our people to this day. They're our own brothers and sisters. We have elders who can still call them. Sometimes we go out in small boats to have prayer ceremonies, and the dolphins come. I swear it! They start jumping all around the boats! They come to pray with us!"

He spoke also of the condor.

"Before the people came to the mainland, the condor ruled here. He's the most sacred bird of all. The condor is to the Chumash what the eagle is to the Plains Indians. He's the eyes of God, the messenger of the Great Spirit."

I told him of my recent experience with a condor in Peru, how the old *curandero* had called out, *"Oh, Condorcito . . . Condorcito,"* and how there had been a great rush of wings in the jungle darkness.

Joe nodded, still peering at me with those intensely probing eyes. Being an Indian, he understood.

He continued: "And then there's the owl. The owl is very special to the Chumash people. He's the *observer.* He guides you. He's a helper."

Suddenly his eyes grew bright with some new idea.

"Wait here," he said. "I want to show you something I made. It's out in the car. I'll go get it."

Moments later he returned with an unusual object in his outstretched hands—an inch-thick bamboo shaft about three feet long, trimmed with strips of gray fur. There were several short feathers tied by a beaded red ribbon at one end and a sharp-taloned bird's claw affixed to the other.

"It's an owl's claw power stick," he said. "I made it myself."

He stroked it with his fingertips, holding it under my rapt gaze.

"It has the power of the owl in it," he said. "Go on, touch it."

I touched it lightly, feeling the sharpness of one of the talons with the ball of my thumb. I felt that same tingly chill go along my spine that I'd felt that night in the Peruvian jungle when I'd heard the beating of the condor's wings out in the darkness.

"Here," Joe said, putting it into my hands. "It's yours! I want you to have it, a gift from me to you."

"Oh, but I can't!" I protested.

"Take it!" he insisted. "I'd consider it a slap in the face if you refused."

"But Juanita wouldn't even let me take an arrowhead for a souvenir!" I argued, uneasy at the thought of taking something so lovely from someone I'd known for barely half an hour.

"This stick's no souvenir," Joe said. "It's the real thing. It'll guide you where you're going."

Reluctantly but gratefully, I accepted. My sense of guilt faded at the cool touch of it. I wrapped it inside a rolled piece of newspaper and took it out to my car, setting it carefully in the trunk. I had a sense of being suddenly burdened by some new responsibility, and I wasn't sure I wanted that responsibility, whatever it was. But I was deeply touched by Joe's gesture. "I'll take it for now," I told him. "But I don't consider it mine. It's still yours, Joe. I'll just borrow it awhile. I'll be bringing it back."

Joe seemed delighted by that. "I'll be waiting," he said.

With my usual opacity of spirit, I didn't even think at the time of Two Trees' prediction about Steve and me receiving signs.

The whole notion of signs, so seemingly quaint, had still not come through to me, though it was coming.

Chapter 4

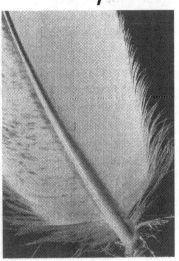

WHILE Harvey was down on the central California coast that summer, I was up on the California-Oregon border. I'd finished the Chattooga River coverage and was out taking photographs for a National Geographic book, *America's Wild and Scenic Rivers*. My coverage at the time was on the wild-watered Smith River. While working on the assignment I stayed for a time at a motel being operated by a Northern Cheyenne-Lakota man named Bob White, a burly, fierce-eyed man with long, flowing white hair. He struck me as sort of a cross between a polar bear and a grizzly. He wore rough Western dress with only a beaded belt buckle and a large silver-and-turquoise ring to suggest he was Indian. At first sight he looked like the kind of guy you wouldn't want to meet in a dark alley. Yet Bob was gentle enough in manner and spoke well on a wide variety of subjects. He seemed to know just about everything.

One night while we were talking he suggested I might like to see his collection of Indian artifacts, and he took me into the next room where he pulled out and unlocked an old weathered trunk. From within he reverently extracted an exquisite full-length woman's white deerskin costume with long fringes and wonderful beadwork.

"That's my grandmother's wedding dress," he said. He eyed me carefully as I looked at it. Beautiful as it was, I felt there was more to come.

Finally, after carefully studying my reactions, he reached back into the trunk, rummaged through it for a while, and at last brought out a folded piece of stained brown cardboard flanked by sections of thin worn balsa wood. Two rubber bands held the folded cardboard closed. Bob White held it up and said, "What's in here can't be placed in plastic or sealed in any way because *it's alive!*" Removing the rubber bands, he opened the folded cardboard as you might open a Bible—and there, almost glowing within, was the most beautiful eagle feather I had ever seen. "Just look at this!" Bob exclaimed, holding it up to me, his eyes shining. "That dark spot surrounded by white you see there, that's considered a sunburst. This kind of spotted eagle feather is used in the most sacred of ceremonies." He said he'd received it just three months before but didn't say from whom. "I wondered why I was getting it," he said. "You don't just get an eagle feather by accident. There's always a reason. I wondered what that reason was, but now . . ."

He sort of squinted at me. I felt like he was casing my soul. He closed his eyes in what seemed a brief prayer, then held the feather in its open cardboard folder out to me. "Now I know what it was for," he said. "It's for you, Steve."

I was stunned.

"You can't own it or even really possess it," Bob said. "You just have temporary responsibility for it. A feather goes where it wants. And when it's ready to go somewhere else, it's gone. You'll see!"

"But . . . Bob," I muttered. "I can't take that!"

He smiled. "You're not taking it. It's taking you!"

I took the feather in my hands and stared at it.

"I can feel its power," I said. And I could.

He nodded, still smiling.

"Take good care of it. You're going to need it for what you're about to do. I don't know what that is—maybe you don't know yourself—but I can tell you it's important and that this feather will help you. It'll be your guardian. What you're about to do will be for all of us."

A charge of electricity ran through me. Every hair on my head must have been standing up straight. Goosebumps covered my arms and shoulders and the back of my neck.

Accepting the feather, I was shaken and moved nearly to tears. In my mind I was hearing what Two Trees had told me earlier: *"You never go on a spirit-journey without a sign that it's time to begin."*

I had not the slightest doubt that this was the sign. I was filled with emotion—elation and, yes, fear. What was going on here? I'd heard of things like this happening but never dreamed I'd be the one to receive such a sign. It carried a terrible responsibility with it, I knew.

I took it with the greatest trepidation. *Now* what? I hardly dared think about it. I knew it was illegal for a white man to possess an eagle feather, but I accepted Bob White's characterization: I didn't have *it;* it had *me.* Never did I consider it mine. And it wasn't. We would be fellow journeyers, that feather and me, and when it chose to go its own way, well, as Bob had said, it would go.

When I later told Harvey on the phone about Bob White's giving me the eagle feather, he seemed typically unimpressed. Only as a kind of afterthought did he mention that a Chumash man he'd met down near Santa Barbara had given him an owl's claw power stick. I could just about hear him shrugging over the phone.

"But that's *your* sign!" I almost shouted.

"Oh, sure."

"Don't you see? It's time to begin!"

"Well, maybe . . . I don't know . . ." His voice trailed off.

That's Old Doubting Harv for you.

Two Trees had no such uncertainty. When I called and told him what had happened, how we'd both received our signs, the feather and the claw, he gave out a loud hoot.

"Ramblin' Tepee's all ready to go!" he announced. "When do we start?"

We made plans to set off in September, after I'd finished the scenic rivers book.

"I can't believe it's happening!" I told him, feeling downright giddy.

Two Trees laughed.

"You don't have to *believe,* Steve. When something real comes along, you *know!"*

Then he told me: "I *knew,* for instance, that you'd get an eagle feather. That's your totem."

"But I don't have a totem!" I protested.

"Oh, yes, you do!" he said with a laugh.

✤

But there weren't many laughs between us after that. In September, Two Trees and I set off in the *Ramblin' Tepee*. It was a strange, even eerie trip. Two Trees seemed really nervous right from the start. I don't think I realized just how difficult this whole enterprise was going to be for him. "You know," he told me, "when a medicine man leaves his home territory, he loses most of his power. The plants are all different from one place to another, so he doesn't know them. And the powers, the energies, are different, too. Everything's different from place to place. Each medicine man has a different medicine, a different power, a different energy. It's his own, and that's the only one he knows. Sometimes it's bad to mix your medicine with another man's medicine. They're like dangerous chemicals. They could explode or, more likely, just not work together."

I'd assumed he would know where to go and what elders to see on this spirit-journey of ours, but I soon realized he expected *me* to find the contacts and make the introductions. The only name he came up with, and that was through a friend of his, was of a Pawnee spiritual elder in Oklahoma. I called Bob White and asked if he could suggest some Indian elders we might see. Bob gave me the name of a Ute medicine man named Charlie Knight out in Colorado. On those slender tips we headed west from North Carolina on Interstate 40. I figured we could stop and inquire about other Indian elders along the way, but when I suggested stopping at this place or that, Two Trees shook his head. "We're only supposed to see precisely who we're supposed to see," he said. "You don't see just anyone when you're on a spirit-journey."

We must have been quite a sight going down the highway in that swaying, tilting old rattletrap of a motor home—dirty and disreputable-looking, dented all over, rusted and paint-chipped, old signs peeling off it, with a long horse-trailer hitch that dragged on the pavement and left a trail of sparks every time we went up an incline. The shock absorbers had given out long ago, needless to say. "Gives you a better sense of the road anyway," Two Trees said. "You can feel every bump!"

And we did, without exception.

"Got everything we need in here," Two Trees announced. "Stove, refrigerator, even a TV!"

There was junk everywhere, piles of things—clothes, rattles, bottles of every color and variety, Navajo blankets, bags of groceries, bulging cardboard boxes, bundles of dry tobacco hanging from a rod, even a buffalo skull. This last item we planned to bring out to a group of Sioux I'd met in Oregon while working on the rivers book. They'd told me they needed one for a sun dance, and I'd exchanged a lever-action 35-caliber deer rifle for it with a friend of Two Trees'. A large and ominous-looking thing, it was tucked under my bed, and throughout the trip I slept uneasily, knowing that skull was staring up at me with those eyeless sockets.

"Don't use those drawers up on top," Two Trees told me. "They've got all my medicine stuff. You've got a whole drawer for your stuff next to the bed."

One small drawer for my three camera bags, a large tripod, and two Halliburton suitcases! Somehow we got it all stowed under and around things. The only way to walk back there was to leapfrog over everything.

I hate sitting in the passenger seat, but Two Trees insisted on doing most of the driving. The swaying and constant bouncing and creaking made sleeping in back while on the road almost impossible.

❋

As we headed west on I-40, the road lost its curves and leveled out to a straightaway. In the rearview mirror I watched the mountain peaks of North Carolina growing more and more distant. Leaving home and facing the unexpected gave me a kind of inner chill. A dark, brooding sky lowered ahead of us, and I could feel its heaviness inside me, a reflection of my own feelings.

I just couldn't shake that sense of unease about what was coming, and I know it showed in my eyes and in my voice. I'm a bad liar. I can feign something for only so long, then I give it away. Two Trees tuned right into it.

"You shouldn't be putting out negative energy like this right at the start," he said. "What's wrong?"

I shrugged. "Oh . . . I guess I just hate leaving B.J. and the kids, going off God knows where."

That was true enough in itself. Hell, I've traveled in thirty-five countries or so over the past twenty-five years, and I've been homesick in every one of them. But that didn't explain this sense of un-ease, even of dread, that I was feeling this time out. Just what had I gotten myself into? It's one thing to suggest an idea like this to *National Geographic* but quite another to pull it off. We were headed into entirely unknown territory, Two Trees and me, and I had fore-bodings. I also had growing doubts about Two Trees himself. Was he really a medicine man? Was he really even an Indian? Harvey's doubts about him were nagging at me, too. I knew if *Geographic*'s edi-tors even sniffed a problem concerning Two Trees' "authenticity," the story would be killed. And Two Trees' often questionable behav-ior was giving me fits.

Wherever he went he handed out spontaneous, on-the-spot, unasked-for diagnoses to just about anyone and everyone, prescrib-ing an instant regimen of various herbs, his all-purpose snakeroot tea, an assortment of natural home remedies and megasupplements of vitamin E, zinc, aloe vera, and so on. I found it embarrassing. It seemed to contradict flatly his stated dictum that a true medicine man has to be *asked first* before he can offer help. He'd told me, "An individual doesn't proclaim himself a medicine man. It's other peo-ple who proclaim him one."

But that's not the way it was going. Two Trees seemed to be pro-claiming himself everywhere. And where was he getting all these remedies anyway? They didn't seem to be particularly "Indian." A lot of them seemed like the kind of stuff you see in New Age health jour-nals and herbal emporiums.

✻

Not only did Two Trees go around proclaiming himself, but, it turned out, he wanted me to go ahead of him to the Grandfathers, set up each meeting, and do the initial proclaiming for him. It seemed like I was supposed to play a combination advance PR man and John the Baptist. I told him, "I thought you said a medicine man doesn't proclaim himself, that other people have to proclaim him."

He laughed at that. "Well, so *you're* other people, aren't you?"

That rankled me no end.

One morning when we got up, he told me, "I saw you coming back into your body last night! Where'd you go?"

I didn't remember a thing. He was just making it up, I figured, just like he made up so much else.

"Hell, I didn't go anywhere!" I said.
"Oh, yes, you did!"
"I didn't!"
"You *did!*"
"Well, then, if you know so much, where'd I go?" I asked him.
"To hell and back!"
Oh, he horse-laughed at that one!

❋

Once he woke me up in the middle of the night, shaking me out of a deep sleep.

"What're you dreaming about, Steve? You've been groaning something awful!"

"Darned if I can remember."

"Lay back down," he said. "Close your eyes. Go back into your dream. Go on . . . you can do it!"

I laid my head back down on my pillow. I sensed that buffalo skull staring up at me from under the bed. Maybe it was giving me bad dreams!

"Go on," Two Trees repeated. "Close your eyes! Dream that dream again while you're awake if you can!"

I tried it. Nothing. I was really getting peeved with him again. Waking me up like that, and now he was even prying into my dreams! Was he working some sort of spell on me?

"Bring that dream on up now," he said. "Go on, bring it right back up!"

Well, it suddenly came back to me. It was a dream I think I've had a hundred times since I was a little boy. It was always the same: I'd be out in the dark, out in a field at night, and I'd be digging with my bare hands at the ground, madly scooping out the loose soil, absolutely terrified at what I'd find. This was something that had actually happened to me when I was nine or ten. I'd been having nightmares about it ever since. It was probably the most terrifying experience of my life. I remember my uncle's dog got run over and killed. We went out in a field and had a little religious rite and buried it a foot or so deep in the loose soil. I was somehow terribly affected by it all. I couldn't get it out of my mind. It kept plaguing me that "Maybe the dog's not dead! We buried it and it's not dead!" I couldn't sleep. I kept having that same thought. So the next night I snuck back out all alone to that field. I just had to find out. I found the spot and, shaking with terror, I dug up the dog with my bare hands! There wasn't any box or anything, just the dog, all covered with dirt. I poked a stick at its rotting carcass. Oh, how it stank! But at least it was dead! Thank God! Then I reburied it. It was horrifying.

I told Two Trees the dream and the story behind it.

"I guess I've been digging up and reburying that dog ever since!" I told him.

"Well," he said, "this is the last time. It's over. Once you bring a dream into your waking state, you don't ever have to dream it again."

And, I have to admit, I've never had that dream again.

Say what you will about Two Trees, call him a phony or a fraud or a charlatan, yet he *knew* things.

❋

Another night he woke me up again. Something made me open my eyes, and there was Two Trees' face looming right in front of me in the darkness.

"Ever wonder about the dead?" he asked as if we'd been talking for hours.

I just blinked at him. This man could whistle in the wind with the best of them, but his tune always had a meaning for someone. He had a way of touching a sore place or a weak spot. Death was one of my soft points, and, damn him, he knew it. Being awakened that way and being asked such a question really shook me up. I felt like letting out a scream and running right out of that accursed motor home. But I kept myself in check.

"Uhhhh . . . what do you mean, Two Trees? Is this personal, or do you have a point to make?"

He made a kind of sucking sound between his teeth. I could smell that sickly smell of wormwood or whatever it was he often had about him. It was a main ingredient of his "Cleansing Indian Bitter Tea." I probably smelled of it myself since, at his insistence, I'd been drinking three cups a day of the stuff since the trip began.

His face loomed over me, eyes darkly aglow.

"The dead are among us," he finally said in a breathy, almost funereal voice.

My whole body ran with goose pimples. Was he being serious or just joking again? You could never tell with Two Trees.

I just lay there, not saying anything.

He went on: "They walk and they talk, but they're not like us. They don't even blink when you wave your hands in front of their eyes. They've got no purpose. They're stranded here in this world. They're trying to get away to that other world, but they can't. Some can see them, others can't. But no matter if they're seen or not, they're here just the same. Ever see any, Steve?"

He made that sucking sound again.

"You remember," he said, "that night last week when I saw you coming back to your body?"

"You were serious? I thought you were just putting me on, you were joking."

"Warn't no joke!" Two Trees declared. "I saw you coming back like a shadow into your body. And I saw something else—a woman, an old woman. She was guiding you back to your body. It was your grandmother."

I'd told him earlier about my grandmother, the one who had told me of my Cherokee great-grandfather Tsiladihi. Strange how we'd both had grandmothers who'd passed on the Cherokee connection. Mine, like Two Trees', had been a huge influence on me. Oddly enough, she was also the one who had convinced me to study for the ministry. "That's the greatest career of all," she'd told me. "It's a calling from God Himself, and you have to surrender to the call if you hear it." Well, I'm not sure I ever really heard that call, but I went ahead anyway and enrolled at a college for Baptist ministers, mostly to please my grandmother and parents. It didn't take me long to become disillusioned with organized religion. Hell, I wanted to be a photographer, not a minister. I wrote my grandmother about it, and she persuaded me to go on. Then one day she up and died. I'd vowed to her I'd become ordained as a minister, and I did. But then I just chucked it all and got a job as a newspaper photographer. I've always had a sense she was looking on disapprovingly from afar.

"She's been watching out for you," Two Trees continued. "She's been trying to get through to you. She wants to help. She knows she made a mistake about you going into the ministry. Ever since she went over to the other side she's realized she was wrong. You weren't meant for the ministry. You had something else to do. So she came and took you on a little trip the other night, trying to reach you, trying to show you everything's all right, that you're doing the right thing."

Was he making all this up? No doubt. I didn't know whether to be mad or scared.

"I thought you said I'd just gone to hell and back!"

He chuckled hoarsely.

"In a way you did! To the other world and back! It was a dream journey, an inner spirit-journey. She wanted to take you and show you things, some really grand sights, but you wouldn't go with her! You kept trying to get back to your body. That's why you were moaning. And finally you got back. But you came back too quick, before she could get through to you. She's trying to get you to forgive her, and you won't! Don't you see how mean you're being, how stupid? You have to give that old lady peace. You've got to forgive her so she can go on her way."

"But I *have* forgiven her!"

"Then tell her, damn it! Don't tell me, tell *her!* What if I told you she was here right now, listening to us! She's hovering right here in this trailer, waiting for you to forgive her! Man, how stupid can you be? Do it!"

"I . . . I can't, Two Trees. I just can't do it! This is too weird!"

He snorted contemptuously.

"You need to get this settled. If you won't talk to her, at least listen! She's here and wants you to know. Damn you, pay attention!"

"Okay. I'm listening. I'm listening."

And I tried. I tried bringing my grandmother's image to mind. I could almost feel her hand brushing my brow like she used to do. But it was just imagination, I know. I guess I drifted off to sleep.

Next morning Two Trees asked me if I'd dreamed about her.

"No, I can't say I did. She didn't come back."

"Maybe she doesn't need to anymore," he said. "Maybe she's finally gotten her release."

"Maybe," I echoed. "I sure hope so."

So what was I to make of it all? Here he was telling me about dreams I didn't even know I'd had! Just who and what *was* this guy?

❦

I grudgingly found myself playing John the Baptist for our visit to Uncle Frank Davis in Oklahoma. A friend of Two Trees' had recommended Uncle Frank as a highly respected Pawnee spiritual elder. Two Trees had never met him. It became my role to go ahead and make the introductions. "You pave the way," Two Trees put it.

While Two Trees waited outside of town in the *Ramblin' Tepee*, I rented a car, took a motel in town, and spent a couple of wonderful days with Uncle Frank, a gentle-mannered and self-effacing man in his seventies. He seemed happy to have a visitor, and we took an immediate liking to each other. Sitting around the coffee-stained Formica-topped table in the kitchen, we spoke of his recently deceased wife, whose presence seemed to hover everywhere in the house. Photographs and mementos of their long marriage filled almost every available space on the walls and bric-a-brac shelves. Heavy velvet curtains were drawn across the windows as if in perpetual mourning.

"I'll be seeing her soon," Uncle Frank confided almost casually.

He kept a telephone book on one of the chairs at the kitchen table. It was covered with a fine dust.

"Don't sit there, please," he said. "My wife always sat there, and I'm saving that seat for her. Sometimes she comes to me and we talk."

Even as we spoke he often looked over at that empty chair as if looking for some confirmation, then nodded, smiled, and turned back to our conversation.

I edged into my reason for being there, not mentioning Two Trees at first. I told him I was on a journey in search of the wisdom of the Grandfathers. "It's a spirit-journey," I told him. That might have sounded sort of inflated, I figured, or even downright corny, but he seemed to understand instantly.

"Yes, that's good. That's very good!" he exclaimed.

That's something I've always liked about Indians. You don't have to hem and haw before getting down to the nub of things. Like Harvey once said about Australia's Aboriginal people: "They always have one foot in the Dreamtime!"

At that moment Uncle Frank happened to be making some sandwiches for lunch. He held up a slice of limp store-bought white bread in his hand, waving it at me.

"Wisdom is like bread," he said. "If you find the right ingredients to make the dough, it'll rise for you and give you life. Also, it's good and it gets passed around for everyone to eat and enjoy! It's meant to be shared!"

He laughed and handed me the slice of bread and took another for himself.

"Eat!" he said.

We ate the two slices of plain white bread in silence, eyes locked onto each other as we shared the spontaneous sacrament.

"My wife made better bread than this," he announced sadly, glancing over at the empty chair. "It had a wonderful crust. I wish I could give you some. This will have to do."

I could see I was going to like this man. But I still had to explain about Two Trees, whom I hadn't yet mentioned.

After lunch and half a dozen cups of strong black chicory-laced coffee, Uncle Frank said he'd like me to attend a special ceremony the next day—"a blessing for your journey"—and I agreed. I could certainly use a blessing, God knew. It was at that point I mentioned that a friend of mine would like to meet him.

"He's . . . a, uh, chief. A Cherokee. Calls himself a . . . a medicine man," I said, forcing out the words. "He's waiting outside of town."

Uncle Frank looked at me, squinting one eye.

"Where's he been? Why didn't he come with you?"

"Uh . . . he's waiting to be invited."

"How can I invite him if we've never met?"

"He's . . . shy, I suppose."

"Well, tell him to come if you like. But I don't know if he'll find anything here he's looking for. We don't have real medicine men around here anymore. It's one thing to be a medicine man to whites and another thing to Indians. Me, I know a little medicine, like a lotta folks, but I'm no medicine man. I'm not even a chief, and I wouldn't want to be one."

Uncle Frank was definitely not a proclaimer.

This was going to be interesting.

✳

Two Trees arrived the next day with a flourish, wearing a tasseled and garishly sequined white buckskin ceremonial shirt that looked like something out of Buffalo Bill's Wild West Show.

"It's my ghost-shirt," he announced. "I put it on for the little ceremony that Steve told me we're having today!"

I could have crawled out the door. Uncle Frank just looked at him, his eyes noncommittal.

Two Trees walked to the kitchen table and picked up the telephone book to sit down on the chair.

I ran over and plucked his white-tasseled sleeve.

"Uh . . . not that chair, Chief. Take the other one!"

Two Trees seemed puzzled but complied. It was an innocent enough mistake—how could he have known? Yet it somehow seemed to betray an unerring instinct to do precisely the wrong thing. His bluff showmanship was just a cover. I could see he was totally out of place here with a real spiritual Elder.

Instead of asking questions and listening to Uncle Frank—the whole object of our journey, I'd thought—he immediately started making pronouncements.

"So Steve tells me you're not actually a chief!"

"No. No, I'm not," Uncle Frank acknowledged.

"Well, don't worry. You *will* be in the near future!"

I was astounded.

"No . . . no, I won't. That'll never happen!" Uncle Frank insisted, leveling a sharp look at Two Trees.

"Well, I can help with the ceremony today if you like," Two Trees volunteered. "You have any children around? I'd be glad to give them Indian names."

Uncle Frank eyed him.

"We already have someone in our tribe who gives names," he said, "someone who's *supposed* to do it."

Two Trees seemed not to catch the barb. He continued blithely on in his boastful way, tossing out the names of local Oklahoma medicinal plants, speaking of the virtues of this remedy and that. He even got in vitamin E. I don't think he asked a single question. It was an ugly display. I was terrified that he'd actually start to diagnose Uncle Frank!

But Uncle Frank was too smart for that. He'd had enough. He stood up suddenly, grabbed his jacket off a wall hook, and walked to the door.

"Sorry, but I gotta be going, you fellas. Got a meeting at the Senior Citizens Center. Forgot about it till right now."

"But wha-*a-at* about the ceremony?" Two Trees asked.

"No ceremony," Uncle Frank said flatly, opening the front door and gesturing for us to leave with him.

Two Trees sputtered, "But . . . I thought Steve said—"

"No ceremony," Uncle Frank said flatly, finality in his voice. "Sorry, I have to lock up here."

I could hear Two Trees whistling through his teeth. I remember he just jerked his head to one side, then jerked it back to the other, as if possessed by some enormous involuntary twitch. Then he smiled weakly and shrugged. He'd been here not five minutes, and the whole thing was ruined.

Outside, Uncle Frank crooked his index finger at me. Aching inwardly, I went over to talk with him and make amends while Two Trees made a beeline for the *Ramblin' Tepee* in the driveway, sharply and emphatically slamming the door shut behind him.

Uncle Frank touched my forearm with his hand.

"You're on the right journey, Steve. I want you to know that. I'll have that ceremony later and give you my blessing from afar. You just got to travel with this man awhile, for whatever reason, and then go

your own way. You and him, you got different paths to travel. I hope you find yours, Steve. I think you will. No point in walking anyone else's path. That'll only get you nowhere."

He gave my forearm a little squeeze, as you would squeeze a child's arm in reassurance.

"Have a good road, my friend," he said. Then he walked off.

Later I realized I'd been too stricken even to say thanks. Before Two Trees and I took off in the *Ramblin' Tepee* that evening, I insisted on stopping at a bakery in town and buying a big loaf of their best crusty white bread. Uncle Frank's house was dark when we went by. Maybe he was in, maybe he wasn't. You couldn't tell with all the curtains drawn. I didn't knock. I just left the bag with the loaf of fresh-baked bread on his doorstep. I figured he'd know who left it.

❋

I decided I wouldn't go on with the John the Baptist routine. It was just too much. I couldn't do it again.

I told Two Trees: "You'll have to tell them yourself about being a chief and a medicine man and all that. I'm just not qualified."

He sort of *harrumphed* and didn't answer. Just a shrug and a hard sidelong glance.

We hardly spoke during the two-day drive out to the Ute reservation in southwestern Colorado. I could see this "flyer" on the Grandfather Medicine Men going down in flames around me—and me without a parachute. My *Geographic* career was in free-fall. If only I hadn't stoked up Garrett on this project, I'd have abandoned it right then and there. I could hear Harvey saying, "Told you so . . ."

❋

"When ya leavin'?" were Charlie Knight's first words to us as we drove up to his sheep camp in the *Ramblin' Tepee*. Charlie's little aluminum trailer, with a blue Chevy pickup parked beside it, sat behind a low red mesa on the Colorado desert plateau. Charlie had been recommended to me as a high-level medicine man by Bob White, who had worked a few years before on the Ute reservation. When he gave me the feather, Bob had mentioned he knew a medicine man who used such an eagle feather to diagnose patients. "He waves it over their bodies like an X ray to find out what's wrong," Bob had told me. "Then he takes a red-hot coal right out of the fire in his bare fingers,

drains the heat from it into his hand, and applies the heat to the affected part of the body."

Now *that* was a Grandfather Medicine Man!

We shrugged off Charlie's odd greeting. It was spoken with a smile and followed by a cautious handshake. No, not so much a handshake as a light glancing touch of the fingers. Charlie eyed us through opaque sunglasses that gave him a darkly mysterious look. At first he denied being a medicine man at all.

"Maybe you got the wrong Charlie!" he said with a laugh. "Yup, that's who you got—the wrong Charlie!"

But he was the right Charlie.

The question was, were *we* the right ones to be here?

Two Trees immediately and unabashedly announced himself to be both a chief and a medicine man. Charlie just nodded. He said he had no objection to our hanging around for a few days—which we did, chasing after wild bulls with Charlie and his son Big Jim up on the slopes of Sleeping Ute Mountain, then attending the livestock auction with the two of them in Cortez, the main local town.

As with Uncle Frank, Charlie seemed to relate much better to me than to Two Trees. He just kept cocking an eye at Two Trees, sometimes suspicious, sometimes merely amused. At least Two Trees didn't wear that white buckskin Wild West outfit. But of course he couldn't resist diagnosing everyone in sight. My heart fell every time he did it.

One day out at the sheep camp Charlie asked me in a whisper, "Is that man really a medicine man? Are you sure?"

I shrugged. "Well, he says he is!"

Charlie just shook his head.

Two Trees seemed at a loss. He tried talking to Charlie about medicine, and the old man just didn't respond. We seemed to be wasting our time. Then Two Trees decided he would prove himself. Charlie had pointed out some wild horses he'd been having trouble roping.

"I'll bring them over for you to rope if you want," Two Trees declared.

"Okay. Let's see you do it," Charlie said.

While Charlie and I stood there watching, Two Trees ambled out a few dozen yards into the barren landscape, then sat down on the stony ground. He lowered his head and pushed his cowboy hat down over his face. For several minutes he sat there immobile.

Well, after a short while, damned if those horses, half a dozen of them, didn't come running toward him, trotting right past Two Trees, then circling around and coming right back past him again. Two Trees didn't move, just sat there rock-still, hat covering his face. The horses stopped a few feet off from him, sniffing the air nervously and inching slowly toward this strange man sitting on the ground with his head down and his cowboy hat covering his face.

I was amazed. I looked over at Charlie. He was watching coolly. The horses came right up to Two Trees, sniffing his boots with their noses. He could have reached right out and touched them. But then, instead of making a gentle movement as you'd expect, Two Trees suddenly flipped up the cowboy hat from his face, jerked back his head, and let out a loud *"Hahhh!"* The horses immediately reared and bolted, scattering back into the immense landscape. Two Trees sat there smiling at us. He waved his cowboy hat as if in confirmation of his powers. Again I looked over at Charlie. He was just shaking his head. No smile. He kicked at a stone.

"Mmmm, he knows horses, all right," Charlie muttered, "but that don't necessarily make him a medicine man."

"Want me to bring them back so you can rope them?" Two Trees called, swaggering back toward us.

"'Nother time," Charlie said, then added, *"When ya leavin'?"*

Two Trees furled his brows for a moment, then flashed a grin. He was determined not to take offense.

Again and again he tried to get Charlie to discuss medicine. Charlie would just shrug. Finally, Two Trees tried a new gambit.

"Say, Charlie," he said, "I've got this groin pain that's bothering me. Got kicked there by a horse years ago. Maybe you could do something?"

Charlie squinted one eye.

"Maybe. But not now. You guys come back in a few days. Maybe Charlie'll look at you then."

"Uhhh . . ." I said, hesitating, "I don't suppose I could take a few photographs while you work on Two Trees?"

Charlie shrugged again.

"Maybe, we'll see," he said.

It seemed a rare opportunity. Many times I've been asked by Native Americans to set aside my cameras at a ceremony, and I've always done so without argument. Cameras rarely belong at a ceremony. I've never taken them out where they weren't wanted. Maybe I could have cheated or bought my way into a phony ceremony, as some do, but I never did. And I never will. It was precisely because of an almost obsessive lust for such photographs—"zingers" they called them at the magazine—that photographers are now prohibited from shooting ceremonies on nearly all reservations. A religious ceremony should not be reduced to a photo-op. I agree with the prohibition, though I suppose it's cost me more than a few zingers over the years. Frankly, I don't want to take zingers. You don't need to photograph the actual ceremony to capture the spiritual essence of Native American people. You can find that essence just as well, and maybe even better, in everyday nonceremonial situations—in a young mother's eyes as she puts her baby to her breast or in an old man's hands, as gnarled and arthritic as the ancient ceremonial cane he carries.

Charlie repeated, *"When ya leavin'?"*

We finally took the suggestion and headed back to our motel in nearby Cortez.

"Well, maybe we're breaking through," Two Trees told me on the way back. "Better call Harvey. Tell him to come on out. Looks like we're gonna have a real live Ute healing ceremony. And you can even get photographs!"

"Maybe," I cautioned. "Charlie said *maybe.*"

"Hey, *maybe*'s a lot better'n *no!*" Two Trees laughed.

❋

I called Harvey that night. I didn't let on about all my problems with Two Trees. Who knew, maybe we were finally getting somewhere. Maybe I could even get a zinger! I told Harvey how Charlie diagnosed his patients with an eagle feather.

"Maybe you can get him to use *yours* in his ceremony!" Harvey suggested.

"Maybe. Who knows? Right now everything's *maybe!*"

"Well," Harvey intoned, "if you can get him on film holding that red-hot coal in his hand, *maybe* you've got a story the magazine will actually publish!"

"Can't you come out and be here with us?" I asked him. I didn't know what was going to happen. Maybe nothing, maybe something. Either way, I wanted Harvey to be there. I figured he'd never believe

what happened—if something *did* happen—unless he saw it with his own eyes.

"I'll see if I can get permission to fly out," he promised. "That red-coal trick sounds interesting. Now *there's* a zinger for you!"

Chapter 5

A grim-faced Steve Wall picked me up at the Farmington, New Mexico, airport, and we drove back to Cortez, Colorado, near the Ute Mountain Ute reservation to meet Two Trees. Steve's jaw muscles worked angrily under his beard, and he bit down on the stem of his pipe like he wanted to bite it right off. Driving with controlled fury, he complained bitterly about Two Trees the whole way.

"He's some kind of egomaniac," he fumed. "He acts as if he's the Messiah, and I'm supposed to play John the Baptist and proclaim his coming. He acts as if I'm expected to do everything: find all the Grandfather Medicine Men, make all the introductions, do all the dirty work. And then, after I set it all up, why, he'll just walk in and play medicine man!"

This was the first I'd heard of any problems. I wasn't pleased.

Two Trees was waiting for us when we arrived at the motel. He immediately pulled me off to one side and whispered, "We've got to get a new photographer! Steve Wall is impossible! I can't work with him!"

With each of them badmouthing the other, I could see that this story was about to collapse of its own weight. I regretted having

flown out, since I'd had to plead for permission to make the trip with articles editor Joe Judge. Judge had looked askance at this story from the beginning, and he was definitely not a true believer when it came to red-coal tricks. I told him how Steve had gotten permission to photograph the old medicine man actually taking the red-hot coal in his bare hand and using it in the healing. Now *there* was a zinger! When Joe still seemed doubtful, I added that this same medicine man could make an eagle feather lift right off a tabletop and hover in the air, then settle back down on the table. Actually, I was mistaken; it had been another medicine man that Steve had told me about, Amonyeeta Wolf Sequoiah, who had allegedly done that, not Charlie Knight. But it helped convince Judge, who was definitely wavering. Finally, shaking his head, he approved the trip. "Well, go on out there," he told me grudgingly. "Find out what's happening with Steve Wall and this Two Trees guy. I smell a fish here." Judge gave me one last piece of cautionary advice: "And, please, Harvey, *don't get into bed with your subject!*"

❋

Next day, leaving the *Ramblin' Tepee* in Cortez, Steve, Two Trees, and I drove a rental car out to Charlie's sheep ranch. We didn't talk much on the way out. Steve drove. Two Trees sat in the passenger seat. I assumed my proper subordinate place in the backseat, as I always do when we travel with the elders. I'd brought along the owl's claw power stick that Joe Parra had given me that summer in California, and so we both had our signs with us—Steve his eagle feather, me my claw. To be truthful, I found this matter of signs more than a little disconcerting, but I let it slide.

When I'd showed Two Trees the claw on arriving the day before, he'd looked at it strangely. I'd tried to hand it to him in the motel room, but he'd backed away.

"Got to watch out for that thing!" he'd admonished. "It's got power in it. Could be dangerous. I can feel it. You want to handle it carefully. It can do you harm."

"Or *good*?" I'd asked hopefully.

"Mmmmm," Two Trees said, a doubtful expression on his face. "Maybe. You never know."

"How about Steve's feather?" I asked him. "Is that dangerous, too?"

Two Trees had shaken his head.

"Nope. Eagle feather's only for good. There's no darkness in it. But that claw, now—it has darkness in it, and you have to be damn careful. The owl, you know . . . sometimes the owl means death. Probably better don't show it to Charlie. He might just pick up on something negative."

I was irked. Here I'd brought the sign he himself had predicted I'd receive, and now he was telling me the blessed thing was dangerous! Vaguely despondent at his reaction, I rewrapped it in newspaper and packed it away.

Steve brought out his feather when we reached Charlie's camp.

"We'll see if he'll use *this* in the healing ceremony," he said.

He seemed so damn proud of himself and his feather! I felt my claw was definitely second best, an inferior miracle.

✻

Sure enough, Charlie's first words to us on our arrival at the sheep camp were *"When ya leavin'?"*

Steve breathed in my ear, "Don't worry, he always says that!"

But this time Charlie wasn't joking—if indeed he ever had been. At our approach he stood in the open door of his little aluminum trailer and waved his hands at us—in a gesture, it seemed, of caution or warning.

Steve barely had time to introduce me, the editor he'd spoken of from *National Geographic*. Charlie seemed uninterested, glancing at me with a perfunctory nod. He said nothing to Two Trees, who stood off behind us, peering aimlessly into space, making that whistling sound between his teeth.

"So," Steve blurted, sensing disaster, "everything okay for the healing today, Charlie?"

"Charlie ain't doing any healing today. Sorry. *When you guys leavin'?*"

"Thought you said you'd look at Two Trees' groin."

"Nope. Can't do it. I gotta tell you guys, it's better for you to go. Get on outa here. Charlie's sorry. But it ain't safe for you here right now. Stick people, they be about—"

"Stick people?" I asked.

Charlie stepped down from the trailer and struck an almost theatrical pose before us, his body twisted and contorted as if he were trying to portray the hunchback of Notre Dame.

"Stick people, skin people," he said, twirling around on one boot heel and lurching toward us with hands outstretched and grasping in a kind of Boris Karloff imitation. "Like big dogs. Stand up like this on back legs. Go running in the night looking for people to eat. Only they be made outa sticks and skin! That's all they be! Skin and sticks! That's why they're so hungry! They need human flesh and blood!" He stopped lurching toward us and stood there in the cloud of red dust he'd stirred up, eyes glowering. He laughed gruffly, darkly, a hoarse gurgle deep in his throat. "Gonna getcha! The stick people! The skin people! They be looking for you. I got a warning. Someone's gonna get hurt if you guys stay. You guys don't wanna be around here after dark when they come out. *When ya leavin'?*"

Was he putting us on? Was he just trying to scare us away? Was he actually serious about the stick people? Damned if I could figure it out.

Some miracle! I could hear Joe Judge laughing.

I looked over at Steve. He turned his eyes away, utterly distraught. I somehow expected Two Trees to step into the breach here and do something, but he just stood there behind us, stone-faced, cowboy hat pulled low over his eyes. He said nothing.

Now Steve stepped boldly forth, trying to save the situation.

"I got something here, Charlie."

He unfolded the piece of weathered cardboard with reverent fingers and, holding it out to Charlie, revealed Bob White's eagle feather. In the bright, beating desert sunlight it seemed to light up and all but lift off the piece of cardboard, like Amonyeeta Wolf Sequoiah's feather.

Charlie was instantly struck by it. He took the feather in his dark gnarled hands, letting it rest across both palms. He stared down at it.

"Mmmmm. That's the real thing," he said, his voice softening. "Yeah, that's it okay."

"I thought maybe you could use it in the healing ceremony, Charlie," Steve muttered uncertainly.

Charlie looked up, brows furled.

"No healing ceremony. Charlie can't do it! I got a warning. Bad things'll happen. Just can't do it!"

He set the feather back on the cardboard and returned it to Steve.

"So . . . *when ya leavin'?*"

I could hear Two Trees whistling through his teeth behind us. This thing was going nowhere. Then I had a thought.

"Charlie, would you give us a blessing with Steve's feather before we go?"

"Well . . ." he said, squinting at us through his dark, impenetrable sunglasses. "Mmmmm . . . You wait a minute. Stand right here. All you three guys together. Charlie'll make a little medicine for you, a little blessing!"

Two Trees came and stood between Steve and me. He'd taken off his cowboy hat and held it in his hands. Bending his head, he stared at the ground. He looked downright remorseful.

Charlie grasped the feather by its quill tip and waved it around the three of us, sort of combing and fluffing the air with it, starting at the ground behind our feet, then working up to our heads, then back down to our feet. He waved it four more times around each of

our heads. For a minute or so his lips spoke some silent prayer, then he stepped back and said:

"Good blessing. Help you find the right path. You gotta go your own ways, you guys. Each his own way. Maybe you come back another time. Right now's the wrong time. Later on the stick people go away and you come back. It'll be safe then. You remember. Follow the right path and take it back here. Charlie's on that path, too, so maybe we meet along the way. You be sure to come. Charlie be waiting."

He stood there smiling at us.

"Okay, now. *When ya leavin'?*"

There was nothing more to say. We left.

That night Two Trees took off in the *Ramblin' Tepee*. We didn't really talk much about it. "I'm gonna split," he told us without rancor. "Gotta go my own way, as Charlie says. You guys, too. Each of us our own way. Steve, you gotta do what you gotta do. I can't do it with you. Harvey, sorry you wasted your time coming out here. Tell Garrett and Judge I'm sorry."

He was going off on his own spirit-journey, and that was it. "Think I'll be heading out to Hopi. Maybe I can pick up the trail again out there," were his last words to us. We watched the *Ramblin' Tepee* with one red taillight recede down the motel driveway and onto the road, spewing a trail of sparks from the dragging horse trailer hitch in back.

We never saw him again.

✳

For us, Two Trees had been the Gatekeeper, not the Guide. He'd shown us the way to the path of the Wisdomkeepers; but he couldn't lead us onto it. Strangely, what had begun as another man's mission had now become our own. It was as if we'd been passed a baton in mid-race and now would have to run with it toward some unknown finish line. At that moment, though we couldn't have guessed it at the time, we became runners.

Steve was utterly depressed.

"How will I ever explain this to Garrett? My *Geographic* career's down the tubes. Why, oh, why did I ever start this whole thing anyway?"

"I'll do the explaining to Garrett," I consoled him. "Hell, I was probably going to ghostwrite it all anyway. Why don't I just ask him if I can take over as the author?"

"He'll never go for it," Steve insisted. "The whole point of the thing was one medicine man going out and talking to others."

"Who knows?" I said. "He might just buy the idea. Remember that Shawnee great-grandmother."

"Harvey, do you really think . . ."

"Hell, at least I'll give it a try!"

Steve's eyes glowed ecstatically. "Man! Wouldn't that be something? Just you and me! No more *Ramblin' Tepee!* No more playing John the Baptist! Hell, what's to stop the two of us from just going out ourselves, two bumbling white guys? Two Trees had to prove himself to them, one medicine man to another, and that was his downfall. We've got nothing to prove. Just be who we are! Just go up and knock on the elders' front doors and ask them to talk about anything they like. You record their words, I'll take the pictures. What's wrong with that? Wouldn't *Geographic*'s readers be interested in *that?*"

I felt myself being swept up by this new idea of ours. Maybe two unlikely white guys would have an easier time than Two Trees had had. We brought no baggage with us—other than our ignorance. We wouldn't be perceived as rivals. We weren't looking for herbal secrets—or, for that matter, any secrets at all—but only for whatever thoughts and experiences those we met cared to share. We would seek them out not as curiosities but as teachers, as guides, as human beings. We weren't looking for ceremonies or red-coal tricks or miracles, though maybe we'd bump into a few of those along the way. We weren't Indian "experts"—historical scholars, anthropologists, sociologists, or ethnohistorians. We would be just a couple of typically uninformed white journalists nosing around, looking for, of all things, *wisdom!* We weren't after *in*formation at all. We were after *trans*formation.

In a deeper sense we weren't even journalists. That was simply our pretext, our context, our worldly excuse for traveling into a mystic otherworld that we sensed calling us—the world of those we've come to call Wisdomkeepers. I remember that word popped out of my mouth one day as we were discussing just who exactly it was that we were going out to see on this spirit-journey. I'd been struck by the frequent use in Indian Country of the word *keepers,* and I was reeling off some variant phrases in hopes of finding a working title for this still undefined work we found ourself doing. Counting on my fingers I reeled off the titles of some of the people we'd met over the years: Wampum-keepers, Arrow-keepers, Firekeepers, Pipekeepers, Faithkeepers . . .

I stopped for a moment at Faithkeepers, a word used by the Iroquois to designate, in English, a ceremonial subchief. Somehow, beautiful as it was, it sounded just a bit too Christian for an overall title for the traditional spiritual elders we had in mind, few of whom would be particularly pleased by a Christian-sounding name. Indians, as I would come to realize, don't need the concept of "faith"—a kind of compulsory belief in something you can't really know about. In particular, Indians don't need "faith" in God; they see God, Wakan Tanka, the Great Holy, the Great Mysterious, in every stone, every tree, every blowing wind, every star. Faith is unnecessary for them; they can see what they believe in with their own two eyes and hear God in every stroke of lightning and thunder.

"God is Nature and Nature is God," Mathew King would teach us. Those who see that as "mere pantheism" may, of course, do so, but equating the world with God is not a "mere" anything. Belief in one God could as well be described as "mere" monotheism. These are all metaphors in any case—words used in a futile but necessary attempt to define the undefinable. Without accepting *some* metaphor, we would be blind to God altogether.

I decided against "Faithkeepers" as the word I was seeking and cast about in my mind for some other word growing out of the concept of "keepers" when, almost as if from a distance, I heard myself speak the word "Wisdomkeepers." It was like one of those lightbulbs going off above someone's head in the comics. The name we'd been looking for—*Wisdomkeepers*—was born. I recognized it instantly, as did Steve, and of course it would become the title of our first book years later.

※

But for now, we couldn't know that the disastrous, just-concluded *Ramblin' Tepee* trip with Two Trees would be seen as anything but a failure, at least from the magazine's point of view. What we'd tried to do had fallen apart. Two Trees, the very centerpiece of the story as originally conceived, was gone, off on his own, out of the picture. It would be tough going explaining to Garrett and the others at *Geographic* that we wanted to go on with this undefined project on our own.

More than a bit confused at just what we were about, yet feeling strangely enthusiastic at what might still come out of all this, Steve and I took a detour through Santa Fe to see my old *Geographic* colleague Fred Kline. Fred had been on the magazine editorial staff with me for half a dozen years back in the '70s. A poet, artist, raconteur, and a bit of a wild man, he'd found *Geographic* too confining for his maverick soul and had gone out west to become a freewheeling art dealer, gallery owner, professional fine-art appraiser, and "blue-sky dreamer," as he calls himself in one of his wonderful poems. I'd kept in touch with him over the years and was hoping for an occasion to visit him.

Fred became instantly excited over this idea of a journey to the spiritual elders. Being a poet, he instantly saw the poetry in it.

"You've got to meet Richard Erdoes!" Fred announced. "He lives right here in Santa Fe. He can give you the names of some Indian elders to see."

Richard Erdoes, author of several popular works on Native American spirituality and probably best known today as the coauthor with Mary Crow Dog of *Lakota Woman,* was already a near-legendary figure at that time. Fred gave him a call, and we were invited over to Richard's house that night. Richard, too, waxed enthusiastic over the project, though he cautioned us: "It's a hard, hard road you're going down. You can't imagine *how* hard." After a lovely dinner served by his vibrant wife, Jean, Richard gave us a list of Native American traditional elders he knew personally. "These guys are all the real thing," he said. "There's not a cigar-store Indian among them. They'll lead you down the right road."

We couldn't have imagined how important that list of names would become to us; of the seventeen Native American spiritual elders we included years later in our book *Wisdomkeepers,* six were on that list and five others grew immediately out of it. Richard told us, "You'll want to start with Chief Oren Lyons up at Onondaga, near Syracuse. He's not a medicine man, but he's a great spiritual and political leader, a Faithkeeper, and an eloquent spokesman for the Iroquois Six Nations Confederacy and for the traditionalist point of view in general. Oren will give you your bearings and keep you from getting in too much trouble. He'll give you introductions to the others—assuming he's willing to work with you fellows, of course."

I was surprised to see on Richard's list the name Frank Fools

Crow, the same Sioux, or Lakota, spiritual elder that my guide Tony Luscombe had told me about that night two years before with the Maestro and the condor in Peru. Seeing it there on his list gave me a strange and vibrant sense of recognition, even confirmation, and a distinct sense that we were doing precisely what we were supposed to be doing, unlikely as it may have seemed.

❈

Before we left Santa Fe that night, Fred gave us a brief tour of his museum-quality gallery in town, filled with exquisite pieces of art, from Western and Native American to ancient Roman. Earlier I'd shown him the owl's claw power stick that Joe Parra had given me. "I probably could get you a good price for that!" Fred had re-marked. "No way!" I'd said. Steve and I were properly impressed with Fred's magnificent collection. Steve particularly admired a bur-nished wooden antique cane with a stylized reptile carved into the handle. "Ahh. Yes, that one's a beauty all right," Fred explained. "It's a Seminole shaman's cane, I'm told. At least a century old." Steve eyed it covetously. On an impulse Fred took it off the wall and graciously presented it to him. "Oh, no, I couldn't!" Steve said. "Please," Fred insisted. "I want you to have it. I have a feeling it'll open some doors for you. It'll give me a sense of going with you. Please, I insist!"

Shaking his head, Steve accepted the cane.

"I guess it means we'll be going to the Seminole!" he said, fondly stroking the cane's beautifully carved reptile-headed handle.

The next day, Steve drove me back to Farmington for my flight home to D.C. The *Ramblin' Tepee* trip may have been a bust, but at least we had Richard Erdoes's list and that Seminole shaman's cane—two items that would prove crucial to us, it turned out, in the years ahead.

When I retrieved my bags at the airport, I realized I didn't have the owl's claw power stick.

"I left it at Fred's! Right there in his gallery!" I lamented.

"Maybe that's where it belongs," Steve said. "Maybe you're not supposed to have that claw with you, Harvey. Maybe *Fred's* the one who's supposed to have it now—at least for the time being."

It was a vaguely comforting thought, though I could have kicked myself for being so careless. I phoned Fred, and he promised to keep it for me.

"I won't sell it!" he vowed.

Looking back on my stupid act of forgetfulness, it now makes sense to me. I hadn't really forgotten the claw; it had simply decided on its own to stay at Fred's for safekeeping. What's more, in a strange sort of way it had been transmuted into something else: the Seminole shaman's cane. The cane and the claw had simply exchanged themselves.

❅

When I got back to National Geographic Society headquarters, I informed Bill Garrett of Two Trees' abrupt departure. I also pitched him on the notion of Steve and I continuing the article on our own. To my amazement he agreed. That Shawnee great-grandmother must have been working overtime whispering to his soul.

Even Joe Judge seemed to show a certain enthusiasm for the idea. He'd never believed in Two Trees anyway. "You and Steve go out and see what you can come up with," he said. "But Harvey, please—don't go *mystical* on us!"

Our journey on the path of the Wisdomkeepers had begun.

T*wo* *Following the Path*

TOWAOC

❈

Chapter 6

CHIEF Oren Lyons, Iroquois Faithkeeper—the first name on Richard Erdoes's list—eyed us suspiciously that wintry night in January 1983 when Steve and I made our first visit to Onondaga, capital of the millennium-old Iroquois Confederacy. We met, as per the appointment we'd set up, outside Dewasenta's Iroquois Souvenirs shop.

"So—we meet in the dark!" were my first words to the shadowy figure who approached us, hand outstretched in greeting, as we got out of our rented car.

"Darkness is our friend!" were his first words to us.

In our blissful ignorance Steve and I had no idea that Dennis Banks, the American Indian Movement militant, on the lam from the FBI, had taken refuge only a few nights before on the Onondaga reservation, just south of Syracuse, New York. The FBI knew he was there, and so did just about everyone else but Steve and me. We were looking for the spiritual, not the political, but were quickly discovering that the two are often one and the same when you're on the path of the Wisdomkeepers. Oren later admitted he'd thought we might be FBI agents ourselves, snooping about disguised as a writer-photographer team from *National Geographic*.

"We had you guys checked out the next day," he told us. "Made some phone calls to *Geographic* headquarters. Sure enough, you were for real. It was almost disappointing."

He led us up to his hideaway log-cabin lodge and took us inside, lighting a kerosene lantern to get a better look at these two unlikely white intruders.

We sat down around a wooden table, and I nervously murmured an explanation, how we were looking for the Elders, the Old Ones, the Grandfathers, and the Grandmothers.

Oren shook his head gravely. "You think we turn our Elders over to anyone who walks in the door?"

He leaned forward almost aggressively, elbows on the table, hands half-formed into fists. (I later learned he'd been a Golden Gloves boxing champion in his youth.)

"We guard them like pure springwater!"

His words rang with a rare authenticity and power. While snow rattled against the windowpanes, he began what was to be for us a years-long—and still ongoing—indoctrination into a new way of thinking, not only about Indians but about human existence itself.

"So what is it you guys want from our Elders? Secrets? Mystery?"

"We'd just like to talk to them about whatever they'd care to share with us," I explained.

"That's good," Oren said, "because I can tell you right now, there are no secrets. There's no mystery. There's only common sense."

He went on: "We're our own law here. This is sovereign territory. There's no BIA here at Onondaga. This isn't the United States. This land belongs to the Haudenosaunee, the 'People of the Longhouse'—that's what we call ourselves. We have our own government, our own Grand Council a thousand years old that meets in the Longhouse right here and it's on an equal footing with your government in Washington. We're willing to deal with you only nation to nation—the Six Nations Iroquois Confederacy and the United States government, both of us equal."

I was amazed. He spoke not tentatively or pugnaciously but calmly and firmly, with a natural authority. He continued holding forth on a wide range of subjects, with an emphasis on something called Natural Law:

"What law are you living under? United States law? That's man's law . . . but there's another law, the Creator's law. We call it Natural

Law. It supersedes man's law. If you violate the Natural Law, you're going to get hit and get hit hard. All life on Mother Earth depends on the pure water. If you kill the water, you kill the life that depends on it, your own included. That's Natural Law. It's also common sense."

He also introduced us to the concept of the Seventh Generation:

"With every decision we make, we always keep in mind the Seventh Generation to come, the generations still unborn. When we walk upon Mother Earth, we always plant our feet carefully because we know the faces of future generations are looking up at us from beneath the ground. We never forget them!"

In one corner of the room hung an array of Iroquois ceremonial False Face masks, their faces turned to the wall. Steve was looking over at them with a photographer's appraising eye. Oren picked up on his thought.

"We show their faces only during ceremonies. And we never allow photographs of our ceremonies. *Never!* So don't even think of asking!"

We returned to the possibility of meeting some of the Iroquois spiritual elders.

Oren simply shook his head.

"I can bring the matter up before the Grand Council," he said doubtfully. "But I can tell you they're a tough-nosed bunch of guys. Not much they all agree on. If even one says no, then it's no. The way our government, our democracy works, each and every one of the peace chiefs has to agree. And, frankly, in a matter like this, two white journalists asking to see the elders, there's not much chance they'll say yes. If they can't come to an agreement, then they just drop it. That's because there's no problem that's important enough to cause divisions within the Confederacy or among the people. The Peacemaker who founded our Confederacy a thousand years ago told us we must be of one mind. Those are good words to remember—today or any day."

"Well," I persisted, "could you ask them anyway? I can promise you the elders will be treated with the greatest respect. We'd like to bring their wisdom and their message to the world."

Oren smiled gently, obviously still a bit doubtful about us.

"I'll try, I'll try," he said. "You guys got a little time?"

We told him we did.

"Have to wait for the right moment," he said. "Too much going on right now. I'll let you know when the chiefs have an answer for you."

We were both more than a little awed by Oren. His words rang with a rare power, more than we could even begin to absorb. On the path of the Wisdomkeepers, we were finding, you need to have not only patience—"You guys got a little time?"—but also an ever-ready openness of mind, an expectation of the unexpected. On Great Turtle Island, learning tends to come not gradually and in an orderly sequence but all at once, spontaneously, unexpectedly, like a sudden shower of meteorites. Oren's words had been like that; he'd all but overwhelmed us with ideas in a forty-minute introductory conversation: "We guard them like pure springwater . . . Natural Law . . . the Seventh Generation . . . We must be of One Mind . . . There's no mystery, there's only common sense . . . The Peacemaker . . . Sovereignty . . . the Six Nations Iroquois Confederacy and the United States government . . . both of us equal . . ." Everything he spoke of was ancient yet seemed shiningly new, utterly original. This was definitely no "quaint" Indian but one extraordinary human being.

❊

Figuring it would take Oren a few days, even weeks, to get an okay for our proposal from the Confederacy chiefs, and not wanting to lose momentum, we decided to grab a plane immediately from icy upstate New York to the steamy Everglades of Florida. During my research in *Geographic's* news clipping archive, I'd come across a yellowed article from the early 1970s telling of an elderly Seminole medicine man named Buffalo Jim, who had taken part in a brief-lived government program to promote the preservation of traditional healing arts. Just outside of Fort Lauderdale, at the Seminole tribal offices in Hollywood, we spoke to Tribal Chairman James Billie, who could have been a movie double for Billy Jack. "Buffalo doesn't speak much English," he told us. "Go see Joe Jumper out at Big Cypress. He's Buffalo's friend and student. He'll take you out to see the old man and translate for you."

We drove out Alligator Alley to the Big Cypress reservation in the Florida Everglades, and, with Joe Jumper at our side to translate, met Buffalo Jim in his small cinderblock house, where a pharmaceutical garden of herbal remedies grew right up to his door. Wearing a

loose-wound red turban like those you see in pictures of Seminole chiefs and medicine men from the 1840s, Buffalo Jim—Jim's his family name, Buffalo his first name—peered at us with bright dark eyes nested in wrinkles. His deep-etched face breathed antiquity. We asked him what he'd like to talk about.

He said, "Ask me questions from your heart, and I'll give you answers from my heart."

"But what would *you* like to talk about?" we asked him, not wanting to direct the conversation.

Buffalo thought awhile, nodded his head at some inward thought, then announced with a smile: "We can talk of birds! Birds have always been important to the Indian because they go where they wish, they light where they may, and they're free. The eagle flies highest in the sky of all the birds, so he's the nearest to the Creator and his feather is the most sacred of all. He belongs to all the tribes, to all the peoples. And then each tribe has a lesser bird of its own. For the Seminole, it's the heron."

I was puzzled at the time. Here we'd hoped to speak to him of the profoundest meanings, and he started off talking about birds! It seemed irrelevant, almost quaint.

"Birds are spirit-messengers," he went on. "They do the Creator's bidding. Always pay attention to them!"

Strange, looking back now over the years, how birds have again and again become meaningful to us. It was an owl's claw and an eagle's feather that launched this journey of ours in the first place. There was the Maestro's condor in Peru, which I now see as another kind of personal foretelling. And there would be others: Frank Fools Crow's miraculous eagle at Wounded Knee, the crows that foretold our friend Lee Lyons's death, the seemingly living eagle in the red coals at the Ute peyote ceremony. You either see and acknowledge such signs, or you don't. They're not true unless you make them so. Like everything else on the path of the Wisdomkeepers, they assume for you the meaning you choose to give them. Disregard them, negate them, and they give back to you exactly what you've given to them—nothing. We create our own meanings.

I remember once, as a child of eight or nine, I casually tossed a stick at a pigeon on a sidewalk in Chicago and, to my astonishment, actually hit it. The bird squawked and flapped its wings and ran around in frantic circles, then simply keeled over, dead. Out of the second-story window of a nearby three-story redbrick apartment building a blond girl my age called out at me, "Killer! Killer! Killer!" I ran away in shame, filled with a terrible guilt and sense of sacrilege. It wasn't simply that I had killed it but that I had killed it stupidly and needlessly, without respect.

Lakota elder Mathew King would later tell us, "You need to respect the animal you kill. It's following God's instructions, too."

We of the "dominant" culture have our ornithologists and our bird-watchers and our parakeet fanciers; but, alas, to us, birds carry no message. We may eat them, shoot them for sport, put them in cages to admire their beauty, but we set no meaning on their comings and goings. To the indigenous mind, on the other hand, birds are natural carriers of meaning. Their comings and goings are no mere happenstance. They are spirit-messengers, signs to be read, intimations of our innermost selves.

Buffalo Jim went on to speak of many things, including the end of the world: "The earth is like an animal. When an animal's sick, it wiggles and it twitches. And just before it dies it shakes even harder, it shakes all over. That's what we call the earthquake and the volcano and the hurricane. Yes, it's already starting to happen. And it'll get worse—you'll see! The world is wiggling and twitching and shaking just before it dies!"

He continued: "The Creator told us there will be three signs just before the world ends. The first sign, He said, is that we would lose our language. And already our young people can't speak the old language anymore. They don't know how to pray. And the second sign, He told us, is that we'd lose our way of dressing, our original beautiful costume of many colors that the Creator gave us. And, you see, now we wear cowboy hats and boots and white man's clothes. Only a few of us wear the old costume anymore. We still weave some of the old colors and patterns into our clothes—like my many-colored vest here—but for most Seminole people today the color has gone out of our lives. And the third sign, the last sign the Creator told us about, is that we'd forget how to make our sacred fire. And, see, we've forgotten. No one really knows how to do it anymore. They may try, but they don't really know if they're doing it the right way. I can barely remember myself how the Old Ones did it. I was just a boy then in the 1890s. Here, let me show you."

He took some dried fibrous material, the inner bark of the cypress tree—the traditional sacred kindling used in Seminole ceremonies—and held it up in the air with the little fingers of his left hand. With his left thumb and index finger he held a small rock he had picked up off the ground. With his right hand he then grabbed an aluminum fork from a table and, with a grunt, sharply struck the aluminum fork against the rock. Again and again he struck the two together as if somehow expecting a spark to shoot out from the meeting of soft metal and soft stone. "That's how we did it in those days," Buffalo said apologetically. "That's how we used the flint and the steel to make the spark to light the sacred fire. It . . . it doesn't work anymore. . . ." His voice seemed infinitely sad.

On another visit we returned to Big Cypress with a piece of red Georgia flint lent to us for the occasion by the Smithsonian Institution. We also brought along the Seminole shaman's cane that Fred Kline had given us in "exchange" for the owl's claw.

Buffalo held the lovely flint rock in the palm of his hand.

"Yes," he said, "that's the kind of flint we used. But there's still something missing. . . . The steel piece to make the spark! Here, maybe this will work."

Again he took a piece of cypress-bark kindling, then lifted a long-bladed steel knife high in the air and struck the blade against the flintstone. He only managed to gash his thumb. No spark. No sacred fire. Buffalo just shook his head, looking even sadder than at his previous attempt. "Can't do it," he said. "Just can't do it."

On an impulse I handed him a pack of matches.

"Here, Buffalo," I said consolingly, "try using this."

Sighing, he struck a match and simply lit the cypress kindling. The fibrous material instantly flared up in his fingers. Buffalo held it for a finger-singeing moment, then dropped it on the ground where it burned brightly for a few seconds before guttering out. It was, to be sure, an improper sacred fire, yet nonetheless poignantly sacred to those of us standing there.

"I'm not sure that will hold off the end of the world much longer," Buffalo said.

"Maybe for a while," I said. "Maybe for a little while longer."

We showed Buffalo the cane that Fred Kline had given us. He

took it across his knees and stroked its burnished length with his fingers, as if it were alive. "Yes, yes, it's Seminole!" he confirmed. "It's very, very old . . . even older than me. It comes from a long, long time ago. It belonged to a chief, a Seminole chief, someone very important."

"What's that carving on the handle?" I asked.

Buffalo squinted at it, turning the handle around and around in his long bony fingers—which, oddly, seemed the same burnished brown color and weathered texture as the cane itself. His fingers seemed to grow right out of the handle.

"It looks like maybe an alligator. Could be he was alligator clan, but we don't have any alligator clan anymore. No . . . it's probably not an alligator. I think it's a snake, a snake with legs. In the old days they used to have that kind of snake. It could walk. We have songs about it. Here, I'll sing you a song."

Buffalo threw his head back and let out a throaty, almost hissing chant, his fingers drumming on the tabletop.

"That's a snake song," he said, "about a snake with legs. See, he can stand up! He's got hands! He steals little children—and their mothers, too! Good thing we don't have that snake anymore, or he might get you guys!"

He laughed with open amusement, making clutching movements toward us in the air with his hands. I was instantly reminded of Charlie Knight's gestures when talking about the stick people.

"But you guys don't have to worry," Buffalo went on. He took the cane back in his hands, fondling it gently as he talked. "This stick was like—what do you call it?—a passport, a visa, like you get to go to a foreign country. A stick like this was given by a chief to a special visitor. He could use it to travel safely anywhere in Seminole country. Nobody would hurt him so long as he had it."

He shook his head slowly, sadly.

"We don't have sticks like this anymore because . . . because today we don't even own our land." His voice trailed off. I remembered seeing a sign as we'd entered the Big Cypress reservation: PROPERTY U.S. DEPARTMENT OF THE INTERIOR. It had been riddled with dozens of bullet holes.

"We lost the land back then," Buffalo continued in a barely audible voice. "Yeah, we lost it. We're still here . . . but we lost the land. Sometimes . . . sometimes I think we're only visitors here, too."

He asked to keep the cane with him overnight. "I can feel the power of the man who made it," he said. "His power's still in it."

When we returned the next morning, Buffalo was agitated. "A man came in a dream to me last night," he told us, "a very old man . . . bent over like this. But he was very powerful. He wore deerskin trousers and a colored Seminole shirt, and he had a red turban on his head. He was a medicine man, a great chief of our people, and, yes, a sorcerer! It was the man who made this walking stick! His power's still in it, you guys, so you'd better take care. It can help you, but it can kill you, too! Yes, a sorcerer! Maybe it was Coacoochee—Chief Wildcat himself. He was the greatest leader. The white men couldn't kill him. He could make a miracle. He knew the old instructions. There won't be any more leaders like that. All be dead. All be dead forever! You'd better watch out, you two. Maybe he wants his stick back! If he does, you'll see—he'll take it!"

We offered the cane to Buffalo, and he seemed about to take it when he hesitated. "Thank you. Yes, I'd like to have it, but . . . here . . . you take it for now, you two. You need it a while longer. It helps protect you. When you don't need it anymore, then bring it back."

In 1990, seven years later, at a moving little ceremony out at Big Cypress with Buffalo and Tribal Chairman James Billie, we would finally return the cane to the Seminole tribe of Florida. Buffalo took the cane gratefully. He nodded, listening to an inner voice, and then looked up.

"Coacoochee's glad to get it back!" he exclaimed.

"Tell him thanks," I said.

Buffalo smiled. "I'll tell him."

Fearing Wildcat might have "worked some spell" into the cane, Buffalo prepared a bitter tea of swampland herbs for us—to ward off evil influences on our continuing journey, he said. He gave each of us a cupful to drink, then instructed us to splash the remainder over ourselves for the next three days. "That way Wildcat won't bother you," he said. It did make us reek a bit for a time, but nothing to compare with Two Trees' wormwood.

❖

The next name on Richard Erdoes's list was Ojibway traditionalist Eddie Benton-Banai, a founder of the American Indian Movement and, at that time, head of the Red School House, a noted alternative high school in St. Paul, Minnesota, providing immersion in traditional Indian ways and philosophy. Oren Lyons had also suggested we see Eddie. "He'll straighten out your thinking for you," Oren told us. We found ourselves, in a sense, being passed on from elder to elder.

Eddie, like Oren, was vigorous and barely fifty, no graybeard by any stretch of the imagination. Many of the Wisdomkeepers, we were finding, are not necessarily "old." Though Two Trees had been right that the Old Ones were dying, as inevitably they must, they are definitely not dying out. Despite oft-heard lamentations about the inevitable death of aboriginal culture, everywhere we would go—at last count some seventy indigenous communities in North America, South America, Central America, and Australia—we would find a new generation of traditionalist spiritual and political leaders emerging, men and women of tremendous ability, dedication, and vision.

These, rest assured, are no vanishing people. Under an ongoing attack, yes, but vanishing no. The very word *aboriginal* means "out of the beginning," and they continue, as they always have, as guardians of the beginning, custodians of the earth, representatives of the aboriginal within us all. They guard not simply some quaint forgotten lifeway, but—for all the assaults upon it—a living and breathing Way.

Just how living a Way was instantly apparent the morning Steve and I arrived at the Red School House, which is housed in an old redbrick parochial school in the backstreets of St. Paul. "Suffer the little children to come unto me" the engraved words proclaim on the lintel above the doorway. The school day begins with a prayer here, but it was no Roman Catholic hymn that we heard as we entered the building. It was the voice of The Little Boy, as the Ojibway call him, the spirit of the sacred Ojibway water-drum—speaking in booming tones through the school corridors.

We followed the drumming to its source, a large open classroom filled with concentric circles of onlookers. And there, in the middle of the centermost circle, sat Eddie Benton-Banai and several youngsters, all flailing away in absolute concentration, beating the taut and vibrant drum skin and spontaneously filling the universe with the voice of The Little Boy. Now the drum was momentarily stilled, and a tiny sacred fire was lit in a ceremonial vessel; the air was suddenly filled with the soul-vivifying aromas of sage and sweetgrass. Eddie crumbled a few grains of Indian tobacco into the little fire, and tendrils of white smoke rose through shafts of sunlight and curled out the open schoolroom window. The chanting prayers of Eddie, his eyes tightly closed as he sang, his ecstatic face gleaming with sweat, rose up the sunlit shafts and through the window, following the rising wisps of smoke—no, not so much following them as rising in unison, in complete oneness, with them.

The spiritual power in that classroom was palpable. Steve and I stood there at the rear of the room, and we could feel it down to our toes. Whatever it might be, however you might want to interpret it, we were damn well immersed in it. Now the water-drum started booming again beneath the flailing drumsticks, and the voice of The Little Boy once again filled the universe. Our bodies, our beings, vibrated with it. Finally, the drumming and chanting subsided. We snapped back into the ordinary world. The morning school bell clanged, the children grabbed their books and headed off to class, and Eddie Benton-Banai walked up to us, hand held out in greeting.

He made that tentative movement traditionalists often make with their hands as, with raised thumb, they test to see if you are going to give them the AIM handshake—grasp the thumb, then clasp the curled fingertips, finish with the short double-pump handshake. I have never quite gotten it right and don't try to. I don't like faking it. I just grab their outstretched hand and pump it soundly, white man's way. I'm not apologetic about it, but I'm conscious of that momentary disappointed look in their eyes as they return my ordinary handshake.

Eddie was brusque but not unfriendly. He made it clear that he had things to do, urgent things. "I'm sorry I won't have much time for you today," he apologized. He ushered us into his little office and gestured for us to sit down. Then for a few moments he sat there in his swivel chair behind his big school administrator's desk, looking us over. I had the sense that I often have with Indian elders—of being a bug on a pin. We white people tend to look away evasively, almost askance, from Indians' eyes, even while the Indians, if they're not looking away altogether themselves, are politely but firmly probing hard into ours. Eddie Benton-Banai eyed us that way, with an enigmatic smile on his lips. His eyes can alternately twinkle or gleam with a dark luster like polished black stones. They weren't easy to look into. I sensed in him the same kind of expectant mystery I'd felt with the Maestro. Certainly he was a man complex in every way, not only a founder of AIM, the American Indian Movement, and of the Red School House but also grand chief of the Three Fires Society, a fourth-level Midewiwin priest, an author, philosopher, poet, teacher, educational consultant, and, for a time, coach of the Red School House football team.

I told him we were hoping to meet some Ojibway spiritual elders.

"Don't call me an elder," he said firmly. "I've yet to earn that honor from my people. But it's still good you've come," he said. "You *National Geographic* types usually go to the Tribal Councils, not to us traditionals. So I welcome you. It's time to draw back the buckskin curtain. Yes, the time is here!"

He went on to tell us: "I'm a full-blood Indian man . . . a *spiritual* Indian man. My real name is Bawdway Wi Dun. It means Messenger and is derived from the Thunder Beings. I was born in a wigwam by natural childbirth, and I was raised in total Ojibway traditional manner. I didn't begin speaking English until age ten. I was chosen, prepared, and taught to be a Midewiwin teacher. Currently I hold a fourth-degree priesthood in the Midewiwin Lodge of the Ojibway people. There are seven levels in all, and I have a long way to go before reaching the seventh level. Unfortunately, there's no one to teach us about the highest levels anymore. We have to pick up things our people left along the trail. Too many of our Elders died too quick back then. They didn't have time to pass the old knowledge down. So we Indians today have to go back and find the things that got left along the trail. We have to educate ourselves to know who we are. That's what the Red School House is all about." He continued:

"Personally, I'm sovereign. Sovereignty isn't something someone gives you. It's a responsibility you carry inside yourself. In order for my people to achieve sovereignty, each man and woman among us has to be sovereign. Sovereignty begins with yourself!"

Eddie arched his dark brows and speared our souls with his hard-probing eyes.

"But right now," he told us, "I'm very busy. My life belongs to my people. There are a hundred other things I have to tend to right now. You come back another time, and we'll have more to talk about then. I appreciate it when people come back. People who come back a second time and a third and a fourth—those are the ones it's worth getting to know. Hey, they're having the tenth anniversary of the Wounded Knee siege out at Pine Ridge in just a few days. I wish I could be there, but I can't. You two should go out there. With a little luck you might even meet Frank Fools Crow and Mathew King. Tell them both hello from Eddie. If you're looking for spiritual Elders, you won't find any any higher than those two. Frank and Mat, two really great men. They're what being Elders is all about. Yeah, if they feel like talking to you, Mat and Frank'll have a few things to teach you, I'd guess."

He stood up. The brief interview was over. We weren't being passed over; we were being passed on.

"There's only one price I ask you to pay," Eddie said somewhat ominously as he showed us out, "and, I'm sorry, but it's a very high price."

I thought to myself, "Uh-oh, this is going to cost *Geographic* a few bucks."

He went on: "I ask you to pay the price of *attention!* If you're willing to pay that price, you may just learn something! I hope you do. Have a good road, you two. And remember, when you're meeting people as high as Fools Crow and Mat King, *pay attention!* You owe them that."

First my guide Tony Luscombe in Peru, then Richard Erdoes in Santa Fe, then Iroquois Faithkeeper Oren Lyons at Onondaga, now Ojibway Midewiwin priest Eddie Benton-Banai had pointed us toward Lakota elders Frank Fools Crow and Mathew King. Yes, we would pay attention. Looking back, I can see now that Eddie's admonition was one of our Original Instructions, one of the inescapable requirements of following the path of the Wisdomkeepers: *Pay attention!*

❊

We flew directly from Minneapolis–St. Paul to Rapid City, South Dakota, a flight memorable first for its turbulence and then for the odd optical phenomenon that appeared outside the airplane window. Steve, I remember, grew bluish during the turbulence episode—as wild a shaking as either of us has ever experienced—and, half sick, had nodded off into a numbed state in the aisle seat. A touch green-edged myself, I gazed out from my window seat at the cloudscape unreeling beneath us, looking for some point of stability out there, only to find my attention slowly focusing on something wondrously strange going on beyond the wing tips.

We were flying directly above a flat-topped layer of pale greenish gray clouds, and I was surprised to see the shadow of our own plane flying along on the cloud tops just below and behind us. Now, to my growing amazement, a small circular rainbow disk appeared off to the right, flying along the tops of the clouds with us. An optical phenomenon of some kind, no doubt. It gave me a weird feeling. Here was the little rainbow circle up ahead of us, and the shadow of the plane flying along on the cloud tops behind us. I'd never seen anything like it.

I nudged Steve for him to get a picture of the strange phenomenon, but, still shaken by the turbulence, he only moaned, "No way, Harvey. I can't even look out the window. You take the picture if you want a picture!"

I grabbed my seldom-used Olympus 2 camera from my shoulder bag under the seat and in several minutes shot half a roll of film, recording the strange visual event transpiring outside the window. The shadow of the plane kept approaching the rainbow, getting closer and closer until it actually flew right into the center of the rainbow! I was utterly amazed. For a minute or more the circular rainbow with the shadow of our plane within it flew along the cloud tops, the two images seemingly fused into one.

"Steve, you've got to see this!" I cried out, shaking him.

"Leave me alone," he groaned, hands over his eyes.

I snapped away. The shadow of the plane flew right through the flat circular disk of the rainbow. I doubt I could describe it credibly even to myself if I didn't have the sequence of images now on film to look at—pale but distinct, the plane's shadow and the circular rainbow slowly approaching each other, converging, then fusing into one astonishing double image, the plane within the rainbow, then the two images gradually separating and, finally, dissolving. No doubt there's a simple scientific explanation, some ordinary trick of optics at work here, but I took it—and take it still—as a sign of protection. We flew right through the rainbow that day, Steve and I, heading out to Great Turtle Island. What's more, we had been given safe passage as we traveled the path of the Wisdomkeepers—or so we choose to see it. Yes, so we choose to see it.

The miraculous dogged us again the next day when we drove out to Pine Ridge and, standing atop the holy hill of Wounded Knee, we watched Frank Fools Crow literally pray an eagle out of the empty South Dakota sky.

Several hundred people had gathered on Cemetery Hill above historic Wounded Knee Creek, where in 1890 the Seventh Cavalry, Custer's old unit, slaughtered some three hundred Lakota men, women, and children of Chief Big Foot's band in the last and perhaps most infamous "battle" of the Indian Wars. Here, too, in 1973, AIM traditionalists seized the little reservation community of Wounded Knee to protest intolerable conditions on the reservation, launching a seventy-one-day siege that became the longest insurrection in U.S. history since the Civil War. Now, exactly ten years later to the day—February 27, 1983—this memorial gathering stood listening to the words of the famed old ceremonial chief. Fools Crow, in

his full ritual regalia, lifted his blue-feathered sacred pipe—central symbol of Lakota religion—to the skies and prayed into the whipping wind in the somber-toned Lakota language as the sweetly pungent scent of sage and sweetgrass wafted over the crowd and the eagle-bone whistle was blown four times in each of the four sacred directions. He was asking, the man beside me explained in a whisper, for a sign that Wakan Tanka, the Great Spirit, the Great Mysterious, still remembered His Indian children.

Moments later a murmur went through the crowd. "Look up there!" voices cried. We looked up, and there, high overhead, circling, circling in that vast empty dome of South Dakota sky, was an eagle!

"Now you know the power of Wounded Knee!" a man yelled out.

A hush fell over the crowd. Steve stood beside me watching, as much in pain as in awe. Here was *the* miracle . . . and no cameras were allowed!

After the ceremony we presented Fools Crow with a pound of fine tobacco and tried to arrange an interview. He gruffly accepted the tobacco but shook his head about the interview. He spoke little English—at least to outsiders. One of his aides told us, "Frank says to go see Mat King in Kyle. He's the one you need to talk to." He told us Mathew King—or Chief Noble Red Man—was Fools Crow's official interpreter and a noted spokesman for the traditional chiefs.

I remember our disappointment at the chief's brusque rejection of our request for a private meeting. Here Fools Crow had given us two extraordinary gifts—a clear glimpse of the miraculous and an introduction to one of the most extraordinary human beings on the planet—and, with typical opacity of vision, we were disappointed. But we wouldn't be for long . . .

We drove out the next morning to Kyle and knocked on the screen door of Mathew King's little government-built house. We'd been told that Mat wasn't a medicine man but a spiritual and political leader, a man revered for his fierce honesty and uncompromising traditionalist attitudes. In recent decades he and Fools Crow had helped bring the long-banned Sun Dance back not only to Lakota territory but to reservations around the country. They stood among the preeminent spiritual leaders of the Great Indian Reawakening that began in the late 1960s. During the 1973 siege of Wounded Knee, Mat and Frank had counseled and supported the AIM militants. Mathew had been marked by the FBI as "the mean one of the bunch." Tough-nosed he was, and implacable when it came to defending the rights of his people, but there was absolutely nothing mean-spirited about Mathew King.

At our knock, an impish gent with short-cropped white hair and a wonderfully sweet if toothless smile came to the door. I started going into my standard introductory spiel again, how we were there seeking the Elders.

Mat waved a hand abruptly in the air. "There's no need to explain," he told us in a gentle but no-nonsense voice. "I know why you're here! White man came to this country and lost his Original Instructions. That's why you're here. You're looking for the instructions you lost. Maybe you figure we Indians have them. Maybe you even figure you can steal them from us like you stole the land. Well, you can't. You can't live someone else's instructions. You've got to live your own. I can't tell you what your Original Instructions were, but maybe there are some things I can explain. Some of God's instructions are for *all* of us. Those are the ones that teach us how to be human. They're the Original Instructions on being human. They're for everyone, even you guys. It's time we Indians tell the world what we know . . . about nature . . . and about God. . . . So come on in and sit down, you two. I'm going to tell you what I know and who I am. You guys better listen. You got a lot to learn."

Over the following days as we sat in his little living room, Mat instructed us on the art of being human. He told us: "God gives His instructions to every creature according to His plan for the world. He gave His instructions to all the things of nature. The birch tree and the pine tree, they still follow their instructions and do their duty in God's world. The flowers, even the littlest flower, they bloom and they pass away according to His instructions. The birds, even the smallest bird, they live and they fly and they sing according to His instructions. Should human beings be any different?"

He went on: "Our instructions are very simple: to respect the earth and to respect each other, to respect life itself. That's our first commandment. That's the first line of our Gospel."

He said, "We don't need your church. We have the Black Hills for our church. And we don't need your Bible. We have the wind and

the rain and the stars for our Bible. The world is an open Bible for us. We've studied it for millions of years."

He spoke of the Three Powers: the material, the spiritual, and the supernatural.

"God put Three Powers into the world for us to use. The material power is the goodness of this earth. The spiritual power is the goodness of human beings. The supernatural power is the goodness of God, the Great Spirit, the Great Mysterious. He made those Three Powers all separate. They're not connected. It's the job of human beings to make that connection.

"The material life isn't worth living. Materialism without spirituality is the curse of this world. It's our job as human beings to use the material in the service of the spiritual. Spiritual power is the power to do good, to follow God's instructions. We don't have to do it. It's up to us.

"That's the spiritual power. It's what makes us human.

"The third power is the supernatural power. You can't use it for yourself. That's sorcery. It's supposed to use you. If you're using your spiritual power, then God will use His supernatural power to help you."

He explained his frequent use of the word *God.*

"In English I call Him God or the Great Spirit. In Lakota we say Wakan Tanka—the Great Mystery, the Great Mysterious. You can't define Him. He's not actually a 'he' or a 'she' or a 'him' or a 'her.' We have to use those kinds of words because you can't just say 'it.' God's never an 'it.'"

He continued: "Everyone is sacred. You're sacred and I'm sacred. Every time you blink your eye or I blink my eye, God blinks His eyes. God sees through your eyes and through my eyes. We are sacred."

I was particularly struck that an Indian, a member of one of history's most oppressed and dumped-upon peoples, could speak the following:

"*Goodness* is the natural state of this world. The world is *good!* Even when it seems evil, it's good. There's only goodness in God. And that same goodness is in us all. You can feel it in yourself. You know when you feel good inside.

"Yes, you're God's child, too. You are good. You are sacred. Respect yourself. Love the goodness in yourself.

"*Then put that goodness out into the world!*"

"That's everybody's instructions!"

Mat taught us that wisdom isn't something you believe; it's something you do. He told us: "When we want wisdom, we go up on the hill and talk to God. Yes, you can talk to God up on a hill by yourself. We use Bear Butte, but you can use any high place you like. When you're up there, you can say anything you want. That's between you and God and nobody else. It's a great feeling to be talking to God. I know. I did it way up on the mountain. The wind was blowing. It was dark. It was cold. And I stood there and *I talked to God!*"

We asked him for a blessing for this spirit-journey of ours. At first he demurred. He thought awhile, then said: "If you'll make me one promise, I'll give you a blessing. I can't really make you promise something you can't do. I'm hoping you'll help Indian people on this journey of yours, but there's no way to be sure you'll do that. So I'll ask you just one thing, and it's this: Promise me you *won't hurt* Indian people. Just promise me that, and I'll give you my blessing."

We promised, assuming a lifetime obligation we have striven to honor. Mat said, "God's making use of you. He's sending you out to reveal the life of the Indian people. That's a good thing. You guys are lucky. You should be grateful He's found a use for you."

He had us set Steve's camera and my pen on a chair cushion in the middle of the living room. He said, "I'll bless them so you don't do any harm with them to Indian people."

Raising his arms, he prayed for several minutes in the Lakota language, talking to God as he'd done so often throughout his life. Finishing, he took Steve's eagle feather and circled our heads with it four times, then "combed" us with it front and back from head to foot. I could feel a charge of energy, like a great wind blowing right through us.

"I told God what you two guys are doing," he said. "He tells me you're going to have a good journey. No harm'll come to the Indian people from what you're doing, and no harm'll come to you two while you're doing it. I asked Him to bless these two men and take care of them."

We've done our best to live up to that blessing over the years. It has carried us this far, and we suspect the journey is still far from over. We'll still be needing it.

At the end of one of our last meetings, while Steve was stowing his camera gear in the backseat and I was already sitting up front in the passenger seat, Mat came up to me, that impish yet somehow angelic smile beaming on his face, leaned his blue-shirted elbow on the car door, looked me right in the eye as if about to comment casually on the weather, and said, "You know, sometimes . . . sometimes I see beyond this world. I see a Great Reality. It's the Great Reality of God, that's what I call it. People like you may not know it's there, but it's there. If you look, you can see it. It's right over there somewhere . . . right where you never thought to look before."

He pointed a finger into the sky.

"Yeah, just keep looking and you'll see it someday. Maybe not clear, but you'll see it. The Great Reality of God, that's what it is. There's no evil there, it's all good. There's no evil in God. This world we're living in comes right out of that world, just like a drop of dew comes out of the night sky and then goes back with morning. It's where our prayers go to when we pray."

He gazed up, eyes misty, shook his head, and half-chuckled. His angelic smile flickered somewhat at that point. His eyes sparked. His nostrils flared. He sniffed, looking at me hard.

"There's buffalo there. Yeah, buffalo. All the buffalo the white man ever killed. And there are spirit-warriors on their horses, too—all the warriors who ever got killed for being Indians. They've gone on to that Great Reality. There's no suffering there. It's where everyone who lives a life with God is headed to.

"My wife's there right now. She keeps calling for me to come on over and join her there. 'This is the best place,' she tells me. She's getting impatient waiting. 'Just wait awhile longer,' I keep telling her. 'There's still things I gotta do in this world.'"

He stepped back, tapped the brim of his cowboy hat with his finger in a fond farewell, nodding to himself as much as to me.

"Yeah, the Great Reality. That's what I call it."

He smiled again and winked at me. Someone watching the two of us would think he had just given me directions to the nearest gas station. In fact, he'd laid out a road map for the rest of my life.

✻

The sheer poetry of this man's rough-hewn and disarmingly simple words set my soul spinning like a weathervane in a high wind. He was giving us a kind of inner compass for following the path. His words became beacons marking the way we were to follow.

I remember Chumash elder Juanita Centeno once telling me how at night, when she was a child, the glowing eyes of owls had guided her home like landing lights at an airport. The path is dark, unseen; something has to light your way from time to time. You sometimes need a guide, occasional assistance. For Juanita it had been the owl, sacred to the Chumash. For me it has been the words of Mat King, guiding my stumbling steps along the path of the Wisdomkeepers, lighting my darkest hours like landing lights, showing the Way.

Though Mat King passed on to what he called the Great Reality in 1989—the same year that Frank Fools Crow passed on—he and I still have a kind of communion. Steve and I featured his words in our 1990 book *Wisdomkeepers*. Then again, in 1994, I dug out my tapes of his words from a dusty file drawer and, with additional materials provided by his family, compiled a memorial volume in his honor entitled *Noble Red Man: Lakota Wisdomkeeper Mathew King*. Mat had always wanted to write a book but never got around to it in his busy and tumultuous lifetime. That I was permitted to help him do it has been one of the great privileges of my life.

❈

It seemed to us we were finally starting to get somewhere along the path of the Wisdomkeepers. But when we got back to *Geographic* headquarters with our tapes and photographs, we were met with indifference, even hostility, by a hierarchy of desk-bound, soul-bound editors. They didn't like Steve's photographs. "Where are the zingers?" he was asked. When I spoke of Frank Fools Crow "praying an eagle" out of the sky, I was met with cool stares. "Harvey," I was told, "you've gone *mystical!*" Somehow, in the hallowed marble corridors of the National Geographic Society, our experiences in the field with Buffalo Jim, with Oren Lyons, with Charlie Knight, with Eddie Benton-Banai, with Fools Crow and Mat King seemed not only unlikely but even foolish. We'd been duped! We'd "gotten into bed with our subjects"! What ever happened to "objective" journalism? We didn't know what to say, how to express what we'd found.

"You have one more chance," we were told, "one more trip. Six weeks, not one day more. If you can't come up with something solid, the story's dead."

Solid? Just what does "solid" mean?

Once again we went out. We revisited Oren Lyons, Buffalo Jim, Charlie Knight, Mat King, Eddie Benton-Banai. More of the same.

Glimpses of the visionary, even the miraculous. Soul-penetrating "wisdom." Enigmatic "signs"—but nothing "*solid.*"

Back at *Geographic* there was no sympathy. We had failed. Our final six-week "flyer" was over, and so was the Grandfather Medicine Men story. Two Trees hadn't been able to hack it, and neither had we. Steve's photographs, including most of those that six years later graced our book *Wisdomkeepers,* were pronounced "unpublishable." Not a zinger in the bunch! No ceremony, almost no beads or feathers or colorful costumes. No red-coal tricks. Nothing newsworthy. No ecological disasters. No armed rebellions. Not even a bloody pow-wow! No—just good, honest, deep-souled pictures of the Elders and their everyday world. Oddly, this negative assessment was made not by Garrett or Judge but by lower-level functionaries who made it clear they didn't like the way Steve and I just went out on our own and "did" a story without their overarching supervision. I never had a chance to write a word of it. No one wanted to listen to the tapes of "wisdom" I'd brought back. Who cared about the ditherings of a bunch of decrepit old men and women? The illustrations editors informed Garrett of our failure. Only Joe Judge, my direct boss as articles editor, seemed genuinely saddened. He'd gotten particularly excited when I'd told him of the amazing Iroquois Confederacy and its demands to meet with the United States government one on one. "Now that would make a hell of an article!" he'd exclaimed. But with no more ado, the Grandfather Medicine Men story was officially killed—a routine happening at the magazine yet always unhappy for those involved. Our flyer—and Steve's and my reputation as "Indian experts" at *Geographic*—went down in ignominious flames. Steve returned to North Carolina, thoroughly depressed. I busied myself with other assignments. I was even asked by one of the illustrations editors to write a kill memo. I was told: "We need some official reason why the story was killed—just for the files." I refused. He asked again. I refused again. He called Judge and asked him to insist I write the memo. Reluctantly, Judge told me, "Do it, Harvey. Put it behind you. It'll never work. Get on to something else." In one of the truly despicable acts of my life, I wrote the memo, somehow managing to put the seeming blame for our "failure" on the Elders, not ourselves. That satisfied everybody. It was the Elders who had failed, not us! Disheartened, I even began to blame Steve's "unpublishable" pictures for the debacle. Why couldn't this guy at least take a few zingers?

Chapter 7

I guess I nosedived after they killed the Grandfather Medicine Men story. I hated myself. I hated *Geographic*. I hated the whole lousy universe. It even seemed as if Harvey had betrayed me with his despicable "kill memo." They told me my pictures were "unpublishable"! God, that hurt. I knew they were the best and by far the most important pictures I'd ever taken. They were the same photographs that would appear in *Wisdomkeepers* six years later, but that was no consolation to me right then. I started actually believing them: Maybe they were right. I was no damn good, a lousy photographer. My doubts and desperation drowned out all confidence and certainty. I just couldn't see what was happening—that I'd stumbled onto some kind of wonderful invisible path I couldn't get off and that, marvelous as it was, it wasn't an *easy* path. When you follow this path, you're as likely to get broken glass or banana peels thrown at your feet as rose petals. The path of the Wisdomkeepers isn't for everyone.

I went back to North Carolina and tumbled headlong into a black hole of depression. One day, I remember, I found myself late at night under the table in my study, a pistol in my hand. I can still feel the steely coldness of the metal barrel-tip against the underside of my jaw, where I was going to fire it. I would later write of that bout with what I now think of as my "inner darkness" in my book *Shadowcatchers,* and I won't dwell on it here. I thought for a while I'd gotten over it, but I don't know. It takes many forms.

❀

A year passed. Harvey and I kept in touch. One day he called with a new idea—a story on ocean pollution in the New York bight, the wedge of ocean directly off New York City, between Long Island and the New Jersey Shore. He said he was sending a proposal on the subject to *Geographic's* planning council. He described the outlines of the story: how barges of sewage sludge were being dumped just twelve miles offshore into the bight.

"The stuff just flows right back into shore," he said. "The fish are poisoned. People get sick swimming. They have to close the beaches. They're finding blood bags and syringe needles and the stuff out of people's toilets right on the beaches. Pleasant subject, huh? This guy Dennis Sternberg—he's a New Jersey dentist and environmentalist—alerted me to it. He thinks a *Geographic* article could help set off a public outcry. I'm sending a proposal on it to the planning council. Want me to cosign your name to it? Wanna take a cruise on a sludge barge, Steve?"

"You think the magazine would give me another assignment after the Grandfathers fiasco?"

"There's probably no other photographer who'd *want* to do it!"

"You mean I'd have to photograph sewage sludge?"

"Seems right up your alley!"

Hell, I was about to sell my Leicas for eating money. I'd hardly worked for a year. I wasn't proud. If they wanted me to photograph sludge, I'd photograph sludge!

"I'm ready!" I announced.

Harvey wrote the memo to the planning council. Out of fourteen possible votes, he got two yeses and twelve nos. But darned if Harvey didn't go up and talk Bill Garrett and Joe Judge into overriding the planning council and giving us another "flyer." They even okayed me as the photographer. Who else would want to photograph sludge barges? We were given the assignment, and my expense advance got my Leicas out of pawn. Talk about miracles! A couple of weeks later the two of us were riding the sludge barges from the East River out into the bight of New York.

It was actually exhilarating. For all its ugliness and bleakness, this was a "real" story—nothing "mystical" about it. We followed the brown trail of the dumped sludge by helicopter, tracing it to the shores of Long Island and Coney Island and New Jersey, where I photographed the blood bags and needles on the swimming beaches. We circled Manhattan in a dinghy, looking for outflow pipes spilling raw sewage right into the Hudson and East Rivers. We snooped around an oil spill in Jamaica Bay where a local contractor bragged how he was making millions off the cleanup. We spent days climbing around the Staten Island landfill, documenting the incredible masses of garbage being routinely spilled into the nearby waters. We photographed fish with gaping cancers and also the fishermen who, despite constant fish advisories, went right ahead and ate their toxin-saturated catches. We got up at 3 a.m. to watch fish being sold at fancy prices at a local market.

We found a huge illegal dump of toxic dredgings from New York Bay on a beach in northern New Jersey, and despite my photographs, government authorities refused to acknowledge its existence. I marked the site on a map for them. "There's no dump there!" they insisted. We went back and looked again, and it was still there—a mound of ugly muck five hundred yards long, thirty feet wide, and twelve feet high, covering a once-pristine strand of the Jersey Shore. It stretched along the beach like a colossal flattened black slug. From what we could learn from tight-lipped state officials, the Army Corps of Engineers had dumped it there as a "flood-protection and beach-erosion-control project." We reported it again to the Environmental Protection Agency. They didn't return our calls. It was the story nobody wanted to hear about!

Back at *Geographic,* my beloved picture editors looked gimlet-eyed at my photographic coverage. "No way we can publish this stuff!" they said, shaking their heads and rolling their eyes. Shades of the Grandfathers story! Harvey and I went back out to try again. We photographed Dr. Sternberg swimming through the disgusting brown-foamed waters off his home near Asbury Park. I spent a day photographing human turds floating by the thousands under the Hudson River piers of midtown Manhattan. I got one photograph of a turd floating through a little rainbow spray under one of the piers. It was beautiful! We photographed black fishermen with their lines dropped right into the outflow from raw sewage pipes. I got a picture of a seagull with a plastic tampon inserter in its beak; another of a little girl playing with them on the beach, a tampon inserter on each finger like finger puppets; another of a small boy on crutches cavorting in the toxic sands of the dredgings dump that supposedly didn't exist in New Jersey. I even got a zinger of thousands of seagulls hovering over the Staten Island landfill. It turned the whole scene to silvery filigree in my borrowed 600-millimeter lens. I actually made garbage look artistic!

But no matter how you cut it, this was an ugly story. "Can't you get some variety?" the picture editors asked us. "We can't just run a story about sludge and toxic dumps and blood bags and tampon inserters on the beach!"

Harvey had read about an Indian tribe, the Shinnecock, who had a small reservation on the South Shore of Long Island. "We'll go see how the pollution's affecting *them!*" he suggested. And so we drove out to the far end of Long Island and had an amazing few days with Harriet Starleaf Gumbs, a youngish elder of the Shinnecock people. We were back on the path of the Wisdomkeepers!

Harriet took us out for a stroll along the Shinnecocks' lovely beach, directly fronting the bight.

"Our ancestors called this place *Sea-wan-hac-hee,* or Shell Heaven," she told us. "This is where all the tribes of the Northeast came to barter for the purple quahog shells used for wampum. Now the pollution has pretty much killed them off. Once this land was ours for miles around, now we have only these four hundred acres. It's all we have left. When I was a girl, this water here was so clean and pure we bathed and washed our clothes in it. Now look! There's so much pollution that no one wants to set foot in it! That's the difference between the white man's way and the Indian's way. We have lived here since time began, and the only waste we left behind were the oyster shells on the beach. But twentieth-century Americans—future generations will look back and call them the garbage-makers, the poison-producers, the carcinogen-makers."

She arranged a traditional cookout for us on the shore, featuring fresh-caught foods from the bight—raw and grilled oysters, steamed crabs and clams, stuffed scallops, baked mussels, wonderful clam chowder, succulent baked bluefish. For appetizers we dug fresh clams from the surf line, pried them open, and simply popped them into our mouths. I tried not to think what might be in them.

"Delicious, aren't they?" Harriet said. "You don't need lemon or hot sauce. They're perfect just the way they are, the way the Creator made them!"

It really felt good to be with Indians again! They actually have a *conscience,* something we hadn't seen much of lately.

"Oh, Lord, I wish we were still doing the Grandfathers story!" I told Harvey.

"What's over is over," he said consolingly, prophetic as ever.

❀

In the midst of our bight coverage, Harvey received a call from Iroquois Faithkeeper Oren Lyons, whom we hadn't seen since a year and a half before, when he'd asked us, *"You guys got a little time?"*

Oren announced: "It's time for you two guys to come on up. I'll introduce you to some of our Elders, as you asked."

How could we tell him the Grandfather Medicine Men story was dead?

"We're working on a pollution story right now," Harvey tried to explain.

"Well, that's the same story!" Oren exclaimed over the phone. "You should see the pollution up here! Listen, why don't you come right up? We need to talk. Some interesting things are going on. The chiefs would like you to do an article on the Six Nations Iroquois Confederacy. That's the story you *should* be doing."

It seemed a remote possibility, though Harvey mentioned to me that Joe Judge had gotten excited about his reports on the Iroquois when we'd first gone out to see them.

"Let's take a flyer of our own," Harvey suggested. "We'll just drive on up to Onondaga for a couple of days, see what's going on, then get back down to finish the bight."

I wasn't hard to convince. This bight story seemed like a mirror of my own inner darkness. Go out and do a story on the Iroquois? Now, that would be like being back on the Grandfathers story again!

We drove on up to Onondaga and spoke with Chief Lyons.

"The Elders would like to see you do a *Geographic* story on the Haudenosaunee, the Six Nations Iroquois Confederacy," he told us. "They're offering their cooperation. They want the message of traditional people to get out. The time has come!"

Harvey seemed doubtful.

"I'll talk to my boss, Joe Judge, about it," he told Oren.

"You can start today," Oren announced.

"But we're working on the bight of New York right now."

"I told you—*it's the same story!*" Oren declared. "And there's something really important going on. How'd you two guys like to fly out to South Dakota with us?"

"South Dakota?"

"Yeah. We're flying out there tomorrow. Want to come along? You said you wanted to meet our Elders, didn't you?"

"What's going on?" Harvey asked.

Oren looked at us. "It has to do with Dennis Banks."

We knew fugitive AIM militant Dennis Banks had been holed up at Onondaga since a few days before our first visit there in January 1983. At the time he was on the run from South Dakota and federal authorities on charges stemming from a riot he had allegedly provoked at a courthouse in Custer just before the 1973 armed uprising at Wounded Knee. For years he had taken refuge in California, where Governor Jerry Brown refused his extradition to South Dakota and gave him political asylum; but with the election of Republican governor George Deukmejian in 1982, California withdrew its offer of asylum. Dennis had taken flight and hidden out at Onondaga. The chiefs of the Six Nations Confederacy at Onondaga, despite FBI demands for Dennis's arrest, reiterated their centuries-old assertion of sovereignty, which was more than a claim since it had been acknowledged two centuries before by none less than President George Washington. Federal authorities, unwilling to provoke an ugly incident and unsure as well of their constitutional authority to invade a sovereign territory confirmed by federal treaty in 1794, backed off.

"But what would happen if the FBI *did* come in?" Harvey asked.

Chief Lyons answered: "The decision has already been made by the Grand Council. If they cross the line, it's out of the peace chiefs' hands. The warriors take over. And we've warned the Feds: If they come in by force, every Iroquois reservation in New York State will cut power and water lines across its territory. New York City will go dark and dry."

Now *here* was a story!

We knew the chiefs had checked us out the year before to make sure we weren't from the FBI.

"So how do we figure into all this?" I asked, puzzled.

Oren eyed us calmly. "Can you get a plane?" he asked.

"A plane?"

"Yeah. See, Dennis has decided to give himself up. He doesn't want to do it here. He's flying out to Rapid City tomorrow to turn himself in. The plane he's taking is full. We need another one for some of the chiefs. We want as many supporters as possible on hand when Dennis gives up—to make sure he's not hurt, particularly by the South Dakota police who have it in for him. If *Geographic* can hire a small plane for us, we'll let you two guys come out with us! You can be on hand for a moment of real history! Well, what do you say?"

Harvey and I looked at each other. Rent a plane? Fly out to South Dakota in the entourage of a wanted fugitive? It sounded totally bizarre. After all, weren't we supposed to be working on the bight of New York story? No way the magazine would go for it.

I remember Harvey chewing hard at one corner of his mustache.

"I'll call Joe Judge," he said, "and see if he'll okay renting a plane."

I'll never forget the phone call Harvey made to Joe Judge from our hotel room in Syracuse that afternoon. I could hear his voice shaking as he tried to explain, first, what the hell we were doing at Onondaga in upstate New York when we were supposed to be on the Jersey Shore, and then trying to convince the ever-skeptical Judge to let us rent a small plane and fly out with the Confederacy Chiefs to Rapid City. He wisely didn't mention anything about Dennis Banks.

"It's a priceless opportunity," Harvey pleaded. "The Iroquois chiefs want us to work with them. They need the plane for an important meeting. It's a chance to get to know them, win their trust. If it works out, they want *Geographic* to do an article on the Confederacy. Joe, it's a once-in-a-lifetime chance! The Iroquois have shied away from the media until now."

I watched Harvey as he reacted to Judge's response. His brows furled. His face contorted. His lips worked in furious silence. It looked like he might bite his mustache right off! Then his eyes suddenly lit up. He nodded, threw me an uneasy smile.

"I promise," he told Judge. "No funny business. We'll fly out to Rapid City, attend the meeting with the chiefs, then fly right back. I'll report back to the office as soon as I can. Then Steve and I will head back to Jersey and finish the bight coverage."

There was a long pause. Harvey stared into the phone's mouthpiece.

"Uhhh . . . okay . . . okay, Joe. Really, I promise. We'll stay out of trouble. This could lead to one hell of a story! All right . . . I'll do that. You have my word. I'll take the blame if anything goes wrong."

He hung up, looked at me, and smiling as wide as I've ever seen him do, let out a *hoot* that literally shook the walls.

"Judge says okay. He says the Iroquois Confederacy sounds like a great story. He says we can rent the plane."

I gave a resounding hoot of my own. "We're going to South Dakota. Who would've believed it!"

"I didn't mention anything about Dennis Banks to him," Harvey said, "just that we were meeting the chiefs and the Elders."

❋

What we didn't realize was that we were actually being set up as a decoy. The first plane didn't contain Dennis Banks, and neither did ours. Both planes were to keep the Feds distracted while Dennis actually made it out of Onondaga at night in a battered old station wagon and headed on back roads to Rapid City. Oren took us over to meet him in the wooden shack he had been living in for the past year and a half. That was the first time we met Tadodaho Leon Shenandoah, who seemed amazingly unassuming for the presiding chief of the Six Nations Iroquois Confederacy. I photographed Dennis's last hours at Onondaga before he fled into the night. They had him strip off his shirt so I could get some photographs showing that there were no marks on his body before he gave himself up— just in case he got beaten up after his arrest. He knew if the Feds spotted him, they'd collar him immediately and spirit him off. He wanted as much publicity as possible for his "surrender"—to bring national attention not only to his own plight but to the plight of the many AIMers and traditionals who had been harassed and hounded and jailed on virtually any pretext whatsoever since the Wounded Knee siege of 1973 and the Incident at Oglala in 1975 when two FBI agents were shot dead in a gunfight. AIM activist Leonard Peltier would ultimately be pinned with the guilt for the latter incident and still languishes in prison more than two decades later—the Native American Nelson Mandela in the eyes of Indian traditionalists and millions of supporters around the world.

Of all this Harvey and I had only the foggiest notion at the time.

The two planes took off from Syracuse for Rapid City the next morning. The first had a few chiefs and clan mothers aboard. Ours, a cramped five-seater—the only plane available at such short notice—left a couple of hours later. Aboard with Harvey and me was Chief Leon Shenandoah—Tadodaho, or presiding chief, of the Six Nations Iroquois Confederacy—and his chaperone, a soft-spoken young Iroquois man named Andy Fish. We would be picking up Eddie Benton-Banai in Minneapolis–St. Paul, then flying on the following day to Rapid City, where Oren and the others would meet us. Our pilot, who seemed instantly suspicious of our activities, stuffed us all into the tiny interior with our gear. I hadn't felt so claustrophobic since riding cross-country with Two Trees in the *Ramblin' Tepee!*

"How will we ever get Eddie in here?" Harvey asked, sitting in the tiny rear seat, surrounded by luggage.

Tadodaho Leon Shenandoah looked back at him and smiled. "Don't worry. There'll be plenty room!" he declared.

Andy Fish sat up front with the pilot, and I, well, I got to sit in the middle row with the Tadodaho himself. For the next few hours I sat there casually chatting with a man who held a title of spiritual and political authority more than a thousand years old. I couldn't have been prouder if I'd been sitting next to the Pope!

When I told Chief Shenandoah that Harvey and I were in the middle of an article on water pollution, he reiterated Oren's words: "It's the same story!" He went on: "It's prophesied in our Original Instructions that a monster, a great monster, will rise up from the water and destroy mankind. It's coming. It's already here. A great wind will come, a wind that'll make a hurricane seem like a whisper. It'll cleanse the earth and return it to its original state. That'll be the punishment for what we've done to the Creation.

"We're just visiting here, we human beings. We're the Creator's guests. He's invited us to stay for a while, and now look what we've done to His Creation. We've poisoned it, we've made a wreck of it. He's bound to be mad—and He is."

He stared into my eyes.

"I'm working for the Creation. I refuse to take part in its destruction!"

❉

Because of plane noise, we spoke to each other on the intercom. Our pilot overheard the conversation and twitched his nose as if he smelled something seditious. No doubt he'd been reading in the newspapers about the Dennis Banks affair. He kept looking over uneasily at Andy Fish.

A couple of hours into the flight he announced: "Got to refuel in Saginaw. Just take a few minutes."

We landed in Saginaw, Michigan, and taxied to the small air-services terminal. "You'll have to wait inside," the pilot told us. "I'll fuel up, and we'll be off in no time."

It was good to get out of that cramped plane for a while. We sat down and waited for the pilot to call us. I saw him go to a telephone and make some calls. Then he just disappeared. He didn't come back. An hour passed. Two hours. Three hours. Leon just sat there serenely, hands folded in his lap, eyes half-closed, almost Buddha-like. Harvey wandered impatiently around the little terminal like a caged animal, his eyes throwing sparks. He never has been good at waiting. I could see our plane through the window. It just sat there on the tarmac, unattended. No one was refueling it.

Finally, past midafternoon, the pilot returned, looking terribly harried and out of sorts.

"We're not going to South Dakota," he announced. "We've got engine trouble."

For a moment I thought he'd said "Injun trouble." That sure seemed more likely than "engine trouble" at the time since the plane had flown just fine all the way from Syracuse.

He said, "You can go up to the main terminal and see if there's a commercial flight to Rapid City—or back to Syracuse if you like. This plane's not flying anymore."

Well, *damn!*

He gave one last hard look at Andy Fish, snorted, and stalked out of the terminal, leaving us there in the lurch with the Tadodaho, Andy, and our mountain of gear, which he'd off-loaded along with ourselves.

Harvey was beside himself. Imagine having to call Joe Judge back and tell him we were stranded in Saginaw, Michigan!

He went over to the main terminal and learned there were no flights until the following day. His eyes were pinwheeling with rage.

"Don't worry," Leon said calmly. "We'll get there."

Harvey had bought some snacks in the main terminal—Twinkies and apples. That was his idea of health food. He passed these around, and we ate dinner, such as it was, while trying to figure out what to do. I got on the phone and started making calls to every rental plane service in the area. No one had a plane on such short notice. I asked at the main terminal if there was anyone who could help us. Finally someone suggested a small air service in a town in northern Michigan, forty-five minutes away by air. I called the number and spoke to the first sympathetic voice I'd heard in hours. "Yeah, I have a plane," he said. "How many in your party? Oh, that's no problem. Hell, she's an eight-seater! When do you want to leave?" I blurted, *"Now!"* And he said, "Well, I'll just drop everything I've got. I'll be down there in less than an hour!" And damned if he wasn't true to his word!

His twin-engine eight-seater landed out of the night sky and taxied right up outside the little air services terminal about 9 P.M. It was twice the size of the first plane, with plenty of room for all of us and our gear, and enough for Eddie Benton-Banai as well.

During all of this, Leon had sat there serenely in the terminal, calmly eating Twinkies and meticulously peeling apples with his little pocketknife. He showed not the slightest impatience. "Don't worry," he repeated again and again. "We'll get there. We'll get there."

Our new pilot was highly appreciative of what was going on. "Hell, this is *history!*" he declared. "I'm proud just to be here with you guys. Can I tag along with you when we get to Rapid City? I don't want to be stuck in some motel. I want to be out there doing what you do! And when you're finished, I'll fly you all the way back to Syracuse!"

❈

We flew to Minneapolis–St. Paul, stayed the night in a motel, picked up Eddie Benton-Banai in the morning—there was plenty of room for him now—and took off again for Rapid City.

"I see you guys have been paying attention!" Eddie said with a smile and a wink.

We arrived at the Rapid City airport a little before noon. As our eight-seater taxied to the terminal, a crowd rushed toward us. I could see photographers' flashes popping. I also saw half a dozen men in dark suits that I took to be plainclothesmen of some kind, probably FBI.

"Looks as if we have a little welcoming party," Harvey piped.

We were surrounded as we got out. The plainclothes boys looked us over. They looked at Harvey. They looked at me. They looked at Leon and Eddie. Then they looked hard at Andy Fish—and looked again. "*That's* not Dennis Banks!" someone yelled out. Then someone else shouted, "Hey, he's back at the main terminal. Just drove in. Come on!"

The crowd made a beeline toward the main terminal tarmac, and we followed. Even as our plane was taxiing in, Dennis himself had driven up to the airport in his station wagon. Apparently he had timed his arrival to coincide with ours. The distraction of our arrival enabled him to get past the security perimeter set up by South Dakota State Police without being spotted. He definitely wanted to be arrested not by the locals but by the FBI itself—and in the full glare of the public eye. The decoy had worked.

By the time we caught up with the crowd, Dennis was already standing on the tarmac at the center of a tight crowd. He had picked up one of his daughters and was holding her paternally in his arms while the press and police swirled around him. I've never seen greater dignity in a man's eyes. I imagine Crazy Horse must have had such a look in his eyes when the Army arrested him, using trickery, at Fort Robinson, Nebraska, in 1877.

I got a few pictures of Dennis being arrested and handcuffed before he was pushed into a police car and driven off. Later we got word that his braids had been cut off at the jail by arresting officers.

"That's always the first thing they did to us at the Indian boarding schools we were forced to attend," Eddie Benton-Banai remarked. "They figured, 'Cut off the braids, and you cut out the Indian.' Well, it never worked, and it sure won't work with Dennis!"

Dennis Banks remarks in a letter, "As a postscript to my jailing, the prison was not successful in cutting my braids off. I still have them and wear my hair long. Waiting for my own 'Stone Canoe,' I will *never* cut it."

Already convicted in 1975 of assault and riot charges, Dennis would spend the next couple of years in prison—almost anticlimactically, it seemed, after nearly a decade of fugitive living and hiding. He has since reemerged as a major spokesman on Indian issues.

Our delighted pilot, after witnessing history along with us, flew us back to Syracuse the next day. Harvey called Joe Judge from our motel and got an earful. "Harvey! What's this I hear that you've been flying Dennis Banks, a fugitive felon, around the country in a plane rented by *National Geographic?*" Harvey's eyes widened. "But, Joe, it's not true!" He managed to pacify his infuriated boss—but only barely. When he got off the phone, he said, "It must have been the pilot of the first plane. I guess he thought Andy Fish was Dennis Banks. That's why he wouldn't take us on from Saginaw. He must have notified his office, and they called *Geographic.* Judge sounded as if he wanted to kill me. Imagine the two of us getting involved in such a thing! He was really miffed, to say the least."

❈

Back at *Geographic,* the illustrations people grudgingly produced a twenty-page layout of our coverage on the bight. They left out the turds going through the rainbow. The magazine's ten million subscribing members wouldn't want to see *that!* But otherwise that layout looked strong, I thought, though certainly not pretty. For sure these were the ugliest pictures I'd ever taken. Bill Garrett came down to the eighth-floor layout room, looked over the layout dummy—I could see him wincing—and then, to my surprise, said, "Wrap it up. We'll go with it!"

The picture editors were appalled. They'd only put the layout of my photographs together in the certainty that the editor would kill it on the spot! Now he'd gone and accepted it! No way they'd let that happen. They immediately deconstructed the entire dummy and surreptitiously deep-sixed the story. On the editorial side, Harvey was having as much trouble with the text as I was having with the photographs. He wrote three versions of the story, all of them rejected. After many months the bight story just died, just as the illustrations editors had hoped. Finally, like the Grandfather Medicine Men, it was officially killed. Two failures in a row. Two years of work down the tubes. Harvey and I were reeling.

As it turned out, the next summer the blood bags and the syringe needles and noxious sludge on the New York–New Jersey beaches be-

came national news. Had *Geographic* published our article—which would have come out right about then—the magazine would have seemed downright prescient. Thankfully, Dennis Sternberg and his fellow environmentalists got the word out about the sludge and how it was ruining the Jersey Shore. New laws were passed. Today the sludge barges have to go out 106 miles and dump their load off the edge of the continental shelf. They are ultimately to be phased out entirely. "New Jersey's waters are blue again," Dennis told us recently. Still, I feel bad that we couldn't have been part of the solution.

�

After our two high-visibility "failures," I nearly went into my black hole and never came out of it. But fate has a way of turning things around.

Although Harvey's boss, *National Geographic's* associate editor Joe Judge, had never cared for the Grandfathers story and was no champion of the bight, either, he loved the idea of doing an article on the Iroquois. Even his momentary displeasure over the Dennis Banks affair hadn't changed that. He told Harvey, "Write up a memo on the Iroquois Confederacy, and I'll present it with my recommendation to the planning council."

Harvey did, and they bought it! The only question was, would they let me be the photographer? After two resounding failures in a row, it seemed unlikely. Harvey had signed my name to the memo as well, but I still had to convince Director of Photography Bob Gilka and Editor Bill Garrett that I was up to it. To prove my worth, I asked for a showing of my Grandfathers pictures in the projection room outside Garrett's ninth-floor office. I chose the tray of photographs myself. All the top editors gathered, grim-faced. I figured they had killed both stories, and now they were going to kill me—or at least my *Geographic* career.

Garrett had hardly looked at my photographs on the Grandfathers story. The illustrations editors had seen to that. He'd taken their word that my photographs were no damn good. The lights dimmed in the projection room, and the screen lit up with all my rejected photographs.

There was Tadodaho Leon Shenandoah and Mat King and Frank Fools Crow and Buffalo Jim and Eddie Benton-Banai and Charlie Knight and all the other Wisdomkeepers we'd met. Seeing their faces shining there in that darkened room on the projection room screen, I didn't know whether to laugh or cry. I just bit my lip. Oh, Lord, how I wanted to do that Iroquois story! I just couldn't imagine Harvey going off and doing it without me.

Finally Garrett finished reviewing my photographs.

"Not bad," he said. "Some pretty good stuff there, Steve. I didn't realize all that you guys had done." He turned around in his chair and looked at the assembled editors. "What do you say? Anyone here for reviving the Grandfathers story?"

I couldn't believe my ears: A volley of moans and "Oh, no's!" from nearly everyone in the room quickly dissuaded him. My heart fell.

"Well," Garrett continued, "at least there's no question of Steve's ability to do the Iroquois. We'll give him another chance."

He gave me a wink and a smile across the room. That Shawnee great-grandmother had come to my rescue again.

And I was assigned! The very same pictures of mine that had been used to kill the Grandfathers story now got me the assignment to do the Iroquois story. You figure it out.

But at least Harvey and I were off to Great Turtle Island again. We were back on the path of the Wisdomkeepers. Just as it seemed we had lost our way altogether, we found the path right there under our feet again. We'd been on it all along! It was like being reborn.

Chapter 8

WHENEVER we head up Interstate 81 to visit the Iroquois—a trip we've taken dozens of times over the past fifteen years—we have a sense of crossing an invisible boundary, of entering a different world, an alternative reality. Steve drives up to D.C. from North Carolina, stops impatiently at my house while I fling my dented Halliburton suitcase into the trunk of the rented car or whatever semi-wreck he's currently in possession of, and we set off—filled with that sense of renewed meaning and urgency we seem to get only when we're on a new leg of this endless journey of ours.

We call it "being on the wind"—that intuitive feeling of being swept along by an unseen current into new possibilities. The journey takes us; we don't take the journey. We try not to do too much planning. There's a way of doing things without forcing them. A deliberate nonstrategy. Letting what happens happen. Not being totally passive, mind you, since great effort is often involved, but being active in the way, say, that a bird is active as it rides the wind currents, assuming a natural oneness with its environment.

"What do you say we go on up to Onondaga and see Leon?" one of us blithely suggests to the other out of the blue, nudged by some inner urge. And we do just that, not even calling to see if he's there. If he's not, we'll see someone else, follow the path to the next Wisdomkeeper. You go where you go, you see the people you see. Pick a road, any road, and let it take you to the rest of your life. That's being on the wind. That's following the path of the Wisdomkeepers.

We've traveled many a mile together on these journeys, Steve and I—several hundred thousand, in fact. He loves to drive; I don't. Hence, almost always he does the driving, and I ride shotgun in the passenger seat. We both like it that way. He has an uncanny knack for rolling right up to the door of whomever it is we're supposed to see, with or without map or directions, in the most out-of-the-way places, down roads without a sign on them, even at night in a pea-soup fog. Some interior compass seems to guide him.

I picture him now, sitting there beside me, a powerful presence of a man, his bearded face a shifting topography of scowls and grimaces and occasional ecstatic smiles. His hands barely hover on the steering wheel, like a pianist's over a keyboard. He helps guide the wheel from beneath with his right knee, which does most of the actual steering. Periodically he grabs his well-scuffed pipe off the dashboard and fires up the bowl with a spurt of demonic flame. He drives on effortlessly, a gracefully aggressive driver, every so often breathing out a sweet cloud of meditative smoke. Former smoker and confirmed tobacco lover that I am, I breathe it in thankfully, dosing on the vicarious nicotine. I open the window a crack to let in a touch of breeze, and the smoke curls out and away into the wind outside.

We leave the ordinary behind. The road unreels before us, inviting us into new possibilities. Flanking the four-lane roadway with its grass divider, the curvaceous green hills of western New York ripple along beside us. Here and there, where a green-shadowed patch of woods intrudes on the domesticated farmlands, you sense a gentle primordial wildness, lurking deer, snakes, rabbits, wood tortoises. Call it Great Turtle Island—the name Native Americans have given to the aboriginal North American continent. It's as much vision as reality—the land as it was before its living body was bound and trussed with power lines and telephone cables, strapped down with interstates, straitjacketed with farms and shopping malls, riveted with cities. No, not the land as it was. As it *is*. Because it's still there, that other reality. You can squint your inner eye and vaguely see it, as if peering through thrashing windshield wipers while driving into an oncoming rainstorm—a mysticized landscape, alive and breathing, just beyond the corner of your imagination.

❄

We began our coverage of the Iroquois Confederacy in April 1985 and worked on it for most of the next two years. The article finally appeared in the September 1987 *National Geographic* under the title "The Fire That Never Dies: The Six Nations Iroquois Confederacy." But what had begun for us as a journalistic assignment would now continue as a kind of personal mission. This assignment, no matter how it kept shifting its shape, was for life. We'd become runners, as Chief Shenandoah called us. Reluctant runners, no doubt. He showed us one of the little strings of wampum that Iroquois runners, or messengers, use when delivering important messages between member nations of the Confederacy. "You guys are doing work sorta like that," he told us. "A couple of runners, that's what you are even if you don't know it. Doing the Creator's work despite yourselves. Hey, that's a kind of holy work, you know? Carrying a message between worlds, that's what you're doing. For a couple of complainers, you're two of the luckiest guys in the world. Did you know that?"

For sure, having Leon Shenandoah for a friend is to be counted among the lucky ones of this world. Leon gives you a different sense of what being human is all about. After a while in his company you begin to see that life is not an entertainment but a holy task. He's one of the toughest and yet gentlest and most unaffected human beings either of us has ever met—and, without doubt, one of the wisest, for he not only showed us we were on a path, a spiritual path, but he showed us how to walk it. He told us: "Everything's laid out for you. Your path is straight ahead of you. Sometimes it's invisible, but it's there. You may not know where it's going, but still you've got to follow that path. It's the path to the Creator. That's the only path there is."

I remember once we were talking about powers, spiritual and otherwise, and Steve asked him, "Leon, what is the greatest power?" Leon squinted thoughtfully, then closed his eyes for several seconds, carefully chewing over his answer before speaking. Finally he said, "I myself have no power. Real power comes only from the Creator. It's in His hands, not ours. But if you're asking me about strength, not power, then I can say that the greatest strength is gentleness."

The greatest strength is gentleness! That's Leon Shenandoah, gentleness incarnate.

Every so often on our journeys to Onondaga, we would convince Leon to take a getaway trip with us for a few hours or a few days. He was usually delighted to go. We'd feel guilty about taking him away even for a short time from his duties as Tadodaho, presiding chief of the Six Nations Iroquois Confederacy, and helpmeet and advisor to anyone and everyone knocking at the door of his little yellow clapboard house.

This time out, reconvening our spirit-journey for a brief trip with our old mentor and friend, we have it in mind to drive out with him to the southeast shore of Lake Ontario, near today's Sackets Harbor, New York. Somewhere in this vicinity the luminous prophet and deliverer called the Peacemaker—founder of the Iroquois Confederacy—came ashore in his magical white Stone Canoe to begin his epochal spiritual and political mission a millennium ago.

"We call it the Second Landing," Leon had told us intriguingly on an earlier visit.

He spoke of Four Landings, or earthly incarnations, of the Creator, of which the Peacemaker's was the second. He described how the Peacemaker journeyed in his Stone Canoe among the then-warring Iroquois nations—the Mohawk, Seneca, Onondaga, Oneida, and Cayuga—and how he established among them a Great Peace based on a Great Binding Law. He traveled in the Stone Canoe as a sure sign that the Creator had sent him.

"He didn't have to paddle," Leon told us. "The Stone Canoe took him wherever he was supposed to go."

Here was a magnificent story and legend, as great as any of Greece or Rome—greater, to my mind.

"We call him the Peacemaker," Leon went on, "because we use his real name, his Indian name, only when we actually want him to come, when there's some kind of great emergency. Other times we just call him the Peacemaker. Funny, you white people use the same word for one of your missiles, something to kill people!"

"And does the Peacemaker come when you call him?" I asked him.

Leon looked at me. There was the slightest flicker of a smile on his lips.

"Oh, yeah. He comes," he said knowingly, nodding very slowly but emphatically, his eyes locking on mine. *"He comes!"*

After an emphatic pause, he went on: "So he was sent by the Creator to save our people. We call it the Second Landing."

"What was the First Landing?" I asked.

"The First Landing," Leon said. "Aaahhh . . . that wasn't a person. That was the Creation itself! The Peacemaker . . . he was the Second Landing. And then the Prophet Handsome Lake was the Third Landing. That was after the Revolutionary War, and our people were bleeding, dying. He brought a new message to add to the Peacemaker's, giving us instructions on how to survive in this modern world."

"And was there a Fourth Landing?" I asked.

Leon paused, as if wondering whether to go on. "The Fourth Landing," he said hesitantly, "well, that hasn't happened yet. But we're waiting. He's coming. And I think we won't have to wait much more. The Fourth Landing will come to save the world, to save the Creation we're destroying. He'd better come soon, or there'll be no Creation left to save!"

※

The Peacemaker, goes the story still told in the longhouse, was born to a virgin mother somewhere along the northern shores of Lake Ontario. He was originally of the Huron people, closely related to the Iroquois. At that time, the Iroquois nations were warring ferociously among themselves—to the point of self-destruction. The young man who would later be called the Peacemaker received a message from the Creator telling him to carve a canoe out of white stone and take it across the waters of Lake Ontario to bring a Great Binding Law of Peace to the feuding Iroquois nations.

His first convert was an Onondaga exile living among the Mohawk, a towering figure named Ayawentha, or Hiawatha (an Iroquois name erroneously used by the poet Longfellow for an Ojibway culture-hero in *The Song of Hiawatha*). With Hiawatha's help, the Peacemaker persuaded all but one of the Iroquois nations to come together into a powerful new Confederacy.

Their final obstacle was the original Tadodaho, a snake-haired ogre with a cannibalistic appetite who ruled over the Onondaga nation. Eventually they persuaded him, too, to join the Confederacy

and become titular leader—a sort of speaker of the house—of the newly founded Grand Council of the Confederacy. Lighting the "Fire That Never Dies," as it's still called, the chiefs of the Grand Council planted the original Tree of Peace, beneath which the warring nations buried their weapons of war, proclaiming that thenceforth all who cared to might take shelter beneath the protecting branches of the Tree.

For more than five hundred years, until the coming of the white man, the Iroquois Confederacy, based on the Great Law of the Peacemaker, established a *Pax Iroquoia* over the Northeast from the Atlantic to the Mississippi, from the Carolinas to Ontario. Over that span of centuries they were the most feared political and military power on the continent.

What is most extraordinary about this Iroquois epic of the Peacemaker and the Stone Canoe, beyond its intrinsic poetic appeal and spiritual power, is the fact that it is still told each year in the Iroquois ceremonial longhouses of upstate New York and southeastern Canada. Among today's Onondaga, Mohawk, Seneca, Oneida, Cayuga, and Tuscarora peoples (the latter became the Confederacy's sixth nation in the early 1700s), the Six Nations Iroquois Confederacy is still very much alive. The Grand Council still meets, the Central Fire still burns, the Great Binding Law is still followed, and the Tree of Peace still sends out its White Roots of Peace in the four sacred directions.

The name Tadodaho, the snake-haired Onondaga ogre, has become an ongoing title carried to this day by the presiding chief, or "Keeper of the Central Fire," of the Confederacy's Grand Council. In 1969 that title devolved on Chief Leon Shenandoah. As Tadodaho, Chief Shenandoah would become revered and renowned not only among the Iroquois but also among indigenous peoples around the world, being one of the founders of the United Nations' Commission on Non-Governmental Organizations in Geneva, Switzerland—the chief international forum of the Fourth World of indigenous peoples.

The fact that this remarkable human being agreed to accompany us on this leg of our spirit-journey is in itself the highest privilege. And it's not often you get to hear a thousand-year-old story told from the lips of one of the principal characters in the story itself.

❋

Just before dark we reach the Nedrow turnoff, about five miles south of Syracuse. Back in January 1983, the first time we came up here, there was no sign on I-81 indicating that this was the exit to Onondaga, capital of the Six Nations Iroquois Confederacy. There was only a highway sign saying "Nedrow." Today, I'm happy to say, there's an official green highway sign just before the turnoff declaring "Onondaga Nation Territory."

In 1971, along this same stretch of I-81, Leon—then in only his third year as Tadodaho—stood at the center of a tense confrontation between Iroquois traditionalists and New York State troopers. The incident was triggered when state highway crews, without Indian permission, started widening I-81 where it cuts through the Onondaga Nation Territory. Leon organized a sit-down in front of the bulldozers to stop this intrusion onto sovereign Onondaga territory. Heavily armed state troopers soon arrived at the site. Standing at the entrance to the reservation, Leon drew a line on the ground with his ceremonial eagle-headed condolence cane—the Tadodaho's symbol of office—and defiantly declared, "The United States stops here!"

Threatening to have power, gas, and water lines cut on all fourteen Iroquois reservations in New York State if the highway project continued, he compelled New York authorities to back down. The next day the same New York State troopers he confronted hurriedly left the scene to put down the now-infamous riot at Attica State Prison, which left more than forty inmates dead.

Leon later told us: "Those prisoners at Attica took the killing instead of us. They died and we lived. That's how it was with the buffalo in the old days. They took the killing instead of the Indians. So we can thank the buffalo and we can thank the prisoners at Attica who died instead of us. They've all got a place with the Creator up in the Sky World . . . a better place than this."

Now, taking the Nedrow turnoff and heading onto State Highway 11A, a narrow and curving two-lane blacktop, we leave the United States and enter Onondaga Nation Territory, a small holy enclave of Great Turtle Island—and a place like no other. You'll find no Bureau of Indian Affairs office here and no BIA-authorized Tribal Council. Onondaga, to my knowledge, is the only Indian reservation in the country with a single government run by traditional peace chiefs and clan mothers. The longhouse here, home of the Confederacy's Central Fire, serves not only the Onondaga Nation but the Six Nations Iroquois Confederacy as a whole. Here, as in other long-houses throughout New York State and southeastern Canada, the *Gaiw'iyo* is recited each year, recounting the deeds and Instructions of the two great Haudenosaunee (Iroquois) prophets and deliverers, the Peacemaker and Handsome Lake—the latter a reformer who re-shaped the Peacemaker's message for modern times after the devastations of the American Revolution.

We drive through the center of the Rez, past the house of Dewasenta, Leon's sister and a wonderful Wisdomkeeper in her own right. The house's neatly painted red-and-white trim was applied by none other than Dennis Banks himself during the months he took refuge here, protected from federal authorities by the Confederacy's peace chiefs and clan mothers. It was here, when it was still Dewasenta's souvenir shop, that we first met Faithkeeper Oren Lyons that icy night in January 1983. Just up the road is the dirt lane leading to Oren's secluded lodge, where he keeps the ceremonial False Face masks turned respectfully to the wall.

We pull into the graveled driveway of Leon's little yellow clap-board house, right next to the elementary school. We knock on the back door, the only door anyone ever seems to use. And, bless him, there's Leon! He's had an eye operation, back problems, and a few other ailments lately, but for an octogenarian he looks hale and bright-eyed as ever.

"So you guys are back!" he chortles. "Just like chewing gum on the heel—can't get rid of it!"

"Yeah, like two bad pennies! Always coming back!" Steve laughs.

The same words are spoken almost every time we get together.

Leon ushers us into the cozy confines of the house, through the kitchen, and into the dining room where we've had so many of our conversations over the years, imbibing endless cups of his wife Thelma's good strong black coffee. The walls, tabletops, and shelves overflow with mementos, ceremonial objects, piles of news clippings, books, letters, frayed magazines. Leon's magnificent eagle-headed cane of office, the so-called condolence cane, leans against the wall. Atop the tall china cabinet, beneath the raised right wing of a large stuffed brown eagle, I see his circular ceremonial deer-antlered, feathered peace chief's bonnet, or *gastoweh,* perched up there like a sleeping bird. The sounds of his grandchildren and great-grandchildren playing upstairs drift through the thin walls. The TV is on in the parlor, just off the dining room. I've never been here when it was off. No one ever seems to be watching it.

Leon grabs a small overnight bag, and minutes later we're heading into the night, Steve and Leon up front, me in back. Next morning, after checking out of our motel at Sackets Harbor, we drive out to the nearby shore of Lake Ontario. A pink-gold light ignites the broad waters of the lake, casting a magical glow over everything. The three of us sit on a low rock wall, contemplating the scene.

Leon begins speaking in a low, steady voice: "Right about here," he says, pointing a gnarled index finger to the shoreline, "somewhere along this shore. This had to be about where the Peacemaker came ashore in his Stone Canoe. He made it out of stone so they'd know the Creator sent him."

His voice takes on a gentle singsong quality.

"He was born of a virgin mother. She lived with her mother, the Peacemaker's grandmother, on an island out there across the lake. Just the two of them. Then one day the mother saw the girl was getting big, that she was going to have a baby. She asked her, 'Has any man been here?' She said, 'No!' And yet it was obvious she was pregnant. She got bigger and bigger, and finally she had a little boy. Her mother was ashamed for her 'cause she wasn't married. So she decided to get rid of him. She threw the baby under the ice on the lake to kill him. She watched him go under. But when she went back to the house, there was the baby . . . crying! Next she took the baby out and threw him into the fire, but when she went back to the house, there was the baby again . . . still in his bed, crying. Then she buried him in a deep hole, and the same thing happened. She decided to cut him in pieces then, but a shadow came to her and said, 'Don't try to hurt him anymore. You can't do it. He's here for a purpose!' So she let him grow up, and she watched him. She noticed he was making a canoe out in the creek, but it was no ordinary canoe. He carved it out of stone. White granite. He told her he was going on a mission across the lake in that Stone Canoe. 'It'll never float,' she told him. And he told her, 'It'll float.' He pushed it out on the lake, and sure enough, it floated. So that Stone Canoe was the Peacemaker's sign. It showed everyone he was really sent by the Creator."

Leon's voice trails off.

"There's lots more words to the story. It takes days to tell it all in the longhouse each year. Lots of it I can't tell you guys at all."

He continues: "Anyway, the Peacemaker went across the lake in his Stone Canoe. His mission was to bring peace to the people, to stop the Haudenosaunee people from warring with each other. He had to come somewhere right through here in his Stone Canoe to get down to Mohawk country. The Mohawks back then weren't up on the Saint Lawrence, where they are today. Their country was down the Hudson, down below where Albany is today. That's where the Peacemaker made his first disciple, Ayawentha, the one you call Hiawatha. The two of them created the Confederacy and gave the people their Instructions, the Great Law.

"Tadodaho—the original Tadodaho—was the last one they went to. He was the chief of the Onondaga people. He had snakes in his hair, a really bad guy. It took the Peacemaker and Ayawentha a long time, but finally they won Tadodaho over. Then they went and buried their weapons of war under the Tree of Peace, and they made

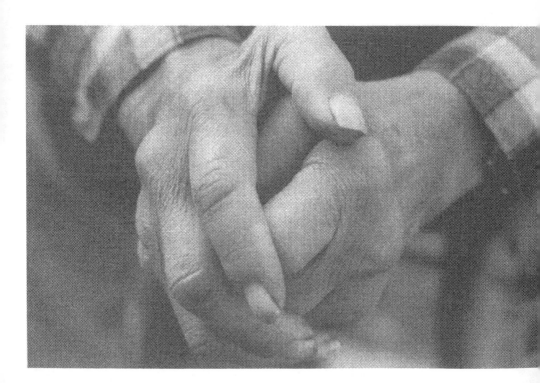

Onondaga the Confederacy's capital. Tadodaho became the presiding chief—not the ruler or dictator, 'cause we don't have those, just the first among equals. And from that time the name Tadodaho became a title. It's passed on by each generation at Onondaga. There's been more than two hundred since then. I was chosen by the clan mothers in 1969. I never thought it would be me."

Leon holds out his hands, oddly shaped hands, seemingly misshapen by arthritis yet still powerful-looking. They glow like burnished bronze in the pink-gold light.

"You see," he says, "if you're a spiritual leader, there's a special marking on you somewhere. See my hands? See how they're shaped different than yours? Look at my fingers, the fourth fingers. See? Look at yours, then look at mine. Notice something different between them? Which is the longest? On yours it's the third fingers. On my hand the fourth finger's the longest. See? That's my marking. That's the sign I'm a spiritual leader. So I was born to it. That's my purpose in the world. Everyone's got a purpose, and that's mine."

We drive back to Onondaga and drop Leon off at his yellow clapboard house in the center of Great Turtle Island, the center of the universe. Then we hit the road back down to North America and the ordinary world again.

Chapter 9

OUR Stone Canoe took us next as near to the land of the dead as I hope to get in this lifetime. Not long after we finished the Iroquois Confederacy story, Leon phoned me and suggested another article he thought *Geographic* might be interested in.

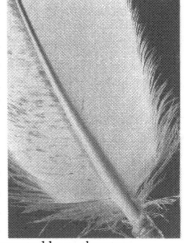

"It's about bones," he said.

Bones?

He told me he'd been asked by some Shawnee people to go down to Kentucky to give a proper ceremonial burial to the exhumed bones from an old Indian cemetery that had been desecrated by pothunters.

"It's an important story, Steve," he told me. "Imagine if some Indians had dug up a white cemetery and sold the skulls to devil worshipers. That's what's happening to our Indian cemeteries!"

National Geographic Editor Bill Garrett agreed to take a flyer on still another Indian story. This one had an alluring Shawnee connection, which no doubt made it personally irresistible to Garrett. The Shawnee people, driven west from their Ohio homeland in the late 1600s, had settled for a time in Kentucky before crossing the Mississippi River to eventual resettlement in Oklahoma. Both Shawnee National Forest and Shawneetown, Illinois, bear telling witness to their former associations in this area.

An angry delegation of traditionalist Shawnees and their supporters, on learning of the burial ground desecration on a farm overlooking the Ohio River near Uniontown, Kentucky, had driven over from Oklahoma to demand return of their ancestors' bones. Among them was Cherokee spiritual elder Jess Bluebird and his Shawnee-Delaware wife, Mary, a vibrant couple in their seventies, much revered by all the Indians. Harvey and I fell in with them shortly after we arrived.

Jess was visibly disturbed by the sight of the scattered bones and the cratered cornfield where the pothunters had done their grisly work, tossing aside thousands of human bones—fingerbones, forearms, thighbones, jawbones, teeth—like so much sewer pipe.

He lamented: "Those are our ancestors they've dug up. The Ancient Ones. Their journey to the spirit world has been interrupted. They're mad! They've been let loose, and they don't know

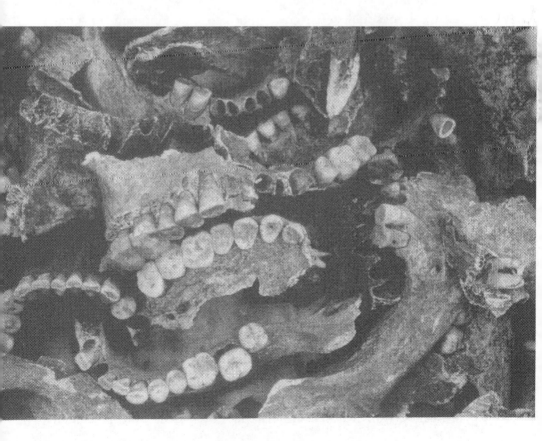

where they are! We've got to pray for them. We've got to rebury their bones and let them continue their journey."

The archaeologists who were cleaning up after the pothunters had quite a different viewpoint on these bones. To begin with, they refused to acknowledge that the bones were Shawnee—or, for that matter, that they belonged to any other identifiable modern tribe. "They're Mississippian" was all they would admit, "and they date at the latest from around A.D. 1600, which predates Shawnee occupation in this area." This only infuriated the Indians, who have a standing feud with archaeologists and anthropologists—as well as with pothunters—over their routine exhumation of Indian bones and grave goods. "Anthropologists are just grave robbers with college degrees!" I've heard Indians say. These same anthropologists are reluctant to admit any direct connection between so-called prehistoric peoples such as the Mississippians and identifiable modern tribes.

"They won't admit it because if they did, they'd have to give back all the bones and stolen grave goods in their museums to today's Indians," an angry young Oklahoma Shawnee AIM activist named John Thomas told us when Harvey and I arrived on the scene of the desecration.

Tempers were hot. The Ancient Ones were aroused.

The Indians had set up a small encampment replete with ceremonial tepee and sweat lodge at the site of the desecration—a Kentucky cornfield overlooking the Ohio River. There they monitored the work of the archaeologists. An uneasy peace prevailed between the Indians, the anthros—as the Indians called the archaeologists—local police and authorities, the owner of the cornfield, and other local farmers who didn't like the notion that they could be stopped from planting or harvesting if their plows happened to unearth a few Indian bones.

As any local pothunter will tell you, the bluffs of the Ohio and Mississippi rivers are studded with the remains of hundreds, even thousands of "prehistoric" Indian settlements. "Prehistoric—that's what you whites call everybody else's history," one Indian told us. Here once rose impressive cities of Mayan-influenced pyramids, such as the extraordinary ruins now partially rebuilt and on display at Cahokia, in nearby southern Illinois. This Kentucky cemetery, however, had simply been part of the site of a series of medium-sized villages that had occupied this pleasant Ohio River blufftop over the centuries. Even these modest villages originally had featured dozens of twenty- and thirty-foot-high mounds, some of them temple-topped, to withstand the periodic floods. Burials had been made right between the wood-and-wattle houses. Leveled in the mid-1800s for farmland, these village sites have long been the weekend hunting ground for souvenir hunters and, in recent years, as prices of Indian artifacts and grave goods have soared, of an army of professional pothunters.

The site of the desecration itself was shocking in its total disrespect for human feeling. Imagine visiting the graves of your grandparents to find them dug up, their remains looted for sale to collectors, study in laboratories, and display in museums. This was worse—not simply a few graves but a massive excavation of more than four hundred waist-deep holes and trenches, dug by a professional team of grave-robbing pothunters who had stumbled on this centuries-old Mississippian cemetery and meticulously looted it for weeks before being stopped by alerted state police, who arrested them on charges of violating an obscure Kentucky law: desecration of a venerated object. The same statute covers infractions ranging from Ku Klux Klan cross burnings to the toppling of tombstones on Halloween.

The place looked as if a squadron of bombers had been using the cornfield for practice. Those holes had yielded unknown "treasures" for the thriving international black market in Indian grave goods. An unbroken pot can bring at least a few hundred dollars, some carved pieces in the thousands. Occasional special items—say, a hammered copper mask—can bring hundreds of thousands. Even a moldy old skull will bring a hundred or more from devil worshipers and curio collectors. Harvey and I visited one local collector-dealer who proudly toured us through his multimillion-dollar collection of museum-quality pieces, kept in an armored garage. He boasted of his escapades over the years raiding Indian cemeteries. He figured we understood. We didn't.

The archaeologists likewise patiently explained all the historical details to us—how this was a site that could explain a whole period of America's history and that it was now virtually obliterated by the pothunters. Outraged local politicians, sensing an opportunity, came down to make poignant speeches—and, indeed, new state and federal laws would be passed based on this and similar incidents, giving new protection to Indian sacred sites. Of all this we reported in our March 1989 article for *Geographic,* and I refer you there for more details.

What I want to recall here are a few matters that never appeared in that article, things we left out so as not to "go mystical." One occasion I remember in particular. It still gives me chills when I look at the photographs I took that day. It wasn't visionary; it was disturbingly real. It had to do with two sculptured plasticine heads of the Ancient Ones. I know it sounds a little bizarre, but I'll tell it as I experienced it.

✸

I had arranged with Dr. David Wolf, forensic anthropologist with the Kentucky medical examiner's office, to make soft-tissue reconstructions of two skulls, one man and one woman. I wanted to photograph the faces of these Ancient Ones as they'd actually looked when living. Dr. Wolf, who often makes such reconstructions to identify murder victims, made casts of the two skulls—the originals would have to be reburied—and over the casts he molded their likely facial features in plasticine clay. He then added makeup and long, straighthaired, shiny black wigs. The results were startlingly realistic, almost frighteningly lifelike. These faces hadn't seen the light of day for hundreds of years.

I tried several times to photograph the heads indoors, but nothing seemed to work. They looked like two staring clay heads set on a table, nothing more. Artificial lighting only made them seem more artificial. I then decided to take them out to the farm where their originals had been unearthed, hoping to photograph them there in natural daylight. It was midafternoon by the time Dr. Wolf and I drove up to the farm site, with the two heads strapped down in the backseat. The weather was especially warm, and the two still-moist plasticine heads—I noticed—were perspiring slightly.

Tadodaho Leon Shenandoah and Onondaga chief Vince Johnson had been invited to the desecration site to preside over the reinterment of the Ancient Ones' bones, and Dr. Wolf and I arrived just as the chiefs were finishing the third burial in the past two months. I'd already photographed the other reburials; this time I was here for a different purpose.

I'd figured they'd have been done earlier in the day and we'd have the place to ourselves, but they were still saying the final prayers for the reinterred Ancient Ones when we drove up.

As on the two previous occasions, Chief Shenandoah had set a lighted kerosene lantern on the low mound over the new grave. "To light their way to eternity," he said.

"Until the bones completely disintegrate, the spirits can't finish their journey to the spirit world. They're stranded here. They could do great harm if we don't rebury them."

The chiefs and the other Indians in the group were surprised to see us and were even more surprised as we took the two reconstructed heads of the Ancient Ones out of the car. They stared really hard at those, with genuine alarm in their eyes. At that moment, almost as if on cue, the wind suddenly died and the heat seemed just as suddenly to intensify. We all looked up at the blinding sky.

Everyone could sense it: something strangely foreboding seemed to have settled over us.

The wind stopped dead and the heat in the Kentucky cornfield became almost unbearable as we removed the clay figures from their braced positions in the back of the car. In the thick, oppressive air, I felt I could hardly breathe.

Dr. Wolf and I readied the lifelike heads on a card table set up in front of the grave site, positioning the wigs and touching up the makeup. Dr. Wolf was worried the heads would deteriorate in the sweltering sun.

"They've already started sweating," he said, "just like real people—even in the same places."

Fearing they would actually start to melt, I worked furiously to photograph the staring heads. The Indians gathered around at a distance, watching silently, their faces increasingly glum, obviously worried. I arranged the heads now this way, now that, photographing them from every position I could think of. Repeatedly changing lenses and repositioning my tripod, I sought the perfect angle, the most pleasing composition. Sweat rolled down my face, burning my eyes and blurring my focus. My clothes became drenched, and my back ached. Still—I could sense it—it wasn't working. As Dr. Wolf had warned, the heads started to sweat. Distracting highlights from the light of the sun reflected on the softening plasticine faces. Soon the faces would become distorted.

As I continued shooting in that windless and oppressive heat, Chief Johnson came over and stood beside me, motionless, watching intently. Finally, in a soft voice, he asked, "You know why the wind stopped?"

I looked at him, not understanding.

"It's the Ancient Ones," he said. "Something's wrong. They were happy to be reburied, but now they're disturbed. Peace was being restored, but now the peace has been broken. It's those two heads you've brought. The spirit world is upset. They've never seen anything like this. The spirits from the two skulls you used have recognized their own faces in those heads. They're confused. How can they be buried and yet still be out here, separated from the others? If you take these clay heads away from here where they belong, their spirits will be carried away with them. That's why the wind stopped. It's their way of calling out to us."

He said, "Steve, can I make a strange suggestion? Would you let us bury those two heads after you've finished with your photographs? We don't want you to take them away. Their spirits will never rest if you do. They'll be stranded in this world with those heads."

I suddenly felt some great burden falling away from me.

"Of course," I said. "Whatever you want. Just as soon as I'm finished."

Returning to my camera, I continued shooting. Roll after roll I shot. Then, finally, I stopped. I'd done all I could do. I was finished. Photographically, it looked like a failure. They were still just two clay heads sitting on a card table. Maybe it was just as well. Maybe it shouldn't have been done in the first place. "Let it go" something inside me said. And I did.

"Okay, they're yours," I told Chief Johnson.

The Indians gathered around and gently took the heads, carrying them to an open grave pit—one of the same pits the robbers had dug. One of the Indians, a young Apache, stood at the pit's edge, cradling the female head in his arms. Standing there speechless, he gently removed the strands of hair from her staring, wide-eyed face. His eyes welled with tears as he looked into her eyes—eyes that earlier had appeared just a little crossed but now somehow looked at him straight and level.

Chills ran up and down my arms. I suddenly knew what I had to do. Reaching for my camera, I began to photograph the strange scene. Something happened. In their unaliveness, the heads glowed. They appeared alive. Could it be the light of the setting sun? Something in the atmosphere—or in me—had changed.

Now the Apache took the other head, the man's, and lowered himself into the grave to lay it beside the woman's. Holding the head at his waist, he turned toward me. The head stared right into the camera's lens. Without planning, the perfect composition materialized before me. The eyes seemed to plead, "Take the picture, Steve. This is it."

The heads were placed side by side in the grave. They stared up at us for the last time from the darkening pit. One of the Indians went to get a cloth to put over their faces. "We don't want to just throw the dirt in their faces," he said. With that done, we all grabbed shovels and started filling the hole. Within minutes they were buried, back where they needed to be in order to continue their interrupted spirit-journey to the other world. We stood at the graveside, heads bowed. A soft, cool wind stirred, rustling the weeds beside the grave.

The wind! The wind had returned. The oppressive heat had lifted. Suddenly it was chilly. I shivered. I glanced around to catch the questioning glances of the others. Whatever was going on, we all felt it.

Chief Johnson nodded at me.

"Everything's okay now," he said. "They've gone on. We've done our job. They'll get back to the spirit world now."

Once again that chill ran through me, as it does every time I look at these photographs.

Explain it as you will. For me, no explanations are necessary.

Still another matter not mentioned in our *Geographic* article was the "spirit-fog." One afternoon Harvey and I went down to the Indians' cornfield encampment and took a walk among the desecrated graves with elders Jess and Mary Bluebird. The anthros, the police, the politicians were gone. We had the forlorn site entirely to ourselves—or did we?

"Oh, they're here!" Jess announced, walking cautiously among the craters. "The spirits! They're here. You can see them. You can hear them. You gotta have eyes. You gotta have ears. They're calling out to us. They take many forms."

He walked from grave to grave, sprinkling pinches of tobacco from a worn leather pouch into the holes, droning a barely audible deep-voiced prayer.

"Don't step on the bones," he cautioned. "Watch where you walk. Gotta be careful. Let's go on up on the hill," he said. "Maybe we can see them better from there."

We walked up the low terrace edging the cornfield, then sat there looking out contemplatively across the long-shadowed field to the steely lavender Ohio River flowing by, carrying the millenniums in its quiet current.

Directly below us spread the pothunters' holes, most of them covered now by the archaeologists with sheets of black plastic.

"Oh, it's sorrowful," Mary Bluebird said. "It's just sorrowful for me to go out there and see our ancestors being dug up. Do we Indians come and dig up your white cemeteries? Can you imagine what white folks'd do if we did?"

She looked at me accusingly for a moment, then shook her head, smiled gently, forgivingly, and pulled her eyes away from mine.

"Oh, yes, it's so sorrowful," she repeated. "The Old Ones have been interrupted on their journey to the other world. That journey's not over till their bones have turned to dust and gone back to Mother Earth. Those who dug them up and interrupted their journey will have to pay. The Old Ones are mad! We're praying for the Old Ones, yes, but we're praying for whoever did this terrible deed, too. They need God's help even more than the ones they dug up! Just read what the Bible says. I'm an ordained minister, and I should know. Read John Five: The hour will come when we all come to final judgment. Either ye rise from the tomb to resurrection, or ye rise from the tomb to eternal damnation! We're praying for those diggers' souls. They're gonna need it!"

I was struck by her mixture of Christian and Native American metaphors—no, not mixture. Call it a convergence, a union.

"Look out there," Jess said. "Fog's coming up from the river. You usually don't see fog in the afternoon. It's no ordinary fog. The spirits're in it. It's a spirit-fog."

Mary shook her head.

"I don't think it's coming from the river," she said. "I think— Seems to me it's coming right out of the graves themselves! Either it's coming out of the graves, or it's going into the graves, one or the other. But it's not coming from the river."

I offered no opinion. There was a light mist playing along the ground, and whether it came from the river or from the graves was a matter more of poetry than truth, it seemed to me. Being open to both, I'd settle for either.

Mary went on:

"Sometimes, while sitting out here at night, we can hear them, the Old Ones, the ones from the time before. Sometimes we hear drums far off."

"Spirit-drums," Jess said.

"Yes," Mary continued, "and sometimes we hear a sound like gourds rattling. And sometimes we see sparks around the grave holes, like fireflies. But, you know, there's no fireflies this time of year. I've seen them! It's the spirits themselves! They're hoverin' around. They're lost. Oh, it's so sorrowful!"

Now Jess interjected: "They're down there in the shadows. They can see us sitting up here. They can see the grave dust shining on us. We got it on us when we walked down there. They see it shining on our feet and hands and clothes. Even in our hair! In their world that grave dust makes us shine! They see it on us, and they think we're the ones who dug them out! That's why we got to wash it off when we leave here—take a good scrub bath tonight and wash off every grain of grave dust. Tomorrow we'll have a ceremony, a cleansing ceremony."

The sun was going down. The shadows deepened and lengthened, swallowing the open graves in sudden darkness.

"Come on. We better go," Jess said, getting up and walking back down the terrace. "Look at that spirit-fog! It's coming right out of the graves. Mary's right!"

I squinted into the darkness. The mist did seem to be hovering around the plastic-covered holes like some kind of ghostly exhalation.

"They're coming out!" Jess said. "They'll be looking to find who dug them up. They'll see us shining up here with that grave dust. Maybe they'll cause trouble. We'd better go. Remember, wash that grave dust off yourself back at the motel."

And we did, scouring off every grain, imaginary or otherwise. It was hard not to be affected by this stuff! Just thinking about it raised the hackles on the back of my neck. I could see us sitting there up on that hill, shining with grave dust. The mere thought of it could give even an icy-hearted anthro the tingles!

❊

The next day Jess asked us to drive him out to the Garden of the Gods, about an hour's drive away in southern Illinois. He had seen a picture of the rock spires in a local tourist brochure and became instantly excited. "Where's that rock?" he asked. "That's a holy place. I want to go to that rock!"

During the drive out to the sacred site, he told us: "I know that place! Soon as I saw that picture I knew it! I seen it in a dream—no, a vision. Right when I saw the picture of that big rock. It was like a movie starts going in my head. I see a little boy running there. An Indian boy. He's maybe ten, maybe eleven. And he's wearing an Indian girl's dress! And he's got a girl's wig on with long hair in a braid. And he's running—runnin' hard as he can. There's soldiers coming after him. The soldiers, they got blue uniforms. Dark blue. I can see them. They got guns, big long rifles with bayonets on them. They comin' to kill all the Indian men. They killin' even the boys. This boy's mother dressed him up as a girl to hide who he was, but still the soldiers are coming after him. They're shooting at him. He's running. Oh, he's running hard as he can go. Now he falls down. He's been hit! Oh, he's dying. He's dying, that boy. Right there. Right by those rocks. Right there in what they call the Garden of the Gods in that tourist pamphlet. That's my dream-vision. I need to go there. Maybe that boy . . . maybe that boy was buried in this corn-field here. Maybe he's one of them spirits out there. Maybe he's one of them fireflies!"

I didn't know quite what to make of all this. Poetry, yes. But truth? Too far-fetched to get past *National Geographic's* editors, that was for sure. I remembered Joe Judge's edict to Harvey: "Please, don't go mystical on us!"

I could see Harvey shaking his head. No way he could write about this stuff for the magazine!

We arrived at the Garden of the Gods and immediately followed Jess and Mary out into the rock amphitheater. Shawnee John Thomas and his wife, Fay, had come along with their two girls, Redday and Martina. Jess had said he'd have a naming ceremony for little Martina. "We'll give her a spirit-name," he announced. Jess wore a western outfit with a black Stetson-like cowboy hat, an eagle feather stuck jauntily in its bright-beaded band. Mary had wrapped herself in a colorful Indian blanket.

We stood amid the bizarrely shaped spires on a rock platform overlooking the forested valley, draped now in a light morning mist. Jess burned a few pinches of tobacco on the rock, uttering a breathy, low-voiced prayer. Then he brought little Martina to the center of the rock platform, placed one hand on her shoulder, and, closing his eyes and facing toward the sun, raised a gentle singsong chant into the air in his native Cherokee language. Mary stood on the other side of the little girl and lifted her arms so that the Indian blanket seemed to metamorphose into two widespread protective wings. Now she, too, broke into a prayer:

"O Lord, this is your daughter, Sister Mary, and your son, Brother Jess. We ask you to bring us together and heal us with your love. We ask that you help the Old Ones, the Ancient Ones, who were so cruelly dug up from their graves. Help them find their way back to You. Please light their way, Lord. We ask that you forgive those who dug them up, too, Lord. They know not what they do. They don't know the powers they've let loose. Forgive them, Lord. Please light their way, too. And, Lord, please bless all of us standing here, including these two men from *National Geographic* who've come here to tell the Old Ones' story to the world. Bless them, too, Lord. And, Lord, please whisper into Jess's ear a lovely spirit-name for this beautiful child here."

Now she broke seamlessly into a gentle singing voice, and the words of "Amazing Grace" mingled softly on the air with Jess's continuing chant in Cherokee: *"Amazing grace, how sweet the sound, that saved a wretch like me . . . "* Mary's bell-clear notes entwined contrapuntally with Jess's low-droning tones. For a minute or more Christian hymn and Cherokee prayer came into lovely convergence, an exquisitely poignant union. Then, abruptly, Jess let out a loud *whoop!*

Then another. Then another. Five *whoops!* in all. The entire rock amphitheater resounded, setting up a chorus of softly muffled echoes. Five distant answering *whoops* seemingly came from the mist-draped wooded valley below. And through it all Mary kept up the words of "Amazing Grace": *"I once was lost, but now am found, was blind, but now I see."*

Their moving duet became a many-voiced chorale with the murmuring echoes that seemed to swirl around us. I was tingling from head to foot. We'd stumbled headlong into the visionary. We'd gone mystical!

After a couple of minutes the singing and the chanting and the echo-murmurs gradually faded away. The air was still.

Jess finally opened his eyes. He turned to little Martina.

"I have your name," he said. "Your name is Angel!"

She smiled a smile as bright as sunlight. It seemed perfect.

Jess went on: "Did you hear the spirits calling? See that spirit-fog down there? See how bright that mist is? That's the light of the spirits. They're shining down there. They've come to hear us. They've come to pray with us. They called up your name to me. I heard them. 'Angel,' they called. 'Her name is "Angel"!' And that's what you are!"

"And, look!" Mary exclaimed. "Look at the eagle feather in Jess's hat. It turned around! See? It turned right around during the ceremony!"

Jess took off his cowboy hat and looked at the feather in the band. The pale underside of the feather was turned outward. I vaguely remembered having seen it before, with its outer side—whitish at the base, brownish black at the top—turned outward. Now it did seem to be in there backside out, though I couldn't have sworn it hadn't been that way before.

"Oh, Jess never wears the feather backwards," Mary said. "He'd never do that. The spirits did that. They turned the feather around in Jess's hatband. They gave us a sign—just a little sign, but still a

sign. A tiny little miracle so we'd know they heard our prayers. Oh, thank you, Lord. Thank you for hearing our prayer."

With a twist of his fingers Jess turned the feather frontside out again. He set the hat back on his head and looked out into the valley. I expected him to say a prayer of thanks or start chanting again, but he abruptly let out the loudest whoop yet, a whoop that answered itself in several muffled echoes from the misted valley floor.

"Yep, they hear us," he announced. "They happy we come here to be with them!"

"And that little boy in your vision," Harvey said, "is he one of those spirits down there?"

Jess cocked one eye and smiled darkly.

"Oh, sure," he said. "He's the one who whispered 'Angel' in my ear!"

Chapter 10

JUST recently, seven years after our article on the grave desecration was published in the March 1989 National Geographic, Steve and I drove out to Oklahoma to see Jess and Mary Blue- bird again. "The door to our little house is always open," they'd told us. We'd always remembered that standing invitation. And I had a gift I wanted to pass on to them this time, something that had come into my possession—an old 1886 high school graduation autograph book from Oklahoma's famed Chilocco Indian School and an exquisitely beaded Shawnee moccasin top from the same period. These had been turned over to me years before by *National Geographic* Editor Bill Garrett, who had received them from a reader in the mail with the hope that they would be "returned to a proper place." Bill had sent me a note along with the package: "Harvey, see if you can find the right home for these." The box had been gathering dust in a file drawer since then, and this new journey seemed the perfect occasion to return the moccasin and the book to a proper place—as well as an excuse for stopping by to spend a few hours with Jess and Mary again.

That day at the Garden of the Gods in 1988 had stuck hard in our memories over the years. It was one of those experiences that stays with you, a recurring memory imbued with a special personal meaning. It had hardly been an earth-shaking miracle to be sure, no more than the merest turning of a feather. But for us it was one of those small confirmations of at least the *possibility* of the miraculous, hardly more than a fleeting and uncertain suggestion, perhaps, yet enough to pull us in the direction we were meant to go. Miracles, even the smallest miracles, have a purpose. They're never wasted. They're a form of Original Instructions. "We live by miracles," Mathew King had told us, and we were beginning to see what he meant.

✤

Our visit with Jess and Mary became a kind of ceremony in itself. We pulled up to their little house in Sperry, Oklahoma, and there was Mary, standing on the front steps in a bright red dress, almost as if she'd foreseen our coming and was waiting out on the stoop for us to arrive. As a matter of fact, it took her several squints and a long uncertain shake of her head before she recognized us.

"Oh, now I remember," she finally said, nodding with a smile, "that time in Kentucky when they dug up those old Shawnee bones. Of course, you're those two fellas from *National Geographic*. Well! Imagine! After all these years! What brings you boys all the way out here to Sperry?"

"We're on another one of our journeys," I explained. "We're hoping you and Jess could give us one of your blessings," I told her.

Her eyes brightened. She clapped her hands silently.

"Of course!" she exclaimed, her face beaming, "It's always the perfect time for a blessing!"

"And we've brought a little gift for the two of you," I added.

"Oh, come on in, you two!" she cried excitedly, "I'll call Jess!"

She called back into the house. "Jess! Jess! You hear me in there, Grandpa? Two old friends are here to see us!"

A dark face appeared at the half-open door behind her.

"Who? Who is it, you say?"

"Hello, Jess," Steve announced brightly. "Remember us? We went with you to the Garden of the Gods that time."

Jess peered at us uncertainly. Mary took his hand and squeezed it fondly.

"Don't you remember, Grandpa? The two men from *National*

Geographic that time we reburied those bones of the Old Ones over in Kentucky? They took pictures of us that day, remember? The time the eagle feather turned around in your hat at the Garden of the Gods?"

Jess finally nodded in recognition, squinting at us.

"Oh, yeah. The feather! Yep, it turned around. I remember now."

Mary winked at us. She steered Jess back into the house and motioned for us to follow.

"Don't worry," she whispered. "He remembers. It just takes a little while, that's all. Jess is a foreseer, you know. He sees the future better than he remembers the past! Come on in, you boys. Welcome to our little house. Come on in for a blessing!"

She ushered us into their cozy living room. Jess eased himself into a stuffed armchair in one corner. We sat facing him. From my camera bag I extracted the small tooled antique cardboard box containing the old autograph book and moccasin top from Bill Garrett, holding it out to Mary.

"I know you're Shawnee," I said.

"I'm Shawnee-Delaware-Cherokee-Creek-and-Scotch-Irish!" Mary declared, saying it all in one gulp as one long word, smiling proudly, eyes sparkling. "And Jess here. Jess is Cherokee. Full-blood!"

Jess stirred in his chair. "Full-blood, hell. I'm *over*full!"

That got a laugh. The ice of seven years instantly melted.

"The reason I mention it," I went on, "has to do with this little box."

I opened the box and took out the autograph book and moccasin top. I explained how Bill Garrett had given them to me to be passed on. "He's part Shawnee himself," I told Mary. "I know he'd want you to have these."

Her eyes opened wide.

"I went to Chilocco Indian School!" she exclaimed, taking the little autograph book and riffling through its faded pages. "Oh, my. Oh, my. Look at all these names! Their own signatures from 1886! I know those families! Oh, what a treasure! What a wonderful treasure! I'll put it in a little Indian museum we're planning to build. Oh, my . . . thank you! Tell your Mr. Garrett, *thank you!*"

"And there's also this moccasin top," I said.

Jess leaned forward in his chair and took the lovely beaded artifact in his hands. He stroked it lovingly. "Mmmmm," he said. "Yep, that's the real thing, all right. Real buckskin. Real Indian beads. Yep, probably Shawnee, I'd say. How much you say you want for this?"

"No, Grandpa!" Mary broke in. "They're not *selling* it."

"Oh, too bad," he murmured.

"They're giving it to us, Grandpa! Isn't that right?"

Mary looked at me for confirmation. I nodded.

"Givin' it?" Jess asked with genuine surprise. "Really? It's for us? Why . . . Well . . . Thank you, boys!"

"No thanks necessary, Jess," I said. "This is where it belongs."

He seemed genuinely moved. He continued stroking the moccasin top.

"Look here," he said, holding it out for us to admire. "This is only the upper. There's no bottom, no shoe-sole. It's a spirit-moccasin, that's what it is. They buried it with the dead. That's so they could walk in them on their journey to the other world. They didn't need shoe-soles, they just wore the tops. There's no ground in the spirit world so you don't need shoe-soles. Yep, a spirit-moccasin. That's what it is. Well! I think I'll just hang it up on the wall right here. That's a beautiful thing. Yep, a holy thing, that's what it is."

"We'll put it with that autograph book in our little museum of Indian history," Mary said. "These two items will be part of the collection. Everyone will be able to look at them. Oh, my. Once again, thank you!"

The moccasin and the book had found a proper home.

Jess sat back in his chair with a pleased look on his face. He looked me square in the eye and nodded. I felt that suffusion of warmth I experience on those rare occasions when I actually do something right.

"Mary says you're a *foreseer*. That right, Jess?" I asked him.

"Oh, yeah," he intoned, his face turning serious. "Yep, I see things."

"What kinds of things?" I asked.

He stroked the moccasin top with his fingertips. His eyes grew dreamy.

"I see . . . I see what's coming," he said in a thick, breathy voice, very hard to understand.

In order to make out his words I had to lean right up to him, almost knee to knee. He leaned forward with a kind of urgency. His mystic face loomed only inches in front of me—a complex conundrum of a face, dark copper and cast bronze with inner glints of lavender and purple, deep eye sockets lost in inky shadow, mobile mouth continually flickering with transient smiles and grimaces. A face somehow serene for all its mobility and lurking complexities.

"I see the end o' things," he breathed. "Yep, the end. It's coming. Yessir, it's coming!"

"The end of what things, Jess?" I asked.

He took a deep breath and eyed me hard.

"Everything . . . everything on this Mother Earth. All gone. All wiped away. God'll wipe all this wicked world away, that's what He's gonna do. Wipe it all away like you wipe dirt from a dirty window with a wet rag. Only God won't use a rag. No. God's gonna use the tornado for a rag. He's gonna use the hurricane for a rag. He's gonna use the earthquake for a rag. He's gonna wipe away all the wicked world. Wipe it all away like you wipe a dirty window. Yep, wipe it clean. All the wickedness wiped right away. Only the sky be left. Blue sky all over . . . up above . . . and down below . . . all over. Just clear blue sky . . . like a clean window.

"Yep, God's mad!" Jess went on. "He's *very* mad at what people are doing to His world."

"But He's a *loving* God, too, Jess," Mary interjected, a certain alarm in her voice at Jess's dire words.

"Yep, He's loving, okay, but He's still mad," Jess continued, his eyes darkly incandescent. "He's giving us signs. We've got to see them. Last year, a few weeks before those floods we had on the Mississippi, I told people, 'I see coffins coming down the river, floating down the river like boats.' I foresaw it . . . the river full o' coffins. And then when the floods come a while later, it happened! The river . . . it dug the cemeteries out, and all them caskets came right out of the ground and went floating down the river! They showed it on TV. It was the same thing I foresaw. Yeah, all them coffins with all them people in them, all those corpses, sailing right down the river! That's God paying them back, them people, paying them back for digging up those Indian graves. That made God mad!"

Jess still had the moccasin top in his hands, and he stroked it fondly as he spoke.

He rapped the tabletop three times sharply with his knuckles, then rapped it three times again.

"I'm calling Him. I'm calling God," he said. "See, God's right here. He's here in this room right now! There—He's in that smoke from my cigarette! He's in that light there on the ceilin'! He's all over, not just here. He's everywhere! Those church people say they have the only God, and He's there in that church with them. They think they got Him all to themselves. But they don't. They *don't!* God's right here with us, right here now, right in this room with us. He's sending His signs. He's sending His life. But then—watch out! He's sending the tornado!"

He leaned back, smiling softly, serenity glowing on his dark-burnished face like firelight reflected from an inner mirror. The foreseeing was over.

Jess leaned forward, reached a hand under his armchair, and plucked a pack of cigarettes from a carton he kept there.

"You guys like some holy smokes?" he asked.

"Holy smokes?" I asked, puzzled.

"Yeah," he said. "If you like, I'll make you some holy smokes. You can use them in a ceremony while you're traveling sometime. Or just smoke them. Make you feel good. Bring you luck. Think of me when you smoke them, and I'll be there with you!"

"Well . . . why, sure, Jess. Go ahead. We'd be honored."

Jess banged the bottom of the pack a few times on the surface of the end table beside him.

"Every cigarette's a prayer," he said. "The smoke carries them up to the Great Spirit. Here, I'll say a blessing over each one of them. Later on you puff on them, too. There's a blessing in every one of these cigarettes!"

He chuckled, obviously both pleased and amused.

Steve put in: "Say, Jess, you know . . . Harvey's doctor told him he shouldn't be smoking those things."

"These won't hurt him," Jess said. "Just don't smoke any more after you finish them, that's all. I'll put a blessing on them so they won't hurt him. Once they've been blessed they won't hurt you."

Jess meticulously unwrapped the cellophane and broke open the top of the cigarette pack, tearing off the gold foil to expose the cigarettes within. He sniffed the tobacco appreciatively, then held the pack upright in one hand and with the other gestured over it with a repetitive circular motion. A deep-toned hum emitted from his throat. Rocking back and forth in his armchair, he blew lightly on the cigarettes . . . once, twice, three times. He waved his fingers over them, then tapped the top of each cigarette with his fingertips. He blew again, waved his fingers over the pack again, then tapped again. He continued rocking back and forth, eyes half-closed, seemingly seeing into some other world, some other dimension. The hum in his throat rose into a soft chant. He was singing now, rocking and singing as he blew repeatedly on the cigarettes, waving his hand over them, tapping them with his fingertips. This went on for two or three minutes. Finally he let out a soft little "whoo-oo-oop!"

"There," he said, handing the pack back to me. "Now they're holy smokes. Won't hurt you. You smoke one every day till they're gone. Remember, they're prayers. Praying can't hurt you. Tobacco can't hurt you when it's used for praying."

He went on: "It's not the tobacco that kills people, it's the poison they put into it! That's what does the killing. White man's poison! He's poisoned the cigarettes like he's poisoned everything else!"

He held the newly blessed cigarettes out to me.

"Now I'll get addicted to praying!" I said, laughing.

"Well," Mary chimed, "you could certainly do a lot worse than that!"

I held the pack of cigarettes up in the air and intoned: "I hereby christen thee the Holy Smokes!"

"Now it is time to have our other blessing," Mary announced. "You boys put down your cameras and your tape recorder there. Come right around here in a circle with me and Jess. Join hands now. It's time to pray *my* way! We'll raise the spirit right here and now, just the four of us. We'll have a little talk with God."

We stood in a circle in the middle of the living room, hands joined, the spirit flowing almost palpably through our fingertips.

"Yes," Mary began, "let's have a prayer here. Let's shut the world out and get our minds upon the power of God. Everybody pray now. Grandpa Jess, you pray in your own language."

While Jess murmured softly in Cherokee, Mary continued, face lifted, eyes gazing upward right through the ceiling, squeezing our hands as she intoned:

"Almighty God, our Creator, we call upon your mighty power and infinite mercies. We're calling on you right now for these two brothers you've sent to us. Touch these brothers with your mighty power. They're on their spirit-journey, Lord, doing your work. And we're calling on you right here, Lord. We know you're here in our presence. Yes, we can feel your fire coming down on us! Touch these brothers with your fire, Lord. Send your fire right on through them—from the tops of their heads to the soles of their feet. Yes, I can feel it, Lord! Your fire! *Hooo!* Oh, thank you, Lord! Yes. *Hooo! Hooo-oo!*"

Now Jess, too, let out a gentle echoing *whoo-oo-oop! whoo-oo-oop!*

"You feel it?" Mary exclaimed. "The fire! The fire! It's flowing right through us now! Oh, feel it! Hoo! Thank you, Lord. Thank you! *Hooo!*"

I didn't fight back the tingles. I let them flow right through me like an electric current. I could see Steve with his eyes closed, his face contorted. Now he tilted back his head, opened his eyes, and smiled beatifically. I almost expected *him* to let out a loud and piercing *whooop!* himself.

Mary continued, her voice bell-clear: "Guide these two men, Lord. They've set out to tell the people of the spiritual way. Yes, help them with their work. Oh, I know you will! We're placing them in your hands. Wrap your arms around them. Light their path and meet their needs."

She paused, nodding emphatically at us, then went on: "Yes! Yes! They're now being blessed at this very moment! Hooo! Feel the light come down upon them, upon the four of us here. Oh, thank you for sending your fire to us, Lord! Hoo! Thank you for sending your light! Lord, we give you all the glory. Amen."

"Amen," Jess echoed.

The prayer ended, but the tingling subsided only slowly. I felt prayed out, drained. Mary and Jess walked out to the van with us.

Mary laughed. "Well, I really cut loose in there, didn't I! Sometimes that happens—when the spirit's really strong, you know? That's why people come to us for healing. We've got *double* power, Jess and me. Both of us were struck down and then lifted up! We both had terrible accidents.

"See, Jess here was hurt in a terrible car accident back about 1960. He had brain damage. His head was crushed. He couldn't speak, he couldn't walk, he was almost blind, but God *saved* him for a purpose. He was healed by the power of God! What happened—what Jess did—was, he decided he'd go up the mountain near where he lived and talk to God, ask God to cure him. There was snow on the ground. He had to crawl on his hands and knees up over this mountain. And up on top of that mountain he kneeled—there on his hands and knees in the snow. He lifted his hands up and prayed to the Creator. He told God, 'If you'll help me speak and walk and see again, I'll serve you the rest of my life.' And God *touched him!* Jess said it was like a bolt of lightning hit him."

"Yeah," Jess said, "just like lightning. It hits me, then I see . . . I can walk . . . I can talk the first time. Up to then I couldn't speak. Nothing!"

"That's the power of God," Mary went on. "God touched him with a bolt of lightning. God gave him this power through the lightning and thunder. That's where Jess's power comes from, through the lightning and thunder. That's one of the most powerful powers you can have. It wasn't man-given. It was *God-given* right then and there on that mountain! That's why Jess is so powerful in his work. He's a medicine man and a foreseer by God's will! True medicine comes not through tradition or studying but directly from God. It can't be handed down. It's got to come *direct!*

"And, see . . . what's strange—back as a young girl I was almost killed in a car accident, too. A car hit me while I was walking down the road right here in Sperry. I was torn head to foot. My leg was crushed. My hip was just hanging on by the skin. The pelvic bone was sticking right through the flesh. And I was internally injured. They expected me to die. I was in the hospital for a year. But God came down and touched me! I lived! God saved me for a purpose, same as He did Jess. We're both living witnesses to what God can do. Then God brought us together, Jess and me. He led us to each other. God saw us as a team! And that's what we are—a team with double power!

"People come here for their healing and other needs, and they say they can feel the power here, the *double power!* So that's what God did for us both. He brought us together so we could help people, so we could serve humanity.

"Yes, God saved us for a purpose. And I can see you two men have your purposes, too."

We said our good-byes. Mary and Jess stood in the driveway as we got into our car. I rolled the passenger window down. Jess came over and leaned right inside, his face only inches from mine. There was still an apocalyptic gleam in his eyes. He smiled sweetly.

"You smoke those holy smokes when you get a notion, and you two'll be okay. You think of Jess when you smoke them. I'll be there praying with you. I'll be looking at you through the smoke! You won't see me, but I'll be there!"

Chapter 11

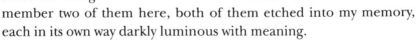

CERTAIN scenes keep returning to my mind, not so much for the words that were spoken as for the way things happened. Sometimes the message isn't in the words, it's in the fine particulars of the event itself. Things happen that can't be caught on tape or in a photograph and yet have a meaning beyond the verbal and the visual. Reality itself becomes the message. What happens is the Instruction.

Such events, like recurring dreams, insist on being re-remembered. I remember two of them here, both of them etched into my memory, each in its own way darkly luminous with meaning.

The first has to do with our humiliation at a peyote ceremony, the second with the death of a friend. Both had their nonverbal lessons for us.

❋

First, the peyote ceremony. That, for sure, was one of the strangest and most memorable moments in any of our journeys. Old Ute medicine man Charlie Knight honored us with an invitation to a Native American Church peyote ceremony after I'd brought my old friend, white spiritual chiropractor Dr. James Chastain, up to the reservation, and he healed Charlie's bad leg. Charlie had fallen off his horse—got thrown due to sorcery, he said—and hadn't walked for months until James came up and did his chiropractic miracle-working. One holy man curing another. It was quite a sight. Charlie was really grateful, and after having disappointed Harvey and me that time with the "red-coal trick," he now arranged for us to attend the Native American Church prayer meeting.

"I had to ask everyone who'll be there, and they all said okay," Charlie told us.

It was dusk when we arrived for the ceremony. Charlie took us up on the side of a mountain where a white canvas tepee had been set up on a rock ledge overlooking the tremendous wide-angled landscape. Sleeping Ute Mountain faded in the distance against a darkening sky bright with new stars. Charlie had told us the legend of how the Sleeping Ute had once been a warrior when the Utes were a race of giants. He was left behind by a hunting party to stand sentry over the land until they returned. But they never did. Finally, after many centuries of standing guard over the land, he fell asleep. "The Creator got mad," Charlie told us, "so He made all us Utes smaller, like we are now, and the Sleeping Ute—why, for punishment, He turned him to stone. You can still see him now." Charlie pointed to the horizontal massif of Sleeping Ute Mountain, lying prone on the horizon. "Those are his feet, see? And that's his belly and chest, there in the middle. And over there, that's his head. See his nose? Someday he's gonna rise up, that Sleeping Ute. Someday he's gonna rise up and take back the land!"

He led us over to the ceremonial tent, a Northern Plains tepee illuminated from within. The shadows of the already gathered participants danced on the canvas walls. I wanted so much to grab my camera and shoot that wonderful scene of the glowing white tent with the shadowed figures against the immense topography of the high Colorado plateau, but Charlie had told us flatly, "No cameras. Ain't allowed." I could almost feel my Leicas twitching with disappointment in my camera bag, but I'd have to live with it.

I could see Harvey chewing at his mustache with frustration. We were out there on assignment from the magazine, and he, loyal staffer that he was, wanted Charlie to pose in front of the tent for a photograph. Charlie just shook his head, adamant in his refusal.

Harvey came over to me, fuming. Frustration was written all over his face. Here, right before our eyes, was a powerful photographic image—a real "zinger"—and we, the two intrepid white journalists, weren't being permitted to steal it with our cameras so as to show our millions of readers how "quaintly" spiritual the Indians are.

Harvey muttered under his breath at me, "If only he'd raise his arms in a kind of prayer in front of that tepee, you'd have one hell of a picture!"

No doubt he was right. And yet he coudn't have been more wrong.

He kept shaking his head and grimacing, glancing at me sharply, as if it were *my* fault . . . as if I should just take out my cameras anyway, despite Charlie's orders not to, and start shooting away without permission. I wasn't about to do it. Harvey and *National Geographic* with him could go jump off the nearest cliff. I wasn't violating Charlie's trust. And I didn't. And so one more zinger, which I'm proud *not* to have taken, remains embedded not on film but on the emulsion of my memory, where it belongs.

❈

"Road chief's already here," Charlie told us, referring to the itinerant preacher of the Native American Church who would be leading the peyote ceremony. "Name's Jerome. Asked him if you could come. Said okay. Asked all the others, too. Got to ask them all. No cameras or tape recorders, remember. And no talk. You boys just sit there in the circle where they set you. Do what Jerome says. Just do it. If they give you something to take, you take it, hear? You'd better be sure, you two. Once you go in there, you can't go out!"

The tepee glowed eerily against the gathering darkness. A fire had been lit within, and the shadows of people moving around inside danced weirdly on the glowing canvas walls. Charlie pulled aside the weighted door flap, and we entered. A circle of men and women sat within, perhaps two dozen in all. We walked counterclockwise around the circle, then took a place just to the left of the door, sitting crosslegged on the dirt floor like the others. Charlie sat on the far side of the circle. He had spiffed himself out in a neatly pressed Western suit and polished black cowboy boots with tooled silver tips, but no cowboy hat or sunglasses like he usually wore. He had a serious, even somber look on his face for a man usually filled with easy laughter. He seemed totally absorbed and gave us not another glance.

Just off center of the circle a burly man in Levis and a red plaid shirt carefully laid small pieces of split cedar wood on a bed of glowing red coals. They called him the "fireman." He used a long-handled rake to move the wood and coals around, ceaselessly rearranging them. Whenever a spurt of flame shot out, he sprinkled water from a bucket on it and tamped out the flame with the rake. The heat from the flameless incandescent coals, only three feet away from us, seared our knees and faces. Only gradually did we realize that he was methodically shaping the coals into the form of a glowing red eagle with wings spread wide.

Jerome, the road chief, a dark-eyed man in a worn black frock coat, stood up and said a few words in English, welcoming Charlie's "two white friends." Then he began a soft chant, accompanied by the light beat of a water-drum played by another man across the fire. Soon others picked up the chant, sometimes singly, sometimes in chorus. Every so often the drum was passed around to be played now by one, now by another of the participants. The chanting and the drumming would continue almost without letup for the next ten hours. All the while the fireman patiently tended the central fire, adding wood when necessary, repeatedly tamping out the flames, and continuously shaping and reshaping the glowing red eagle, which became a living presence in the center of the tent.

A man and a woman stood up, the man carrying an open cocoa tin, the woman holding a small silver spoon. Slowly they moved around the circle clockwise, pausing in front of each participant. I watched with a sense of growing dread as the woman dipped the spoon into the tin and brought out a heaping spoonful of some grayish granules. This she put to the lips of the person sitting before her, who swallowed as everyone else watched. Again she filled the spoon, again they swallowed. This was repeated until all around the circle had partaken but Harvey and me.

Finally it was our turn—first Harvey's, then mine. There was no avoiding it. We partook. One spoonful of the terrible granules, then another. All eyes were on us. There was no chance of spitting it out unobtrusively. Harvey took his granules with a confident smile that almost instantly disappeared. He gave me a sidelong look, his eyes wide and terrified. He made a gagging sound, gathered himself with obvious inner effort, then swallowed or tried to swallow. I saw trickles of granule-laden saliva come out the corners of his mouth. Even as he was struggling to get the stuff down, the girl was now in front of me, smiling ever so sweetly, ladling two spoonfuls of granules onto my outstretched tongue. I closed my eyes like I do at the dentist's. The less you see, the better, I've always figured. But this time it did me no good. I saw the problem Harvey was having. Those ghastly-tasting granules stick to the roof and sides of your mouth like sandy peanut butter. They seemed absolutely unswallowable. You can't swallow them, and you can't spit them out. They hang there in the far back of your throat, wedged against your tonsils, refusing to go down, like a clot of muck clogging a drainpipe. Our eyes must have been bulging. The honor of the magazine, of all intruding white journalists, was at stake. Would we be able to swallow the stuff or not?

Then to our great relief another girl came around with a bucket and a tin cup. Thank God! A chaser! She offered us each a cupful of some brownish drink, which we seized gratefully only to realize that this lukewarm "tea" was only more of the drug in liquid form. Even so—thank God!—it washed down the granules. And then it all began again.

Repeatedly the granules and the tea came around the circle. We lost count of how many times. The chanting and the drumming went on. People occasionally rose to speak, often weeping or screaming. It was all in Ute or Navajo, so we understood not a word. Yet we found ourselves repeatedly moved to tears by what they were saying. We seemed to understand without actually understanding, as if equipped with some inner organ of perception.

At one point some of the granules were mixed with tobacco and rolled in corn husks like huge Jamaican reefers. These, too, were passed around the circle. We smoked. Shadows of the drug-bearers were thrown by the firelight onto the sloping walls of the tepee, creating a grotesquerie of dancing forms on the stretched white canvas wall. The tepee, so small when seen from the outside in that huge landscape, now seemed as large as a cathedral within.

Then the bearers brought around the fourth and final form of the drug: an olive-sized ball that reminded me of dirty Silly Putty. Each of us took one, popped it back in our throats, and swallowed it whole, like an enormous pill. An especially large ball, what olive fanciers call "super-colossal," was presented to one woman across the fire from us.

She popped it back in her mouth with ease but then obviously couldn't quite get it down. Her eyes widened with a kind of horror, then shut tightly as her whole face contorted violently. Her throat constricted. Her body quaked. To vomit it out or even gag would be impossible, a sign of spiritual weakness. Stifling every instinct, she somehow held it in. Pearls of sweat formed on her forehead. She simply had to swallow it. Then, abruptly, she opened her eyes. Her face relaxed. She smiled sweetly once more. She'd gotten it down!

I'm not sure just what our physical and chemical reaction was to this hours-long ingestion of the drug in so many forms. Were we supposed to get "high" or what? I've never been a druggie. I'm just not into it. After a while I felt both nauseous and dizzy. I must have hallucinated. I felt myself drawn out into the air like one of the sparks from the fire, swirling around, looking down at ourselves. There was Harvey, slumped on one elbow beside me, his head nodding to some unheard rhythm. The faces of people across the fire seemed to swim out toward me, then recede, then loom right up to me again.

Just beyond our scorched knees, the fireman worked feverishly, continuously creating his eagle from the incandescent ashes. The eagle pulsed and throbbed like a living thing that has been tied down and is trying to escape. With my mind unmoored from its accustomed perceptions, I fully expected the glowing eagle to flap its wings of fire and fly upward in a whirlwind of sparks. I could see Harvey staring into it, mesmerized. He was swaying, bobbing back and forth, his head rolling. The hours dissolved. Time itself dissolved. At one point I found myself floating in a sea of iridescent chartreuse light. I seemed to be swimming, my hands forming breaststrokes as I pulled myself through the glowing green sea. I felt buoyant, self-propelled, detached from all thought, immersed in pure physical sensation, every one of my senses going off like the exploding lights in a pinball machine.

Suddenly there was a great roar—a roar that finally resolved itself into an enormous booming voice. *"YOU,"* it boomed, as if in an echo chamber. *"YOU TWO GUYS . . ."*

I was leaning against something. My head swam. I opened my eyes. I realized I'd been asleep. I looked over at Harvey. He was slumped in a heap beside me. The two of us had been leaning against each other in a double heap on the dirt floor, sound asleep. We blinked our eyes open, utterly dazed. The booming voice was the fireman's. He was pointing the handle of his long-handled rake at us and shouting out angrily:

"Hey! You! You two guys better wake up! We don't fall asleep in your white man's church, and *you* better not fall asleep in ours!"

We jerked immediately upright, mortified. Shame scorched our cheeks more than the fire. I righted myself, sitting up in a daze. Damn! What fools! I gave Harvey a sharp jab with my elbow. He pulled himself off the floor and sat up shakily. He definitely did not look happy. He was staring angrily at the fireman, and the fireman was staring angrily at him. They both looked mean . . . murderous! I grabbed Harvey's sleeve and tugged it sharply. I swear, he was just about to lunge at that fireman! I could feel him trembling, his body growing taut. "Cool it!" I breathed. Later he told me he'd had a momentary impulse to leap up, shout some obscenity, knock the fireman down, and lurch out of there. Somehow he contained it. Lucky he did. That fireman was twice his size and probably ten times tougher. But gradually the anger and the embarrassment subsided.

Hours later—how long I've no idea—the chanting and the drumming came to a stop. The eagle's red glow had faded into lifeless gray ash. The people in the circle rose and started talking pleasantly to one another. The door flap was opened, and we all stumbled out into the clear cold light of morning. Everyone was smiling, even grumpy old Harv and me. In the distance the Sleeping Ute, etched against the horizon, seemed like he might rise up from his prone position and stride over to join us.

The fireman came over to Harvey and me, smiled, winked, nodded knowingly, and with a loud booming laugh walked back into the tepee, holding the door flap open for us. Within we shared a communal meal of hot fry bread, corn soup, and coffee. We exchanged good-byes with our fellow participants, thanked Road Chief Jerome, then walked back down to the car with Charlie.

"You guys were real funny," he said. "Made Charlie laugh. Good we laugh with each other. Means we're happy." He chuckled a chuckle bright as morning sunlight.

"If you want to remember Charlie," he said, referring to himself in the third person, as he often did, "then remember he's a funny man. That's what you tell them. Tell them Charlie Knight, he's a funny man! But not so funny as you two guys!"

Charlie Knight, for sure, was a funny man as well as a serious man.

He taught us that you don't have to be one or the other. You can be both. You don't have to be grim-faced to lead a spiritual life. A good belly laugh at your own expense is a great spiritual purgative. And it can be a revelation in itself.

�֍

And now from laughter to one of the saddest memories of our lives. During our travels among the Iroquois we were befriended by Lee Lyons, younger brother of Faithkeeper Oren Lyons. Lee, a wonderfully warm and vibrant human being, gave selflessly of his time and wisdom, alerting us to pitfalls and, when necessary, taking these two stumbling white intruders by the hand and leading us personally along the path. Oren called us one day with a terrible message: Lee had had heart bypass surgery and had never woken up. He had gone into a terminal coma. The doctors had declared him brain dead. After weeks of prayerful waiting, the family had come to a decision. Keeping Lee's physical body on life support would only tie his spirit to a hospital room. He needed release. They told the doctors to disconnect him from the breathing and feeding apparatus. Oren asked us to be on hand.

Lee was barely past fifty and looked hardly thirty-five. To those of us who knew him, his passing was unthinkable. A "runner" for the traditional chiefs of the Six Nations Iroquois Confederacy, he had been so exuberant, so filled with life and passion. On a previous visit we had watched him jump naked, wildly laughing, into the frigid waters of Lake Skeneatles—a year-round morning ritual for him—after which we shared a mammoth-sized buffalo steak that he cooked with great gusto and reverence on his backyard grill.

Lee had invited us over to show us a manuscript he was working on. *The Stealing of America,* he'd called it. It was about the way the white man had legalized the theft of a continent, the destruction of a world, and the obliteration of Great Turtle Island. Lee was really hot about it. To him, these dark events of the 1700s and 1800s were the latest news. His bulging cardboard file boxes were filled with photocopies of maps and treaties and documents he had garnered over the years, most recently through the use of the Freedom of Information Act. He was particularly looking at the moment for certain documents of the 1840s that he said would prove beyond a doubt the theft of Iroquois lands around Syracuse. "We actually *own* the city of Syracuse to this day! They're still hiding the *really important* papers that prove it!" he had exclaimed, pounding a fist on the table, eyes sulphurous with fury.

❆

Now, just months later, Harvey and I drove up to Buffalo to witness Lee's final moments. It was an appropriately somber and wintry day, the clouds leaden with coming snow. Just where Interstate 681 curves out of Syracuse onto the New York State Thruway, I saw it for the first time—a shining black crow perched on a roadside fence post. I don't know what made me notice him. He seemed to be eyeing us as we drove by. I eyed him back. I felt some kind of connection between us.

And then a few miles farther on we saw it again, or so it seemed—at least it was another crow, poised over our heads on the railing of a viaduct overpass. I nudged Harvey. "You see that crow?" I asked him. I figured he'd scoff as usual, but for once he seemed on the same wavelength as I was. "Yeah," he intoned. "I see it."

We saw it next on a barbed-wire fence just off the highway, then again on another fence post a few minutes later. It must have happened seven or eight times until it finally became too dark and snowy to see anymore.

Oh, I know, it was simply a lot of crows. Nothing visionary about it, just an irrelevant coincidence. When you have crows on the mind, you see crows. And yet they seemed to be saying something to us, those crows, sitting almost metaphorically on fence posts every few miles out of Syracuse. Not a specific message, mind you, but simply a kind of confirmatory sign. You give heed to such matters, or you don't.

When we neared the Rochester turnoff toward dusk, a snow-and-ice squall blew up suddenly, racing straight east at us down the New York State Thruway from Buffalo and Lake Erie, abruptly transforming the six-lane highway into a skating rink. We found ourselves blind in the whirling interior of a dense white cloud, with only occasional veiled glimpses of the red lights of other cars, all going fifty, sixty, seventy miles an hour. The road became instant ice. For me to touch the brake meant a sure skid; even worse, the car or cars directly behind us would surely plow right into our back end. We were fishtailing wildly. The lanes were invisible. Total whiteout.

"Can't you pull over and stop?" Harvey pleaded. I could see him jamming his feet against the floorboard and locking his knees as if that would somehow help.

"No way," I yelled, peering out desperately into the opaque whiteness. "Worse to stop than keep going. Traffic's heavy behind and ahead. Don't want any mass collisions!"

We had vague fleeting glimpses of cars around us on the highway spinning every which way. Fearing to stop, I eased down to maybe thirty miles an hour. My knees were trembling. My hands clutched the steering wheel, white knuckled. I prayed.

Finally, the squall subsided. We'd come through. Whiteness turned to darkness. It was night. Not a crow to be seen, thankfully. The road, still sheeted with ice, reappeared before us in our headlights.

"Made it!" Harvey cried out, his voice triumphant if a little shaky.

"So we did," I acknowledged with all the nonchalance I could muster.

Drained, I kept my foot steady on the pedal and leaned back into the cushions of the seat, taking a deep gulp of air. Yes, by God, we'd come through.

And then it stepped in front of us, as if out of a dream: a deer. A twin-antlered buck, huge and statuesque, materializing with a sudden leap hardly a dozen yards straight ahead of us, transfixed in our lights. His body was sideways to us, his great head bent our way, ears alert, huge bright brown eyes staring right into my soul. Ah, those eyes . . .

We drove right through him. His body catapulted directly over the front window with a loud thump, and for one eternal moment I saw his rear hooves flick by over my head. Then *whoosh*, it was gone.

It was another hundred yards or more before I managed to bring the car to a cautious halt at the side of the road. I turned off the motor.

All I could say was "I've killed it. *Oh, Lord!* I killed the poor thing. I killed it! Harvey, there was nothing I could do! Suddenly he was there, and just as suddenly we were through him! If only I'd had a second or two to react . . ."

"You just saved our lives!" Harvey said consolingly. "If you'd swerved on the ice or hit the brake, hell, we'd have hit that ditch or another car."

We walked back along the dark ice-crusted highway to make sure it was dead. For a hundred or two hundred yards we searched the highway, the shoulder, and the off-road ditch and nearby bushes. No deer. We looked for fifteen minutes or so. Not a sign. We walked back to our rented car and examined the front end. The passenger-side fender and hood were pretty badly dented, but it was drivable.

We drove on to Buffalo at a steady, unadventurous forty-five miles per hour.

❈

I'll not forget those terrible moments the next morning as we gathered around Lee's bed at the VA hospital with a few close family members and friends, including Oren and Tadodaho Leon Shenandoah. No one spoke for a while, not even a whisper. As if in a dream we looked down at his inert form, connected with tubes and wires to the life-support system that kept his heart and lungs pumping. He was curled in a nearly fetal position, his face serene, smiling slightly, almost sweetly. On a digital monitor above his bed a pulsating blue line traced his heartbeat, and on a small screen next to that a glowing red digital number flickered: 78 . . . 80 . . . 78 . . . 76 . . . 78 . . . marking his pulse beats per minute.

He looked so peaceful that I felt I might have touched him and he'd have awakened, yawning and stretching, rubbing the sleep from his eyes. I hesitantly reached down and touched his fingers; they felt cool. I pressed them with mine anyway, as you would press a child's hand in comfort. No response.

I had to pull myself away from the bed and go stand over by the wall, facing away from the others. Directly on the wall in front of me hung a framed color photograph of a leaf-strewn path winding through an autumnal woodscape at sunset. It was there to comfort the grieving—a visual metaphor. I immediately saw Lee walking down that path, and it was all I could do not to call out to him. I remembered one of the last times I'd seen him—playing a wild pickup game of lacrosse next to the cemetery behind the longhouse at Onondaga. Oh, Lee loved lacrosse! He'd told us how lacrosse isn't simply a game. "It's sacred, really. They say for every lacrosse game played here on earth there's another being played up in the Sky World. It's not a game. It's a kind of prayer."

I pulled myself together for Lee's final moments.

All of this was doubly unbearable for me since my Dad had only recently died after spending much of his adult life in a VA hospital just like this one. Both hospitals had that same sort of sickly medicinal smell, a smell that had haunted my entire childhood. My Dad had been bedridden for seventeen years, unable to walk or, in later years, even sit up in his bed due to complications from war injuries. His ship had been torpedoed in the Atlantic during World War II, and he had received severe shrapnel wounds. In the Navy hospital he had contracted tuberculosis, and they had had to remove one of his lungs and collapse a lobe of the other. His whole body got thrown out of balance, and that triggered degenerative arthritis in his vertebrae. He was twisted. His back was sort of in an S shape. He was always in pain.

Even with his infirmities he'd many a time found the strength to lift a heavy belt and whack it across my backside for any infraction—and my childhood seemed like it was nothing *but* infractions. Still, I loved and worshiped him—and feared him, yes.

I remember the time my mother, my younger brother, and I went up to the VA hospital near Asheville to visit him. I was maybe six years old. They wouldn't let little kids into the hospital, so my Mom went to see my Dad for a few hours and left my brother and me at the guardhouse. We played in the hills there around the hospital. I remember, a few times my Dad would come to his window and wave at us, and we could barely see him. He looked so small, so tiny, so far away. God, I wanted to see him so much! Well, I left my little brother at the guardhouse and went back up the hill by myself. I decided I'd try to sneak into the hospital and make it up to his room. The guard saw me, chased me down, and warned me not to try again. But I just wouldn't listen. As soon as the guard's back was turned, I tried again. Did it half a dozen times. Each time he caught me. It was like *he* was the one who was keeping me from my Dad! I gave that guy more grief. He was just trying to do his job, but I hated that guard as much as I've ever hated anyone in my life! I never did make it up to my Dad's room. I can still see his little figure waving at us from the window. He seemed so far away. He'd always seemed so far away. I still feel that separation. I guess it's the one thing I fear about death—not the pain or the dying but the *separation*. To me, separation isn't a condition, it's an emotion, an unbearable emotion. It's pained me all my life.

I'd visited my Dad in the VA hospital a few weeks before his death, knowing he was getting low and feeling bad about my going off for a couple of months on an assignment. "Don't feel bad," he'd told me, lying there in the bed, looking pale and waxy. His voice sounded like a scratchy old phonograph record. "What you're doing is important," he said. That was comforting, since he'd always seemed disappointed in me since I'd left the ministry and become an "unholy photographer," in Harvey's phrase.

Then, I don't know why, I asked him, "Dad, do you believe in reincarnation? In coming back after you die?" Maybe I was trying to cheer him up with the thought that it wouldn't all be over. He lay there and thought a while. He closed his eyes, then opened them and looked right at me. He had a way, when he got emotionally upset, of his chin tensing and kind of puckering up into a ball, a quivering ball. And right then it puckered up that way and started quivering, and tears came up in his eyes, and he said, "When I was in the Navy, I could find all the old waterholes in all the ports of Europe by the back alleys. No one told me where they were. I just knew. I could find them in the dark. It was like I'd been there before. I don't know . . . Maybe if I lived in some other life, I was a seaman in that life, too. Guess I never progressed much from one life to the other. I don't know . . . I just don't know."

His chin puckered and quivered some more. I know mine was quivering under my beard.

Then he choked back the tears. My Dad would never, *ever* cry, no matter what, no matter if it killed him. He looked me deep in the eyes and said, "I . . . I've thought about this reincarnation thing. I'm glad it's not the Christian way. I hope it's not true because . . . *Steve, I don't ever want to come back again!*"

His last words to me were "I'm tired. I'm really tired."

I never saw him again. He was sixty-two.

Now, in almost the same setting and with many of the same unbearable feelings, I was confronted by the terrible fact of my dear friend Lee Lyons's imminent death. A doctor and several nurses and technicians came into the room. The family gathered at Lee's bedside. I had to lurch out of the room and watch the final moments from the doorway. Chief Shenandoah spoke a brief prayer in the Onondaga language. The technicians performed the necessary disconnections of Lee's tubes and wires.

Lee seemed utterly peaceful throughout, smiling that tough-sweet smile of his to the end. I don't know how long it took. Ten minutes? Twenty? Down into the 50s went the red digital pulse number, then slowly into the 40s, 30s, 20s. Finally, a collective gasp of lamentation shook the room. I looked back at the monitor: The blue line was as flat as death; the red digital number stood at 0. It was over.

We attended the wake at Lee's mother's house. There was little overt grieving—these people are all too familiar with untimely death. But the loss was there in their eyes, in their voices. Lee's coffin was set on a simple bier in the parlor. The dining room table overflowed with foodstuffs. Before anyone ate, Lee's mother took the best pieces from the table and set them on a plate on top of the coffin with a napkin and silverware. "Lee always loved to eat," she said, "and he's not missing this meal for anything!" I went over to

Lee's coffin and rested my hand on the cold polished wood. The lid was open. Lee's arms were crossed over his favorite lacrosse stick, which would be buried with him.

Leon came over and told me: "We all have a day to die. But the Creator, He was very thoughtful. He didn't tell us the day so we wouldn't worry."

As we left the wake that night, Oren warned: "Take care. There are a lot of powers around right now. Lee's spirit . . . He's looking to find a way out. He doesn't want to stay here now. But he's confused. He doesn't know what's happened. Lee's more powerful now than he ever was in life. More powerful than anyone here. He might accidentally hurt you. Or those other powers that are out tonight might cause some harm. Beware as you go out. Don't go out alone. Stay in twos."

I told Oren about the crows we had seen. "Oh." He nodded. "That's the Death Bird!"

Leon added: "Lee's going hunting for a while, hunting for his ceremony. When he finds it, he'll have a ceremony of his own up there in the other world, a ceremony with the Creator, just the two of them!"

We attended the funeral in the Onondaga cemetery, where we had watched Lee running with his lacrosse stick among the grave markers. Now one of those markers was his. It bears his Indian name, Joyondawde, meaning "on the other side of the hill." It was comforting to know, at least, that he had—*has*—his lacrosse stick with him, ready for that eternal game in the Sky World.

Oren told us as we left, "Don't sentimentalize him, you hear? He wouldn't want it. Not Lee. He was one tough-nosed Indian. A real warrior. Anyone who ever got hit by his forecheck in lacrosse knows that!"

Chapter 12

OUR purposes continue. This journey is ongoing. Periodically the wind picks up under us, and we find ourselves heading out again to Great Turtle Island. The path of the Wisdomkeepers, we've found, is sometimes circular, sometimes spiral, sometimes sinuously wandering and circuitous. Only rarely is it straight, a logical path. If you keep walking straight ahead, you're likely to walk right off the path and find yourself hopelessly lost, disconnected from both yourself and the world. Let intuition be your compass. The path dives into the earth at your feet and suddenly disappears, like a river going underground. Then, just as you've given up all hope of ever finding your way again, it reemerges abruptly beneath you like a rushing torrent, sweeping you along once more.

Our paths—Steve's and mine—diverge, then reconverge. This past year, intersecting once again, we set off together on an eight-thousand-mile, seventeen-day journey to return the eagle feather and the owl's claw—the signs that Two Trees had predicted would launch us on our spirit-journey. Call this one a journey of personal closure. Each journey creates its own purpose, its own meaning, its own metaphor. Returning the feather and the claw seemed the perfect way to complete the circle begun so long ago. They had done their work. Now we felt they should go back home.

Simple enough, yes; but problematical. Bob White, who gave Steve the feather, had died some years back, and I had completely lost touch with Joe Parra, whom, in any case, I'd known for only an hour or so when he gave me the claw and whom I hadn't seen or spoken to in the fifteen years since.

What's more, both the feather and the claw themselves—physically—were gone. The feather had been held for us for years by Chief Shenandoah, who had "brought it back to life" with a resanctification ritual and used it in Iroquois ceremonies. When Steve told Leon we'd like to return it where it had come from, he was perfectly agreeable. But when he went to retrieve it from its usual place on top of the china cabinet next to his ceremonial antlered *gastoweh*, it was nowhere to be found. "I'm really sorry, Steve. It's taken itself off somewhere," he lamented, promising he would keep looking and get it to us somehow.

Similarly, when I called my old friend Fred Kline in Santa Fe about the return of the owl's claw, which I hadn't seen since it had "exchanged" itself for the Seminole sorceror's cane so many years before, he confessed: "Harvey, I don't know how to tell you this, but it's been eaten by our cat!" This had happened only weeks before. All that was left of the power stick, it seemed, was the bamboo shaft, some scraps of rabbit fur, a snippet of red satin ribbon, and three scraggly feathers. The owl's claw itself was gone, talons and all. Fred was really loath to tell me. "Oh, that's okay," I lyingly reassured him, hugely disappointed.

Somehow it seemed absolutely essential that this new journey of ours revolve around the return of the feather and the claw, the two signs that had begun it all, and now the claw was gone and the feather had disappeared! But gradually it came to me that, claw or no, we could still return the remains of the power stick to Joe Parra and thus "complete the circle." And likewise with the feather. Even in the event Leon couldn't find it, we could still return it symbolically. "You can return the spirit-feather even if I can't find the real feather," Leon told us. That at least would show a proper respect. And this new journey, if it was anything beyond mere spiritual windmill-tilting, was to be a journey of respect, a journey honoring sacred metaphors, of others and of ourselves.

Through the years Steve and I had invested meaning in the feather and the claw, and they had returned that meaning to us a thousand-fold. We chose to see them as sacred, and they became sacred. By accepting them as metaphors of our own, we found ourselves infused with their metaphorical power. They gave us a kind of directional fix in that seemingly directionless world we were entering. Returning them now, even if only symbolically—a spirit-feather and a spirit-claw—made intuitive sense. And yet it was just a bit bizarre. Here we were returning a feather we didn't have to a dead man and an owl's claw that no longer existed to a man we couldn't find!

That, for all its tenuousness, had a certain poetry to it that I liked. Steve and I have often debated just what exactly it is we're looking for when we go out on these journeys of ours. Wisdom? Revelation? Something visionary? Even, perhaps, a small miracle like the turning of Jess Bluebird's eagle feather that time at the Garden of the Gods? Steve tells me that in addition to the sheer headiness of being on the road and on the wind, it's the visionary that draws him on, the expectation of an epiphany of some kind, a showing or palpable experience of what Christians call "the Divine" and old Mat King called Wakan Tanka—"the Great Holy, the Great Mysterious."

I personally have never received my instructions through visions but rather by a gentle nudging, as if of an unseen hand, that sends me lurching, despite every contrary effort I can muster, in the right direction, down the right path. All my life I have pursued not visions but a visionary *way* of seeing the world. I value the visionary as the source, if not of truth itself, then of poetry—the perfect metaphoric expression of truth. Steve was looking for revelation on this new journey. I'd settle for poetry.

Who knew? Maybe we'd find both.

Steve picked me up in his vintage 1980 Econoline van at the Greensboro, North Carolina, airport, and we headed west on Interstate 40 toward Santa Fe. That we had neither the feather nor the claw in our possession hardly seemed to matter. We knew in some way they would come to us. We had even sent a plane ticket to Chief Shenandoah so that he could fly out with the eagle feather and meet us two weeks later in San Francisco. We planned to drive with him up to northern California so he could be on hand to give a blessing when we returned the feather to Bob White's son, Roben. Having Leon join us for part of this journey would be a blessing in itself.

❀

Steve was in an odd mood—odd moods being his usual frame of mind. Just minutes before, when we had set off from the Greensboro airport onto I-40, he was all enthusiasm. "Harvey," he'd told me, "I'm going to have a vision on this journey. I'm telling you, I can feel it coming. A vision!"

Inwardly I winced. I didn't know whether to scoff or humor him. It's not that I don't believe in visions. I do. But I can't imagine predicting I was going to have one. You can be a believer without believing everything—or even most things. "Old Doubting Harv," Steve calls me. He and I have witnessed more than a few phenomena that might qualify as mystical during our travels on Great Turtle Island. So why not this time, too? I just wasn't prepared to give instant credence to every vision claimed, not even Steve's. Not even my own, for that matter.

"You mean like *Close Encounters of the Third Kind?*" I asked him. "A 'sighting'? Extraterrestrials? UFOs? That sort of thing?"

Before us highway I-40 unreeled toward the western horizon, and I half-imagined a sudden apocalyptic brightness out there at the far interface of heaven and earth.

Steve shook his head. Once again I'd failed to understand.

"Uh, no, not that sort of thing, really. Not UFOs."

Shrugging off my half-mocking tone, he took a meditative pull at his scuffed pipe and squinted through the rising curls of sweetly pungent smoke at the eternal road ahead of us.

Gripping and ungripping the steering wheel, he went on in a confessional tone: "I went out to the van the other night. Just sat out there all alone in the dark with the engine off till three in the morning. You remember how old Corbett Sundown used to go out in the car to have his visions? Well, I wanted to see something out there in the darkness, a sign or something. Hell, other people see angels. Why not me? 'Speak to me,' I said. 'I'm here. I'm open to you. I'm listening . . .'" His words drifted off.

"So what happened?" I asked. "Did you see something?"

"Uh, no. Unfortunately. Nothing. Pretty depressing, actually. But still I have this sense. I tell you, Harvey, it's coming! I can feel it. The hairs on my scalp are tingling. I'm going to have some kind of vision, I swear!"

He spoke with all the evangelical fervor of an ordained Baptist minister, which indeed he once was very briefly before lapsing into the blissfully unholy life of a photographer and author. I, for my part, am equally lapsed—as a Jew if not a Baptist—and can claim to be every bit as unholy as he, having for thirty years flourished as one of those professional disbelievers called "objective journalists" even while secretly pursuing, as best I could, my own personal, tentative, behind-the-scenes visionary life.

This was going to be an interesting trip. Not easy—they never are, these periodic inward-outward voyages of ours. But interesting, yes.

Steve seemed miffed when I didn't immediately accept the notion of his having a vision. He started fuming inwardly and hardly talking, just staring grimly down the road ahead. He tossed his pipe up on the dashboard and drove on in sullen silence, fingernails occasionally tapping on the plastic of the steering wheel, his jaw stubbornly clenched, jaw muscles visibly working under his beard. Yes, he was definitely miffed. Personally hurt. No doubt I would have been, too, if he'd just scoffed at something I'd said. I knew he saw me, at least momentarily, as somehow disloyal. Oh, well. I'm used to his moods, just as he's used to mine. He always gets a little nervous when we set off on one of these journeys of ours. So do I.

But now a subtle smile curled the corners of his mouth. His lips worked silently at some inner thought. Finally he spoke:

"Hey, Harvey, I got you something."

"What's that?"

I could feel something lightening between us. He grabbed the pipe off the dash and sucked at the cold stem.

"A little surprise I bought you . . ."

"Yeah?"

He cast a bemused sidelong glance my way. I could see his naturally irrepressible humor bubbling up. His smile at last broke wide.

"Krispy Kremes!" he announced triumphantly. "A dozen glazed! Picked them up in Charlotte! The red light was on. I couldn't resist!"

Steve knows my weakness. At least on this one esoteric matter we can agree. The tension between us melted like a fresh, hot, glazed Krispy Kreme on the tongue.

"Now *that's* visionary!" I exclaimed.

For those who are noninitiates, let me explain. When the red light goes on in the window of the Krispy Kreme Doughnut Shop in Charlotte, it signals the arrival of a fresh new batch of doughnuts— hot, irresistible, unspeakably delicious, almost narcotic in their addictive quality. Combine the sweetness of spun sugar with the texture of a cumulus cloud, add just a hint of a warm summer evening's breeze, and you'll have some vague idea of the salivary ecstasy. This is soul food indeed. Many a time Steve and I have seen that red light blink on as we've driven by and as if some posthypnotic suggestion had been triggered, found ourselves floating almost disembodied into the shop's divinely scented interior, there to be greeted by Reba the waitress, an angel without disguise who ministers instantly to our diabetic longings. We don't mess with the fancy doughnuts, the jelly-filled, the candy-sprinkled, or the custard-oozing kinds. We are purists—glazed, only glazed. The ones with that sweet crusty frosting as transparent as morning sunlight. Reba knows without asking that Steve wants two and I—well, of course, Old Harv wants four. These are not so much eaten as laid reverently on the tongue and allowed to melt there, doused down with long drafts of tongue-singeing coffee, essential antidote to the doughnuts' teeth-cracking sweetness. Ahhhhh . . .

I thought, "If only I still smoked cigarettes!" The very thought of hot Krispy Kremes and a cup of hot coffee can make a cigarette all but materialize on a former addict's lips. Former? Once and always, they say. It had been three weeks since I'd touched one. The smell of Steve's pipe smoke was addictive in itself. This would be a challenge.

"Of course it's been two hours since I bought them," Steve said. "They're cold. You'll have to close your eyes and remember what they're like when they're hot. Reach behind my seat there. You'll find the box."

Sure enough, there on the floor behind the seat was a large, flat cardboard box of a dozen Krispy Kremes. All glazed. Not quite their original selves, perhaps, but still infinitely edible.

"You're a good man, Steve Wall," I acknowledged. "Vision or no."

"Mmmm . . . If you say so. We'll stop for some coffee up ahead. You go on and eat up."

Suddenly he was almost motherly. Maybe he'd forgiven me.

"Want one?" I offered.

"I'll wait till the coffee," he demurred, tamping some tobacco into his pipe bowl and filling the van with a sweetly aromatic cloud. I've always found his pipe smoke comforting.

I leaned back in the commodious Econoline passenger seat, kicked off my shoes, and thrust my legs out full, wiggling my toes in creature comfort in the warm air from the radiator, which Steve had turned on low this chilly mid-September morning. While I was packing that morning for the trip to Greensboro, two stories caught my interest on public radio. One was on the white buffalo calf recently born in Wisconsin—an event of apocalyptic importance to the northern Plains Indians whose prophecies call for the return of the White Buffalo Calf Maiden, bringer of the Sacred Pipe, to usher in a new age. The newscaster also reminded me that it was Yom Kippur, the Jewish Day of Atonement. Good Jews around the world were fasting and praying and preparing their souls, withdrawing from all worldly activity. And here was I, the lapsed one, heading out *into* the world—scorning, some might say, God's judgment and stuffing my *goyische* mouth with a Krispy Kreme! I remember how, when doing a story for the magazine years before ("The Pious Ones: Brooklyn's Hasidic Jews," which appeared in August 1975), an old bewhiskered Hasidic rabbi in his black frock coat looked at me sternly and said, "Harvey, it's because of Jews like you that we had the Holocaust!" Stinging words. Terrible words. I refuse to believe them. Still, as we headed out west on unholy I-40, I was grateful that Jews more devout than I were sending their prayers to heaven at that very moment. I may not believe in the Hasidim's way of life, following every iota of God's 613 commandments as enunciated in the Torah, the Five Books of Moses, but I wouldn't change a hair on their beards or earlocks. Thank God they exist and keep Him on His toes. I thought similarly of my Indian friends. Many of them, too, would have been "praying the sunrise" this morning, sending up prayers to the Sky World on the rising smoke from their ceremonial pipes and sacred sage and sweetgrass. Thank God for them, too. It's such people who hold the universe together.

❖

I'll never forget sharing a sunrise prayer with Eddie Benton-Banai in the driveway of a suburban garage in Sault Sainte Marie, Michigan. Eddie had asked us to be on hand for the first meeting in a century of spiritual leaders of the Ojibway, Ottawa, and Potawatomie—once known collectively as the People of the Three Fires, the major tribes of the northern Great Lakes.

"We're starting a Three Fires society," Eddie told us. "We're trying to reconnect with our past. You guys can come on out and take a few pictures if you like."

Before attending the meeting, Eddie invited us to a little sunrise prayer out in the driveway of a friend's house where he was staying.

"Get here before dawn, and I'll pray a sunrise for you," he told us. Dutifully, we arrived in the predawn darkness.

Eddie and a sizable group of men, women, and children were already outside the house, a typical suburban house in a typical mid-American suburb. They had already set up the water drum—the sacred Little Boy—in the center of the driveway, and beside it was a small brazier, already smoking.

Looking straight down the driveway, I could see a slight brightening of the eastern sky between the two homes across the quiet street. The group gathered, facing in that direction.

Eddie waved down two men who had brought long-handled drumsticks. "Not this morning," he said softly. "People are sleeping. Don't want to wake them up. We're guests here, remember. Besides, you don't have to beat loudly for the Creator to hear. We can make the Little Boy sing without drumming him all the time. Here, give me one of those."

He took one of the long-handled drumsticks—more like flexible batons—and lightly rubbed one along the taut skin of the water drum. He tapped the skin lightly. A kind of humming emerged from the Little Boy. Eddie rubbed and tapped lightly again with the drumstick, and the humming continued, almost like a deep-throated human voice.

"Do it like that," he told the drummers. "Just like that. Rub and tap ever so lightly. The Creator will hear us all right."

The ceremony began like all such Indian ceremonies, spoken prayers and the lighting of tobacco, the scent of sage and sweetgrass on the sweet morning air. Somewhere out at the edges of all this, fifteen or twenty feet away at Eddie's direction, Steve Wall was manning a tripod and focusing his Leica on the scene. In that darkness I doubted he'd get an image at all, certainly not a zinger. I could see his figure hunched over the camera, utterly absorbed. I turned my gaze back down the driveway and immersed myself in the ceremony. At one point a sacred pipe came around and, with the help of the man next to me, I managed a few puffs of the smoke, passing the pipe on.

And then, like a fishing bobbin that has suddenly been released from under water, the sun bobbed up between the two houses across the street. I must have missed its first moments as I puffed on the pipe. It wasn't a ball at first but a molten pool of light out of which the gilded central "bobbin" suddenly burst into view as if a hand were thrusting it up.

The chanting of the Indians, the rhythmic droning hum of the Little Boy, and the sudden emergence of the sun were not three events but one, a single happening occurring both inside us and outside us. For a few minutes no difference existed between inner and outer. That sun rose inside us. Eddie raised his hands and literally prayed the sunrise. This was no quaint Indian belief. This was fact. We prayed that sun right into the sky that morning. You'll never convince me otherwise.

Steve came back to the group. He had folded up his tripod, put away his camera, and joined us for the end of the ceremony. I wondered what kind of pictures he could have gotten. This was one of the few times he had ever been permitted to photograph an actual ceremony—even if at a respectable distance. But now I noticed he was shaking his head and smiling enigmatically to himself.

"What's up? Get any pix?" I asked him.

"Nope, not a one," he said.

"Not one?"

"Not one."

He shook his head again. "Just couldn't do it. I finally got permission to photograph one of these ceremonies, and I just couldn't do it. I wasn't supposed to. I could *feel* that I wasn't supposed to. I know that's what we came here for, but, Harvey, I swear . . . I looked through the viewfinder, and all I could see was an eye staring back at me. My own, I suppose. I just wasn't *supposed* to take a picture, you know what I mean?"

I nodded. I knew. We both knew.

The memory of that sunrise was just for us standing there, those of us who had prayed it into the sky that morning from that suburban driveway. In Indian belief, the sun would never rise without a prayer. Prayers and ceremony hold the very fabric of the universe together. We had done our job as human beings that morning. We had prayed the sunrise just as Frank Fools Crow had prayed the eagle out of the empty South Dakota sky that time at Wounded Knee. No pictures were permitted either time. Nor were they necessary. That eagle and that sunrise were inscribed permanently within us. We were as much a part of them as they were a part of us. Pictures would have been a sacrilege, a display of disbelief, as if somehow we had to "see" those sacred moments frozen in a "picture" to really "believe" in them.

Steve was right. No pictures. He didn't have to be told. He knew.

The real picture lives on in our private memory, in our being.

That sunrise changed us. Every sunrise changes you, just as every ceremony, every moment of attention to the holy now changes you. That was Eddie's primary message for us: *Pay attention!* Yes, even in a suburban driveway.

✤

Getting back on the road now, on the wind again, is like switching from the past to the present tense. Suddenly it's *now* in an almost visionary way. Suddenly we're *here* in a more than physical sense. The ordinary becomes holy, if you only allow yourself to experience it. Highway I-40 takes on an almost mystic glow, seemingly creating itself as it unwinds into the distance, creating the distance itself. The road turns holy before us, a sacred pathway, as solid as asphalt and as liquid as sunlight. We head down it in our Stone Canoe.

I look over at Steve. He's got a sour look on his face. The pipe is out and back up on the dash. I realize I've eaten three Krispy Kremes, and we haven't even stopped for coffee yet. He hasn't eaten one. I feel satiated, my soul saturated with sugar. My doctor says I'm borderline diabetic. That gives me something in common with many of the Indian elders I know. But, still, I'd better watch it. I put aside the box of Krispy Kremes. I yawn. The air from the radiator warms my toes. I crack the window open a couple of inches. The breeze is refreshing. I'm suddenly tired. I lean back in my seat and let the road come at us.

The sky clouds up ahead of us. Nothing apocalyptic, just a gathering rainstorm preparing its passing benediction. A few drops hit the windshield. Steve sets the wipers on low, and they beat out a muffled rhythm, accompanied by the occasional bass rumble of distant thunder. I lower the passenger seat window another few inches and feel the light spray of cool drops pelting my face and forehead pleasurably. A sense of serenity rises in me, like the glow from a sip of fine wine. Maybe this journey is beginning to make sense after all. I close my eyes for a few minutes.

I hear Steve's voice: "Hey, Harvey, you're falling asleep."

"No, just closing my eyes. I'm thinking."

"About what?"

"About . . . about that ceremony with Jess and Mary at the Garden of the Gods that time. You remember how that eagle feather seemed to turn around all by itself in Jess's hat during the blessing?"

"Yeah. That was something."

"You call that a miracle?" I ask him.

"Could be." Steve nods. "I like to think that's what it was."

He breathes out an aromatic cloud. The smoke wafts past my twitching nostrils on its way out the open window.

We've drifted momentarily out of the now. It's memory time.

"Hey, Harvey," says Steve, "remember the time we were out driving through the Badlands, heading from Rapid City to the Pine Ridge reservation, and we picked up that hitchhiker, a young Lakota guy in his twenties?"

"Yeah, sure, I remember."

"And do you remember," Steve goes on, "you offered him a cigarette? He shook his head and laughed. 'I got other ways to kill myself,' he said. Then he added: 'You white people gave us alcohol to do us in. And we Indians . . . we gave you tobacco. To us it was holy, but you turned it into a killer. That's our revenge.' That's stuck in my mind ever since."

"Mine, too."

For all of our differences, even occasional hostilities, there are times when the two of us think almost with one mind.

I can't help laughing. "And do you remember," I continue, "while we were driving back to Cortez from the airport that time you flew out to see Charlie Knight, there was that awful smell in the car? Really terrible. Like a draft from hell. We couldn't figure out what it was."

Steve smiles and blows out another delicious blue cloud.

"Of course," he says. "You kept sniffing and sniffing. Finally it came to me what it was. . . . *Wormwood!* It was from those three cups of Two Trees' cleansing Indian bitter tea I'd been drinking every day."

"God, it was foul! You even offered me some."

"Well, I figured maybe you wouldn't smell it if you drank some yourself. You probably *should* have!"

"No way!"

Our laughter bubbles out and fills the car with momentary effervescence. God, it's good to laugh again. We haven't been doing too much of it lately, Steve and I. We're both depressive types by nature. We're happy only when we're miserable.

The rain continues, soft and intermittent, diffusing the muted daylight into an evanescent mother-of-pearl. The trees lining the highway take on a burning intensity. The beginning of autumn tips their upper branches with daubs of pale yellow, dusty pink, and misty orange. Or perhaps, it occurs to me, they're just dying from some local source of pollution? I remember Seneca chief Corbett Sundown's words from the Iroquois prophecies: "Our prophecies say there will be three signs of the end of the world: We won't be able to drink the water, the trees will die from the tops down, and babies will be killed like dogs. And now it's all happening! Only you white people call it water pollution, acid rain, and 'legal' abortion."

Yes, you see things differently on Great Turtle Island. In a few weeks the full flush of autumn will turn this North Carolina forest into a conflagration of colors. The tourists will drive through, admiring this little annual death—uncaring about any greater death it may portend. Are the trees in their autumnal glory, or are they actually dying from the tops down, as in the Iroquois prophecy? Two views of things, two different visions. I can't seem to shake this split image of reality from my mind.

"The turnoff is just up ahead," Steve says. "We'll gas up and get that coffee. You leave me any of the Krispy Kremes? I'm about ready for one."

We pull off I-40 at the Black Mountain, North Carolina, turnoff. While Steve gases up, I get two large Styrofoam cups of coffee—Steve's black, mine with milk—in the adjacent convenience store. Steve already has the motor running when I come out. He seems distracted and on edge, in a hurry.

"Let's get out of here!" he grumbles.

We roll back out onto I-40 and head west. I glance over at Steve. He seems agitated. Finally, after a minute or so, he speaks: "Did you see him?"

"See who?" I ask.

"Two Trees."

"*Wha-a-a-at?* Two Trees? You saw Two Trees?"

"Yeah, back there . . . in the gas station."

"Where?"

"At the pumps. I don't think he recognized me. He looked right past me."

"Well, hell, let's go back!"

Steve shakes his head.

"No point in looking. He's gone. Just drove away."

"You're putting me on! You didn't *say* anything to him?"

"Hell, no. What for?"

"You're actually serious?"

"Absolutely! Anyway, if it wasn't him, it sure looked like him. I'd know that face anywhere. He's put on some weight. Yeah, for sure, it was him. Cowboy hat. Boots. A worn coat. I'm sure of it. He never saw me, or at least he pretended he didn't."

"Why the hell didn't you tell me? I'd give anything to talk to him!"

"Didn't figure you'd give a damn. You never believed in him anyway. He wasn't real or authentic, you said. Don't you remember?"

"Bullshit!"

I'm mad enough to spit. Steve's lying through his teeth. He no more saw Two Trees back there than he saw the man in the moon.

"Come on. I'm from Chicago, remember? 'Fess up. You're lying. You're playing games with my mind. Admit it!"

I expect him to laugh and admit it. He doesn't. I stare him down hard. He keeps his eyes on the road, away from mine. His fingers grasp and ungrasp the steering wheel. He has that sanctimonious jaw-clenched bulldog expression on his face that means nothing will move him. Nothing. He is the stubbornest man I have ever known.

"It was him, Harvey. Two Trees himself. Believe it or don't believe it. If it wasn't him, it was his double."

I give up. Okay, I'll play the game with him. Sometimes you can work your way through a lie and find the truth concealed behind it. Sometimes.

"His double?" I ask him, swallowing my anger. "Maybe it was his doppelgänger!" I muffle the scorn in my voice.

"Yeah, maybe so. His doppelgänger. His alter ego. Could be. But I think it was Two Trees himself. He was real. Yeah, it was Two Trees all right."

"Maybe this was your *vision?*"

"No. That was no vision. That was *him.*"

"A miracle, then?"

"Uh, no, not a miracle, either. Call it . . . Call it a *visitation*. Not a vision."

"There's a difference?"

"Yeah, there *is* . . . there's a difference."

"What is it?"

Steve shrugs again. "Hell, it's something talking won't explain—or thinking, either. Have a vision, and maybe you'll find out for yourself!"

"I thought it *wasn't* a vision."

"It wasn't. Call it, as I say, a visitation. It was real. Two Trees was real, I swear it. But maybe there's more to reality than we think. In any case, it *happened*."

"Yeah, but why didn't you tell me back there in the station? Why didn't you talk to him?"

"I didn't want to. I only wanted to get out of there and away from him. Maybe . . . maybe I was even a little scared. It was weird seeing him that way. I was in shock. I couldn't believe it, but there he was! You know how he always seemed dark, mysterious, even threatening? A sorcerer, that's what he really was. Not a medicine man or even an herbalist but a sorcerer!"

"You mean he's using sorcery on us?"

"I wouldn't be surprised. At least . . . Who knows? Maybe he's using it on *me*."

We lapse into silence.

He's not an easy man, this Steve Wall. No, not an easy man. Confronting him straight on just doesn't work. He only clenches his jaw muscles tighter. The only way to handle him is to flow around his quirks and outbursts, his depressions and ecstasies. Hopefully, he'll flow around mine. I'm determined to make this journey work. Maybe he *did* believe he'd seen Two Trees? And even if Two Trees' visitation was only in his mind, did that make it any the less real? Mistaken perception or no, outright lie or no, yet, in some sense it still *happened*. That *had* been Two Trees! Real or not, his visitation has become an important happening on this strange journey of ours.

Strange, yes, and getting stranger.

I take my first sip of long-awaited coffee. It's cold and bitter. I drink it all down in a few gulps. Some things you just have to swallow.

Chapter 13

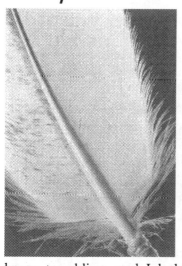

I FEEL like Harvey has painted me into a corner here. Either I produce my vision or I don't. And if I don't, I'm some kind of phony. A fraud. A liar. Oh, well. If I could do it all over again, I think I *would* lie about it. I'd just smile and not mention what I'm thinking, what I'm feeling, what I've seen. But that's just a kind of lying, too.

That *was* Two Trees back there at the gas station. I'm sure of it. Seeing him was a shock, a real shock. My hands are still shaking. My right knee keeps trembling, and I hold it wedged tight under the steering wheel to keep it still. Yes, call me crazy, but it was Two Trees. This was the same damn turnoff at Black Mountain that I'd taken with him onto I-40 when we started off on our *Ramblin' Tepee* trip back in 1982. Mere coincidence? Why do we always call coincidences *mere*? There may actually be some meaning in them. Two Trees' "visitation" at that same Black Mountain turnoff was no coincidence. He was real. Or was I hallucinating? And is there any difference, after all, between a vision, a hallucination, and a visitation?

I was scared, I admit it. I didn't want to talk to the man. This was the same kind of thing he kept pulling on me back on the Chattooga River when I first met him, suddenly showing up out of the blue and then just as suddenly dropping out of sight like a stone. And he made you *see* things! Like the time he held a sweat lodge up on Scaly Mountain, behind the barn. I remember he declared as a group of us went into the tarp-covered enclosure, "Someone here's gonna have a vision," and damned if I didn't see something there in the superheated darkness. The power of suggestion? First I saw or thought I saw a kind of gleaming circle like a crystal ball, then a triangle inside the circle, then an eye inside the triangle. Then it all dissolved and I saw a face, an old man's face, an ancient visage. Then the face became many faces, a phantasmagoria of faces—old men, old women—flowing right up to me and through me. Oh, sure, you say, just an hallucination—or, worse, a lie. Go ahead, scoff, just like Harvey does. For all I know it *was* a hallucination. And for all you know it is a lie. I'm not sure I know myself what I saw. Call it an *imagination* if you like. Afterward, when we got out of the sweat, Two Trees said, echoing his forewarning, "Someone here has had a vision!" I just looked down, keeping my eyes on the ground. I didn't say anything. I kept it to myself—probably wisely.

I should have kept quiet this time, too. But, damn, that *was* Two Trees back there! There he was at the other tier of gas pumps, getting into his brown old Pontiac Phoenix, ducking right inside with his battered cowboy hat on. My mouth must have been wide open. While I stared, he just drove off. Never looked my way. He was gone by the time Harvey got back with the two coffees. I knew he wouldn't believe me. I only wanted to get away from there and back on the road. There's something inescapably dark about Two Trees, a shadow figure if ever there was. But maybe he's just *my* shadow figure, not yours or Harvey's.

I turn to Harvey. His face seems caught in a permanent wince, a frown of disbelief.

"Yeah, maybe it's sorcery," I say. "Maybe this whole thing, seeing him like that, is some kind of sorcery!"

"Mmmmnnn," Harvey grunts.

"Or"—I go on—"maybe it's suggestion, the power of suggestion, like Dr. James Chastain says. That's Two Trees' greatest power."

"May I suggest," Harvey snorts, biting off his words, "that we drop the subject?"

"Okay," I agree thankfully. "I won't say another word about it."

"Good."

"How's that coffee?" I ask him.

I reach to grab my cup.

"Cold as death," Harvey mutters.

And it is. Still, it washes down two equally cold Krispy Kremes.

I'm still unnerved. I can almost sense Two Trees' presence here in the car with us. I even half-imagine I can smell a vague odor of wormwood. It's like he's some kind of shadow figure, haunting me. This guy can be frightening as hell one minute, absolutely hilarious and ridiculous the next.

I remember, shortly after meeting him, I stopped by to see him at a friend's apartment he used in Clayton, Georgia, when he wasn't staying at the horse barn up on Scaly Mountain. I noticed a small un-framed watercolor or tempera painting, about eight by ten inches or so, hanging on the wall. It was a roughly painted portrait of a white-haired man with a familiar look to him, or so it seemed to me. I kept staring at it.

"You paint that, Two Trees?" I asked him.

"Oh, yeah. Painted that years ago."

"Who the hell is it?"

He said, "That guy look familiar to you, Steve?"

I stared at it. There was something compelling about it. It looked sort of Indian maybe. No. It looked more white than Indian. And then I thought, I don't know. It vaguely reminded me of . . .

"You know," I told him, "it almost looks sort of like my Dad."

"Nope. Ain't your Dad." He grinned.

"Well," I said, "it has a familiar look somehow. That receding hair-line, that forehead, that thin chin. But I can't say I know him."

He grinned some more with that leering grin of his. Suddenly I knew what he was going to say, and then he said it.

"That's *you*, Steve! It's *you* twenty or thirty years from now!"

Man, it was like my heart went cold. It *was* like me, only much older and without my beard. I nearly jumped—as if I had touched an electric wire.

"But *how?*" I asked him. "How in hell could you have painted that years ago? You didn't even know me!"

He just grinned that grin some more.

"Ain't important!" he said. "What's important is that you're here for a reason."

A while later, as I was leaving, I went back and looked at the painting again. Nothing had changed, and yet it didn't look like me at all!

Damn that Two Trees! He was messing with my mind!

And when he wasn't scaring me out of my wits, he had me doubled over with laughter. I remember the time Harvey and I drove to Scaly Mountain to work out our plans for the *Ramblin' Tepee* trip. We had barely driven up to the barn when Two Trees noticed that Harvey was walking with his shoulders slightly askew. Harvey had complained of a pulled muscle in his upper back.

"We got a problem here?" Two Trees asked, walking right up to Harvey and poking an index finger at his breastbone. Harvey winced at the sharp jab. He gave me a look.

Two Trees announced: "You have a digestive problem." He poked Harvey's breastbone again, probing the soft spot just above the abdomen. "And possibly a hiatal hernia, too," Two Trees went on. "Not too serious but still a problem."

He started circling around Harvey, who stood there sort of bewildered, alarm in his eyes. Now Two Trees poked at his lower left abdomen. "Hmmm, a weakness there, too. Incipient inguinal hernia, I'd say."

Harvey laughed aloud. "Hey, Chief, watch it! I'm ticklish!"

But Two Trees was all seriousness.

"We'll have to get to work on you tomorrow. Right now, let me work on that back! Where does it hurt? Lay facedown on the table here."

Harvey reluctantly got onto the chiropractor's table, clutching the sides of the black plastic cushion and holding on for dear life. I couldn't bite back my smile of anticipation.

Harvey gave me another wild look and sighed aloud, consigned to his fate. Now Two Trees grabbed his right arm, pulled it back as if he were going to handcuff it, then gripped his left shoulder and yanked it abruptly backward.

Harvey blurted out a gasp of pain, followed by an unconvincing laugh.

"Need to apply some torque here," Two Trees said, pulling and yanking at Harvey's twisted form.

"Take it easy there, Two Trees!"

"Just relax!"

Two Trees' hands attacked again on the other arm, the other shoulder. Yank. Pull. Heave. Yank again. Harvey's moans muffled

Two Trees' grunts as he applied that twisting torque again and again.

I heard something crack—not loud this time but still painfully audible, like a twig being broken.

"Yow-w-w!" came Harvey's pitiful cry.

Two Trees stood back, a look of satisfaction on his face.

"Okay," he said, "enough for now. Consider yourself cracked. That feel better?"

Harvey sat up shakily on the chiropractor's table.

"Uhhh, I'm not sure, Chief."

"Don't worry," Two Trees said, "we'll work on it again tomorrow."

"I'm not sure I want to be cured," Harvey pleaded.

Two Trees gave him one last poke in the soft spot under the breastbone. "At first I thought you had a hiatal hernia," he told Harvey, "but now . . . That resistance there—I don't know. Maybe it's your pancreas!"

Harvey got down from the table, his shoulders still skewed.

"Fuck my pancreas!"

Two Trees seemed alarmed.

Harvey never did get back on that chiropractor's table. His back hurt for a few more days, then improved. He did learn much later that he had both hiatal and inguinal hernias. In fact, he was operated on for the latter just last year, a decade after Two Trees' diagnosis. As for his pancreas? Last time I asked him, he snarled, "I don't know what it is or where it's at, and I hope I never find out. Damned if I'm gonna ask!"

Maybe Two Trees was wrong on that one. For the sake of Harvey's pancreas, I hope so.

❈

Another time, while I was talking to Two Trees out in front of his barn, this old pickup truck came rattling up the road and stopped abruptly right in front of us. Out hobbled a man in a porkpie hat. Something was obviously very wrong. He had the strangest look on his face: his mouth was wide open, and his eyes were bulging.

He lurched toward us, his hands reaching desperately up around his wide-open jaw.

"Looks like we got someone here who needs a little help," Two Trees said, giving me a wink.

Watching with intense interest, I guessed I would see the healer at work at last.

The man was grunting as if trying to talk. But his words, if that's what they were, were all but incomprehensible. He just stood there in front of us, shifting from one foot to the other, gesticulating wildly, grunting and groaning, his hands playing frantically around his gaping mouth.

"What's that you're saying?" Two Trees asked him, squinting one eye.

Only barely could we make out the man's tortured, muffled words. Try speaking with your mouth locked wide open, and you'll get something of an idea of how it sounded. He mouthed the words in obvious pain.

"Arghhhh . . . I . . . I . . . My jaw . . . arghh . . . I was arghh . . . I was arghh-h . . . YAWNING!! . . . awww-ww! . . . Can't close it . . . can't close mah jawww-w! . . . arghh . . . ! Won't shut . . . ! Ooooh-ohh—ahhh!

Owwww-w! They said arghh . . . Tol' me you . . . you're medicine man! Right? Owrghhh! Can you arghh-h . . . ooo-h-h . . . Can you oooghh-h do something? Owww-h-h, ohhh it hur-r-rts!"

Two Trees and I stood there, gritting our teeth, avoiding each other's eyes, trying to avoid bursting into loud peels of uncontrolled laughter. We did our best not to give in to it. I could taste the blood from where I was biting down on the inside of my lower lip. That man's eyes looked out at us pleadingly. "Oh, no," I told myself, biting even harder at my lip, "don't laugh , don't laugh."

I turned away and got my camera out of my bag. This I had to shoot.

Meanwhile, Two Trees had composed himself, and a look of utter seriousness came into his eyes. He cleared his throat and took a deep breath. Now, stretching his two hands straight out, he clamped the man on both shoulders, as if fixing him in a vise. He stared right into that gaping mouth.

"Now, let's have ourselves a little look here!" he announced with doctorial authority.

The impatient patient stood there, obviously terrified but without any show of resistance .

I caught the man's eyes with mine.

"You mind if I take a few pictures while Two Trees works on your mouth?" I asked him blithely.

"Mmmmmm . . . yaa-a-a . . . anhhhh . . . oooo-OOOH!"

He nodded his assent through his pain. Two Trees was staring intently into his mouth, gripping his shoulders tightly to keep him still.

"Thanks," I acknowledged, circling their strange scene and snapping away with my Leica.

Two Trees set to work on that man's jaw.

"Gotta crack it!" he announced. "Gotta crack that jaw shut, that's what we're gonna do! Ain't no different than an elbow or a knee. Just gotta *crack* it!"

The man's eyes bulged some more, betraying pure fear.

Two Trees slapped him hard on both shoulders.

"Be still," he ordered. The terrified man obeyed.

Now Two Trees placed his two thumbs right into the startled man's mouth. He took hold of the jawbone firmly, gave it a few preliminary turns and twists, then really got to work.

"Okay, here we go!"

Once, twice, five times or more he yanked and twisted and pried and wrenched at the open jaw, trying to force it shut. Each time, with each wrench, the man's body quaked like a shaken rag doll's. The mouth remained open.

"Damn jawbones are out of their sockets!" Two Trees grunted. "Here, come on over to this bench and lie yourself on down. That's it, right on your back."

Now Two Trees straddled the quivering man as you would mount a horse. He sat right across his chest, reached his thumbs back into the gaping mouth, clamped the jawbone with a pliers grip, and, his whole body heaving, yanked and pulled at that lower jaw to bring it back up. Damn if something didn't finally give!

First there was an amazingly loud *CRACK!* It literally sounded like a gunshot.

Then came Two Trees' screaming shout: "*O-oo-oh!* My thumbs! He's bitten my goddamn thumbs!"

He jumped off the old man and hopped around, shaking his bitten thumbs in the air. "Oh, damn! Oh, damn! Nearly bit both of them off!"

The old man lay motionless on his back on the bench, water standing in his eyes.

His mouth was closed!

"Don't open it again, damn it!" Two Trees yelled, groaning in pain, holding out his two injured thumbs, slowly moving and clenching them again. Finally he managed to regather his composure. It was all I could do now not to laugh at *him!*

Two Trees looked at the man.

"Your jaw'll be sore for a few days. Sore like you never felt. Better don't eat for a few days. Just liquids till you can chew some, then real soft stuff. Don't want those muscles tightening up again before they heal, you hear?"

The man groaned what I took to be an assent. Two Trees snorted almost horselike. The laugh caught in his throat as he threw back his head.

"And for God's sake," he said with finality, "*don't yawn!*"

❁

For all his occasional buffoonery, which I see now as a necessary foil to his darker powers, Two Trees *could* diagnose! I remember I took my son Chris along to meet him on one of my early visits. Chris was just a little fellow then, about ten and undersized for his age.

Two Trees gave him a big smile and a handle-pumping hand-shake, then stood back and eyed him. He said to Chris, "You don't run a lot, do you?"

Chris said, "No, not much." He had never been into athletics.

Two Trees said, "Is that because you turn your right ankle?"

Chris said, "Well, yes. How'd you know?" That surprised me; I hadn't even been aware of it.

Two Trees went on: "Well, there's a reason for that. You'd proba-bly be more active if your ankle didn't turn over when you ran. It's weak, and that's gotta come from an injury you've had, Chris." Two Trees looked over at B.J. and me and asked, "Did he fall or have some accident and hurt his head when he was a baby?" We couldn't think of any such accident. Two Trees shook his head. "Well, he had to have had some kind of fall. Think about it . . . because I think there's pressure on whatever side of the brain it was on. Something has weakened that side."

We thought about it, and then we remembered that Chris *did* fall out of the crib once when he was a baby. He used to get mad when-ever we left him alone during the day in his crib. One day he climbed over the railing and fell straight down on his head. And when he went down, he knocked out his two bottom teeth. Thankfully, they were just baby teeth. They were left hanging, so the doctor just went ahead and took them out.

When we told Two Trees about that, he nodded. "I thought so." He put his hands on Chris's head and moved his fingers around, probing gently. "Well," he said, "something's still out of place. It's af-fecting that ankle somehow. Needs work. More than I know how to do, I'm afraid. You'll have to go see Dr. Chastain."

So we took Chris down to Taccoa, Georgia, to visit Dr. Chastain, and that's when we first met that wonderful chiropractor and spiri-tual healer whose life has intertwined with mine ever since. Dr. Chastain worked on Chris, adjusting the plates in his skull. Chris never did turn his ankle after that.

❖

Now Harvey, seated beside me in the car, lets out a muffled laugh. He doesn't believe a word I said about seeing Two Trees back there.

"Maybe," he says, and I can sense him smiling smugly to himself, "seeing Two Trees back there . . . maybe that really *was* your vision, the one you just said you were going to have."

"I sure hope not. That's one vision I'd rather not have! Besides, it wasn't a vision," I say, contradicting him. "Two Trees was really there. At least he was for *me!* Maybe there's something between a vision and reality. I like that word *visitation.* Let's call it Two Trees' visitation. Like everything else about him, there's just no explaining it. Yeah, I like that: Two Trees' visitation!"

Harvey snorts his usual snort of utter disbelief, then laughs.

"That makes it official," he says. "We'll call it Two Trees' visitation from now on!"

Sometimes the ridiculous and sublime seem to intertwine. I know there's laughter in the divine scheme of things. I remember Charlie Knight telling us, "Tell them, Charlie Knight's a funny man." And Mathew King, that wonderful Wisdomkeeper, was famous for making people laugh, for lighting up a room with his impish smile. Among all the photographs of Indians I took for the rejected Grandfather Medicine Men story, I remember there were dozens of Indian people laughing. My picture editor asked me, "What did you do to get those people to laugh?" In his mind was the stereotype of Indians with a tear glistening in the corner of their eye. Indians know how to cry, of course—you're not likely to meet a people who have more to cry about—but most of the time, in my experience, they're about the laughingest people you'll ever meet. Quick to laugh, quick to cry. Maybe that's how human beings are meant to be.

Harvey's nodded off. At least he won't needle me about Two Trees' visitation for a while. The Stone Canoe carries us magically onward. No expectations this time, just infinite possibilities. I can feel the wind picking up under us again.

We head on toward Santa Fe to retrieve the owl's claw from Fred Kline.

Chapter 14

FRED'S down in the arroyo," his wife Jann told us when we arrived at the Klines' hilltop home overlooking the glittering sweep of Santa Fe. "He's down there with the dogs. Some teenagers went through the other night and knocked some of his sculptures down, so he's gone down there to start putting a few of them back up."

"Hey-y-y, Fred-d-d!" she called out musically from the veranda. Her voice carried down the steep-sided arroyo, thick with scraggly piñon and juniper brush. From far below came an answering call. I recognized my old friend Fred Kline's voice. "I'm coming on up!"

I could hear dogs barking.

Jann led us from the broad stone veranda overlooking the arroyo through the open French doors and into their expansive living room, a veritable art gallery in itself.

I remembered, on our last visit to Fred's, the time after he had given us the Seminole sorcerer's cane, I'd noticed a bizarrely grinning red-painted Iroquois False Face mask with shining copper eyes hanging on the living room wall. It had had its face out—unlike those I had glimpsed with their faces turned to the wall in Oren Lyons's lodge.

"That's an Onondaga False Face mask!" Fred had announced with curatorial pride.

"Hell, we were just out at Onondaga!" I'd told him. "I bet Oren Lyons would love to have that! What's it sell for?"

"Not cheap," Fred had acknowledged. "I'm asking five thousand."

Even my *Geographic* expense account wouldn't cover that. I dropped the thought. But that mask kept staring at me. I could see why Oren kept them turned to the wall. For all their wild and twisted, almost Picassoesque features, these False Faces have a poignant individuality: eyes that rivet directly onto yours, grotesquely grinning mouths that seem to be laughing at you, shifting facial expressions that somehow seem to come and go, morphing in and out of each other right there in the brightly painted carved wood. Their contorted visages represent certain forces, both demonic and benign, in the Iroquois supernatural world. They figure prominently in Iroquois ceremonies.

"They're alive," Oren had told us. "We feed them real food in our ceremonies, and they eat it. They're our relatives, our cousins and uncles. We know each one of them like we know the members of our own families. But they're for us, not for outsiders. They're not secret, they're private."

And now here I'd found myself eye to eye with one of Oren's wickedly smiling relatives, hanging there face-out on Fred's living room wall, an object of fine art for white men's appreciative eyes. I looked at the little identification label on the back of the mask: "Carved by Patterson Homer, Onondaga, 1935." The year I was born! Damn, Oren would love to have that! I'd stood back and gazed at it. That False Face eyed me, transfixed me, mocked me, laughed at me, wept at me, screamed at me: *"I want to go home!"* I could all but hear it.

"How about five hundred?" I could hear my crass voice saying to Fred. Hell, he'd already given us the Seminole shaman's cane on our previous visit. I could hardly expect him to bestow his entire inventory on us.

Fred had smiled at my absurd offer. "Harvey, this is a treasure. It was deaccessioned at a museum, and I traded another dealer my best piece of African art for it, a rare eighteenth-century Benin wood sculpture. I can live for two months on the sale. Why don't you get *Geographic* to buy it—I'll give it to you at cost—and then they could return it to the Iroquois?"

I knew the magazine could never justify such an expenditure. Still . . . I could see in Fred's eyes that he was half-tempted just to give it to me. With a bit more subtle nudging on my part he probably would have done so right then and there. But I didn't want that. This was his business, his living, after all.

A few weeks later Fred had called me. "Harvey," he'd all but stammered. "That False Face mask keeps staring at me. It makes me uneasy. It's like those copper eyes are looking at me and accusing me of some terrible crime. Do you have Oren Lyons's address at Onondaga? I'm shipping the mask to him today!"

And he did. Oren later told me he'd had no idea who had sent the mask; it just arrived in the mail one day. "We were amazed!" he said. "The Elders here at Onondaga remember that mask. It just disappeared one day years ago. It was like a long-lost uncle coming home. We resanctified him, and he's part of our ceremonies again."

Yes, it was the False Face mask that wanted to go home, and it did!

Looking back, I'm amazed at the multiple ways in which Fred became quintessentially involved in this spirit-journey of Steve's and mine over the years. He was the custodian of the owl's claw as well as the generous donor of both the Seminole sorcerer's cane and the Iroquois False Face mask. He had also introduced us to Richard Erdoes, who had led us in turn to Oren Lyons, Leon Shenandoah, Mat King, Frank Fools Crow, Eddie Benton-Banai, and many of the other Wisdomkeepers. Though Fred hadn't actually traveled with us, he was a co-journeyer in spirit from the start. Our relationship is simply one more proof, to me at least, that life *does* have a structure and a meaning and a purpose, expressed through a certain poetry of events. There's a literary hand unquestionably at work in the universe: "The play of things in the poem of the world," as Fred expressed it in one of his poems.

❉

Now Fred himself burst out of the piñon bramble with his three dogs—two massive pit bull labs and a shaggy golden retriever. All four were panting mightily.

"Harvey! Steve!" Fred called out. "God, it's good to see you guys!"

We were both immediately bear-hugged by Fred and simultaneously slobbered over by the dogs. If I have one archetypal image of Fred from the old days back in the '70s, it's of him jogging through his suburban Maryland neighborhood with his dogs romping along around him like a canine protectorate. Back then he had two dogs, now three. I recall only too vividly the time one of them tried to gnaw off a piece of my rear end. Fred had found that enormously amusing. Thankfully, I survived, suffering only some scratches and the loss of a pair of trousers along with my equanimity.

"I see you still go jogging with the dogs," I remarked.

"Oh, they're the terrors of the arroyo," Jann piped in. "Fred goes out running with them every chance he gets. He'll spend hours out there, jogging with the dogs and stopping to build his sculptures."

"I'll take you out there to see what I've been doing these past five years," Fred announced. "I've turned the whole arroyo into a natural art gallery. I'll take you guys on a tour!"

We sat in his living room and discussed the specific purpose of this visit. Fred, it turns out, had given the claw to his son Aren ten years before as a kind of coming-of-age talisman.

"I gave it to him on his thirteenth birthday," he recalled. "To tell you the truth, I thought it was an eagle's claw, not an owl's, and Aren's name means *eagle* in Norwegian. The claw seemed the perfect gift for his journey into manhood."

Aren had come in to join us—a strapping young man, tall, lean, handsome, with the face of a poet, a far cry from the little kid I'd known a dozen years before. That claw certainly hadn't hurt him any.

"Yeah," Aren said. "All these years I thought it was an eagle's claw. The eagle's my symbol. I really feel terrible the cat got it. He somehow jumped up and got it off the wall where it was hanging. We hated to tell you. I know what it means to you—and to me, too. That claw's been my good-luck piece, my personal talisman, since I was thirteen. I've meditated with it many times. When the cat ate it, I was devastated. It was like a sacrilege. I felt guilty, personally responsible for destroying something holy."

"Well," I consoled him, "the claw's still here, Aren. It wasn't really destroyed. You can't destroy these things. It's become a spirit-claw, that's all. You needed an eagle's claw for your symbol, so that's what the claw became for you. For you it *was* an eagle's claw!"

"That claw's been his helper," Fred said. "I know it's helped him over the years because Aren certainly believed in it, and so did I. So, Harvey, I want to thank you for leaving it with us."

I shook my head. "I didn't *leave* it, remember? I just forgot it like a damn fool. It was the claw's doing, not mine. It wanted to stay behind, and it did!"

Aren nodded, smiling. "I'll get the claw," he said, leaving the room and returning moments later with a rolled-up newspaper.

"Harvey," he announced, holding out the newspaper in both hands and presenting it to me, "I want you to know . . . this claw's meant a lot to me. The time's come to give it back. Here it is—or what's left of it."

I raised one hand. "No, not just yet, Aren. You hang on to it for a little while longer. Just set it down on the table there."

I didn't want to rush this. We were dealing with the sacred here, pure metaphor in physical form.

Aren unrolled the newspaper and set the bedraggled remains of Joe Parra's owl's claw power stick on a small table—just the foot-long bamboo shaft, trimmed with gray rabbit fur and a few splayed feathers, yet still somehow radiant with power for all its sorry condition. I gazed down on it. The back of my neck crawled. It was the first time I'd seen it since the claw and the cane had exchanged themselves that day back in 1983.

I was beginning to see the value of such notions as a spirit-claw and a spirit-feather. They enable you to keep alive something otherwise lost or destroyed. This is a real power, a palpable power. Such notions, such metaphors, aren't softheaded mysticism. They're entirely practical, even essential. Great Turtle Island itself is such a notion, a spirit world kept existent by the life-giving power of metaphor. All conceptual worlds—yes, even America, if we could only see it, even the universe—are, in the final analysis, metaphor, poetry, figures of language and thought created by the human mind to seize meaning and spiritual sustenance from the Great Mysterious, itself a metaphor. *Metaphor*—from the Latin *meta,* beyond or outside of, and *pherein,* to bring or to carry—a transference of meaning out of one context into another, a superimposition of layers of thought. Meaning within meaning, metaphor within metaphor. All is metaphor. That's the poetry that draws me on.

Aren stroked the remnants of the owl's claw—still an eagle's claw to him. He had accepted the metaphor and was filled with its power, its breathing reality. I could see it had done important work here during the past dozen years. There was a reason it had stayed behind, just as there was a reason the cat had eaten it only a few weeks before and a reason I had now arrived to retrieve it and take it back home. You create your own reasons, your own metaphors.

Aren told me: "I'm really glad you're taking it back where it's supposed to go, back to the Indian people. I guess it's got work to do back there with them. Everything's happened just the way it was supposed to. But, still, I could have *killed* that cat Tigger! And he acted really strange after he ate it—ran off into the arroyo. I could hear him howling down there. Then he finally came back, looking guilty as hell!"

Tigger sat sphinxlike on the veranda, soaking up some warmth from the sun-splashed flagstones. I eyed him. He eyed me. His eyes were yellow, unfathomable. He's what's called a Texas tabby, almost raccoonlike in his sleek plumpness, the picture of pure self-satisfaction—no doubt at having played a key role in this spirit-journey of ours. It was Tigger, after all, who had turned the claw into a spirit-claw. Never underestimate a cat with such powers.

Just to take back the remains of the claw now, rolled up in a piece of newspaper, somehow struck me as anticlimactic, even inappropriate. Something more was needed. This was to be a journey, above all, of respect, wasn't it?

"Why don't we have a little ceremony down in the arroyo?" I suggested. "Aren, you can return the claw to me down there. I've got Jess Bluebird's Holy Smokes with me. We'll light them up and take a few puffs, say a prayer or two, sanctify the occasion."

"I'll bring along some sage a friend gave me," Aren said, picking up on the idea.

"And I have a braid of sweetgrass I got from an elder a while back," Steve added.

Our ceremony was composing itself, assembling its own pieces, its new and borrowed metaphors.

"Great idea!" Fred exclaimed. "I've built a special temple out there in the arroyo. I call it the Temple of the Hills. Made it out of huge boulders, sort of like Stonehenge. It's the perfect place for a ceremony!"

Minutes later, dogs in tow, we were striding down a tangle of dirt paths five hundred feet to the floor of the arroyo. Fred gave us the grand tour, pointing out every subtle wonder of the extraordinary world he had created down here.

"It's called the Arroyo of the Stone—*El Arroyo de la Piedra,*" he explained, leading the way. "Water and rocks wash down from the Sangre de Cristo Mountains."

"*Sangre de Cristo,*" I repeated, savoring the beautiful words, "the Blood of Christ! That's a wonderful metaphor right there!"

"The whole arroyo is a metaphor!" Fred nodded. "Beautiful, isn't it? I'm hoping to get it turned into a parkland. It's like a strip of natural parkway right here in the city with houses all around. I'd love to see it turned into part of an Arroyolands National Park."

We reached the floor of the arroyo, the dogs romping joyously around us, suddenly filled with a new energy.

"Come on," Fred said, "I'll show you my world."

He led the way up the arroyo.

"No water down here right now," he said, "but I've seen it filled with whitewater after rains. Sure works hell on my sculptures!"

He pointed out his hundreds of works, many of them hardly visible at first among all the rocks and brush and scattered deadwood. It was as if a band of gnomes had been at work in the arroyo, building secret little shelters of rock and deadwood, piling stones and rocks on top of each other in whimsical constructions, building sacred circles out of boulders, hanging bird feathers and dried wildflowers and odd pieces of driftwood in the crooks of gnarled juniper trees. Under every little rock overhang there was revealed some exquisite arrangement of natural objects, each a kind of miniature chapel.

"I call them earth sculptures," Fred explained, kneeling before each and having us peek into the little world within. "Each one is a shelter, a refuge for insects and birds and all the little animals that live in the arroyo. Yesterday I looked into that one, and there was a little lizard looking up at me with beady yellow eyes! He blinked at me, and I blinked at him. I told him, 'Sorry to bother you, brother Lizard.'"

Fred Kline, brother to the lizards.

He continued: "Some of the sculptures I just toss together quickly. Others I work on for days, even weeks. Every time I go jogging by with the dogs I stop and make a little change here, an improvement there. Sometimes they get knocked over by animals or storms, sometimes by freelance critics who see something they don't like and just knock it down. Sometimes it's just teenagers knocking something down because it's there. I got mad as hell at first, but I've become philosophical about it. It's telling me something. I build them again, in a different way each time. There can't be anything permanent out here, of course. It's all a kind of exercise in *im*permanence, just like life itself, right? Now look at this juniper tree over here."

He led us over to a large arthritic juniper with a kind of natural sheltering hollow at the juncture of its lower trunk and exposed roots. Rocks had been arranged around it, as had several large pieces of lovely deadwood.

"Sometimes I'll stop here and go inside," Fred said. "I'll just sit in there and meditate. It's my own little chapel inside a dead tree. I love the idea of walking *into* a tree! The other day I was going to go in there, and damned if I didn't spook a coyote!"

Nearby stood a figure of sticks, a free-form deadwood being poised in an almost dancelike pose.

"I call it a presence," Fred said. "I've built them all over the place."

"Reminds me of Charlie Knight's stick people," I recalled. "But they were malevolent beings."

"Not *my* stick people!" Fred insisted. "They're built with love. They're my friends. No malevolent beings down here. This is a holy place. Bad spirits wouldn't be comfortable here. Now look at this."

He fell to his knees and peeked into a little circular arrangement of stones and sticks. "Come on, look in here. It's my ant coliseum."

I knelt beside him and peered into the miniature world.

"See the little ant hills in there?" Fred said. "They're right in the middle of the arroyo. People kept walking on them. So I set up this protective wall of rocks around them. Ants have a right to live too, right? I even put a little dish in there to catch the rainwater. Hmmm, it's dry now."

He leaned over and spit into the dish. "There! I usually stop to spit in there on dry days. You should see the ants! They come in here and start drinking it, and they go crazy! Start turning in circles. The nicotine gives them a high, I guess!"

Fred Kline, brother to the ants.

We continued our visionary hike. Over there was an arrangement of boulders in the form of a running man. Over here was a small bottle filled with sand, a tiny cactus growing in it. Each step brought us to some new little sanctuary.

"I call this place the Hawksgrove," Fred said, ducking into a group of closely spaced junipers. "There was a nest with two adult hawks and a baby when I first noticed this place. See, there's the nest up there now. I watched them raise the baby for weeks. One day the adults flew away and left the chick alone. He'd gotten used to my being around—

and even the dogs. I began to whistle to him, and darned if he didn't fly down and circle around my head. It was amazing! I whistled the next time, and he came again. Happened every time I came by. He used to bring his kill in there, and I'd find pieces of rabbits and piñon jay and bits of feather. Finally one day he flew off, too. I've missed him. Maybe he'll come back next year. I hope so!"

Fred Kline, brother to the hawks.

Like a latter-day Saint Francis, Fred moved among his creations, extolling the inner living wonders of each. I followed along, enchanted at his profligate artistry. He had turned this arroyo into a gallery of the soul, filled with sacred presences, instilling dead wood and cold stone with life, intelligence, humor, compassion. Transforming space into poetry. In a recent letter to me, he wrote: "Here I am, infusing art into life. The first thing I see I'll become—the stones, the bones, the flying singing bird, the deadwood, the blue sky, the tree. And I dream like God, who knows everything that is beautiful."

Yes, *everything that is beautiful*. This Arroyo of the Stone is Fred Kline's Dreamtime, his own personal Great Reality.

I remember Mat King telling me: "We don't need your church. We have the Black Hills for our church. And we don't need your Bible. We have the wind and the rain and stars for our Bible. The world is an open Bible for us. We've learned that God rules the universe, and everything God made is living. Even the rocks are alive."

Fred hasn't made this place sacred. It was already sacred. He's simply called our attention to it, revealing its sacredness to the otherwise unseeing eye.

I remember Mat King also saying: "Everyone is sacred. You're sacred and I'm sacred. Every time you blink your eye or I blink my eye, God blinks His eye. God sees through your eyes and my eyes. We are sacred."

Yes, Mat King and Fred Kline, two kindred souls. When they blink their eyes, we *all* see.

We rounded a curve of the arroyo, the dogs leading the way, sniffing out the Dreamtime.

"There it is," Fred exclaimed, "the Temple of the Hills!"

Before us loomed a Stonehenge-like group of large rectangular rocks arranged in a circle on a small knoll. Compared to Fred's other arrangements and earth sculptures and presences, it was enormous. (And *Art in America* [August 1995] selected "Temple of the Hills" one of the country's notable public sculptures.)

"The owner of this property," Fred explained, "wanted some kind of gateway for his new housing development. It's just up over the rise there. I told him I'd create a structure for him at cost, and he agreed. Imagine, after working with all these smaller pieces, to have the opportunity to build something really monumental! It's the realization of a lifetime dream. We moved those rocks up here with a rented crane. Took weeks. Aren helped. His energy's in it. And Jann's, too. Her input was really strong. We worked on the model together, and then she came down every day with a picnic lunch during the weeks I built it. Jann's my muse. God must love me because He sent me an angel!"

He led the way through the open gateway into the circle of rocks.

"Quite a place for a ceremony," I remarked, amazed at the scale of it.

Fred continued: "The whole thing's a metaphor for Mother Earth. See, we've walked right into her womb! Those two rounded boulders are her breasts. These two rocks are her hands. The large boulder is her head. The grass and wildflowers are her hair. See, she's reclining. And those shafts of rock just outside the entrance are phallic guardians. Do you notice how it somehow seems quieter in here? And on hot days, I swear, it even seems cooler inside the circle."

We had our ceremony. First Aren lit the sage and sweetgrass, and a heady pungency wafted onto the air. Each of us leaned over the smoke and fanned it into our faces, inhaling deeply. Then we lit four of Jess Bluebird's Holy Smokes. The three dogs sat on their haunches and watched us wonderingly.

"Jess Bluebird told us each one of these Holy Smokes is a prayer," I said, "so let's smoke them with reverence."

We did, standing there in the womb of Mother Earth. Somehow—to us, at least—it didn't seem silly.

"He also said," I recalled, "that he'd be looking at us through the smoke when we smoked them."

I half-expected Jess's mystic face to come floating up at us through the smoke. It didn't, but it did come to mind—and I guess that was enough.

"Now," I continued, "Aren, it's time for the claw to go on its way."

Aren stepped forward, unrolled the newspaper, and presented me with the claw.

"This claw's been a protector to me," he said. "But now it's time for it to go home, as you say. I'll sure miss its power."

"The power is still inside you," I reassured him. "Nothing's being taken, Aren. Thanks for keeping it all these years."

Now we heard a shrill *kwa-a-a kwa-a-a* above our heads.

We looked up.

"Isn't that a raven circling?" I asked.

"It sure is!" Fred exclaimed. "Brother Raven comes to say hello!"

He cupped his hands and returned the call: *"Kwa-a-a! Kwa-a-a!"*

The raven answered once—*kwa-a-a!*—and wheeled out of sight over the Temple of the Hills, disappearing into a stand of junipers.

"Ravens are one of the dominant birds around here," Fred said. "They use the arroyo for a flight path through the city. Glide through here all the time. I have their calls down real well. Aren does, too."

"Yeah," Aren said, "they'll circle over my head, calling down to me. And I call back up to them."

Aren and Fred Kline, brothers to the raven.

Chapter 15

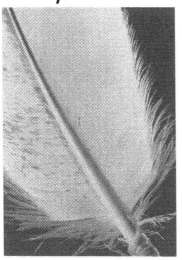

FRED Kline's generosity in returning the False Face mask to Faithkeeper Oren Lyons was one of those truly human acts that have hidden repercussions. It was a factor, certainly, in the trust bestowed on Harvey and me by the Iroquois, a trust that proved essential to our keeping our feet on the path. That False Face mask became a kind of messenger for us, showing the Iroquois that we cared, that we were affected. And you'll see no photographs of that or any other False Face mask in these pages because, quite simply, they weren't intended for your eyes. As Oren told us, "They're not secret, they're private. They're alive. They're our relatives. We feed them in our ceremonies. They're not for outsiders to see. Don't even *think* of asking to photograph them!"

There are some pictures I'm proud of *not* having taken. Like the picture I didn't take of the eagle that Frank Fools Crow prayed out of the sky. Or the picture I just couldn't allow myself to take, even from a distance, even with permission, of Eddie Benton-Banai's sunrise ceremony. In fact, I'm proud of all the zingers I never took. They remain inscribed in memory, where they belong.

But there's one picture I *did* take that I'm especially proud of because in a way it was my reward for not taking all the others, for never intruding my lens into situations where it wasn't wanted, for never stealing a picture from Indian people. And it, too, had to do with the False Faces.

Just as we were wrapping up nearly three years of coverage for the Iroquois Confederacy article, we got a call from the Mohawk chiefs at Akwasasne, on the St. Lawrence River, that we would be welcome at their annual midwinter ceremonies. The invitation came as a result of my request two years earlier to photograph inside the Mohawk longhouse, something that hadn't been done, we were told, since a photographer twenty-five years or so before had sneaked a few photographs and published them in a newspaper with demeaning captions, making these holiest Iroquois ceremonies of the year seem "quaint." They told me I was to be the first outside photographer allowed in the longhouse since then. I had no hope—or, for that matter, the slightest intention—of photographing the ceremonies themselves, only the flow of people and events surrounding them. Instead of making something holy ordinary by photographing it, I've tried to photograph the ordinary activities surrounding ceremonies and see the holiness, the sacredness, in *them*.

When we arrived at Akwasasne, Harvey was pulled off to one side by one of the elders for a discussion concerning our limited participation in the midwinter rite activities, and I was escorted to the home of one of the faithkeepers. I was to witness and photograph, they told me, the preparation of the ritual cornmeal that would be used in the Longhouse ceremony. I was ushered into the main room, which was filled with bustling activity, and I sat down as unobtrusively as I could on a folding chair and photographed the sequence of the men grinding into meal the large white-kerneled sacred Indian corn.

Suddenly the usual talk and laughter subsided. I could hear a loud rustling outside the room and some deep, almost animal-like grunts. The ladies set down the cornmeal and the utensils and looked around uneasily. More rustling, more grunting in the other room. I knew the men of the medicine society were out there, the ones who would soon change clothes and be transformed into humpbacked ash-blowing spirit-beings. Soon they would don their sacred living masks and begin their rounds to the homes of the traditional Mohawk. It was time for the Hadoui, the False Faces.

But there was a problem: me. The Hadoui were out there, apparently getting into costume, and I, the photographer, the outsider, was not supposed to be there. Photographing the cornmeal preparation would have been all right, but not photographing the Hadoui, the False Faces. They'd forgotten that the Hadoui would be there when I was invited. I saw instantly what was up. "Maybe I'll come back later," I told the faithkeeper. He nodded with relief and gave me directions to another residence nearby, home of a young chief, where I was to wait. I gladly followed his advice, walking through the cold January night to the other house.

And that's where I got a glimpse of the otherworld.

In the other house, they had no notion who I was. My cameras were put away. I was just a visitor in a room crowded with men, women, and children, all of them getting ready for the ceremonies. I was told to sit down on a chair in the corner of the kitchen, and I figured I'd wait there until the Hadoui had done their thing, then go back and photograph the cornmeal preparation. But now I heard those menacing rustlings and gruntings again. The Hadoui were here! I'd tried to get away from them, and they'd come after me!

Suddenly children started screaming wildly and running from room to room in every direction within the confines of the small house. Their footfalls pounded on the floor, shaking the wood-frame building. And there were even louder, more ominous bangings.

"The Hadoui are here!" they screamed. "Hide! They're here!"

I jumped up, ready to bolt out of there. I knew I wasn't supposed to be part of the ceremony, except the ceremony kept following *me*. The young chief whose house it was raised his hand and emphatically gestured for me to sit back down.

"If you're here now it's because you're meant to be here," he said calmly. "Sit on down there and let the Hadoui do their work!"

The entire house shook. Walls trembled, as did I. I searched out the source of the disturbance. The noise was everywhere and no place in particular. The rumbling was like the sound of hundreds of cardboard boxes rolling over and over, hitting each other and tumbling about, all in one gigantic mass of motion.

A child screamed, *"Hadoui!"* And in through the back door barged the men. But they were not the men I had been with only an hour or so earlier. By putting on the carefully crafted sacred masks, they had been transformed into the "beings" they represented. Not that they weren't the same men; they were, but now in some mystic way they had become the Hadoui. They weren't just pretending to be them—they *were* them!

❈

Mohawk Wisdomkeeper Cecilia Mitchell had told me how the Hadoui come out this time of year because they come from the stars, and the stars seem closer in the winter sky. As I've heard it from Cecilia and others, the story of the Hadoui goes like this:

> The Creator was walking around the forest, visiting all the beings he had created when he created Mother Earth. He saw one strange creature he didn't know and asked him his name and who he was. The creature, smiling wickedly, declared, "I'm Hadoui, the most powerful being in the universe!"
>
> Amazed by such a boastful declaration, the Creator asked Hadoui to demonstrate just how powerful he was. Hadoui grinned and pointed to a mountain. "I can move that mountain you see out there," Hadoui declared. "I can do it without even moving from this spot, just by my powers of concentration!"
>
> "Okay," said the Creator, "let's see you do it."
>
> So Hadoui closed his eyes, concentrated very hard, and after a while the ground began to shake and that mountain, with a great roar, moved several feet on the horizon. Then Hadoui turned around to face the Creator, and said: "There! I did it! Let's see you match that!"
>
> The Creator nodded. He told Hadoui: "All right. But take care! Don't turn around!"
>
> Hadoui scoffed, disregarding the warning, and turned around to look, and at that second the mountain came rushing right up to him, smashing his nose and twisting his mouth into a perpetual evil smirk. Realizing the Creator's power was far greater than his, Hadoui henceforth used his own power to help others instead of hurting them. His one demand was to be given tobacco and food, and the people see that he gets these to this day.

Now, as I found myself suddenly confronted by this incarnation of the Hadoui themselves, a strange sensation spread through my body, beginning at my toes and slowly crawling to the top of my head. I tried to keep from looking at them directly, as if fearing that in some way they might see into my own dark crevices and find some kindred demons or evil spirits lurking there—maybe even the same kind of shadowy spirits they were now rambling noisily through the house to scare off.

When the chief touched my hand to ask, "Do you have any tobacco?" I jumped, almost in panic, thinking that one of those tortured entities had found me and wanted to climb into my body and share it with me.

"What? Tobacco?" I stammered.

"Everyone has to give them a gift. Tobacco. Do you have any?"

Just as he finished his question, the Hadoui were back and opening their bags for offerings. Making sure I satisfied their wish, I grabbed my pouch of pipe tobacco from my coat pocket and dumped all of it into the bag of one of them. His wild-eyed masked face nodded at me, almost as if in recognition, and then with a snort this figure out of a nightmare seemed somehow to grin even more widely, then backed out of the room and, like a puff of smoke, was gone. Within seconds all the Hadoui were gone, and the phenomenal whirlwind was over. A strange silence settled in after them. No one said a word for a long time.

For my Mohawk friends I was sure there was reflection, a sense of cleansing and, certainly, a spiritual experience, as well as the sheer delight of pure harmless terror being brought under control by a ceremonial act. For me, I was moved emotionally, all but wrung out.

"They must have gotten to you," the chief said with a laugh, his words erupting out of the quiet like a volcano.

"Why–y," I stammered in surprise, "why do you say that?"

"Hey, you gave them your whole pouch of tobacco! You're just expected to make a small offering."

"Well, I figured that if a little bit was required, then a lot would appease them even more and do a whole lot more good. Besides, I didn't know how much to give. I didn't know what I was doing, anyway."

"It's okay. You can't give too much to the spirits, and you always get something back. Hey, it's time to go to the longhouse. The Hadoui will be there, too. Come on."

The longhouse was already almost full when I arrived. I saw Harvey sitting on one of the stair-step benches lining the wall, made my way up there, and sat down next to him.

"What've you been up to?" he asked.

"You'll never believe it. I don't know if I can even describe it."

Just as I was about to attempt a retelling, what seemed to be the early stages of the ceremony began. I thought I could hear some more of those rumbling, banging noises of the Hadoui just outside the longhouse door. They were following me!

"Tell you about it later," I said to Harvey, and he nodded his approval, saying nothing more.

I looked around the longhouse. That's when I noticed that everyone else, maybe two or three hundred people, were all looking at us. Harvey seemed oblivious to it.

I jabbed him. "They're looking at us," I whispered. "All of them. They're *all* looking at us."

He looked around. He looked back at me. "You're right! What's going on? I thought we were invited."

For a couple of minutes the whole longhouse grew strangely quiet, almost expectant. The rustlings and rumblings outside the door subsided. Nobody spoke. There were several hundred pairs of eyes trained intently on Harvey and me. I could feel myself almost twitching under the weight of that communal scrutiny.

"I think we're not supposed to be here," I said to Harvey.

Just then our old friend Chief Jake Swamp silently made his way over to me. Whispering in my ear, he said, "You guys want to go out and get a cup of coffee?"

"Oh, I'd love a cup," I said, "but I don't want to take you from the ceremony."

In the kindest way he could—and without a doubt Jake is one of the kindest men I've ever met—he whispered back, "I think we should get a coffee. There's a little problem here, I'm afraid."

"Are we a problem?" I asked.

"Well, Steve, you're no problem at all. But, you see, one of the clan mothers . . ."

My heart sank. I wondered about the photographs, but he didn't have to say another word. I knew that if one person objected to our presence, we would have to leave. And a clan mother had done just that.

Leaning over to Harvey, I said, "We've got to go."

"*What?*"

"Someone's asked us to leave. Jake's going to take us to the Bear's Den for a coffee."

On the way to the car Jake informed us that the ceremony was very sacred and that no pictures could have been taken during it even if we'd stayed, but that, if I liked, I'd still be able to take some photographs at the social dance in the longhouse after ceremonies the following night. That suited me fine.

❀

The following night Harvey and I returned to the aging whitewashed longhouse. The old building was filled to capacity. A single blindingly bright lantern hung from the ceiling, casting sharp-edged shadows around the large room. Even in the semilight I could feel the eyes of the celebrants turn our way and fix on us, the two strangers, the two outsiders, the two intruders. It looked as if we might be asked to leave again. And then a girl giggled. The silence was broken. People started chattering. The eyes turned away from Harvey and me. It was okay. We'd been accepted. We could stay.

The drumming and the dancing abruptly began. I grabbed my camera from my bag, popped in a roll of Kodachrome 1000—brought along for really difficult lighting situations—and started shooting without a flash, which would have been a sacrilege in there. I figured there was no way *Geographic* would ever use these pictures because there was hardly any light. I had to get up on a low bench to see over people's heads, and I was jostled almost continuously. Holding the camera up as high as I could, I shot at a downward angle at the crowd of circling dancers, with only the slightest idea what I was shooting. It seemed as if we'd gone to an awful lot of trouble—not to mention two years of waiting—just to get a lot of blurred, unusable pictures. The room had such low light—only a single lantern hung over the singers in the center of the room—that I had to slow my shutter speed to the point where it was almost impossible to hold the camera without creating meaningless blurs out of the dancers as they moved around the circle.

"It's impossible," I thought, "not enough light, so much vibration, so much movement." I was ready to throw up my hands in desperation. At the very instant when I'd given up, a sudden and unexpected peace and calmness settled over me; it was as if I had gone inside a quiet little sanctum or chapel of my own and was looking out at all the near yet distant activity. I knew I was at the right place at the right time and that this time it would work.

Careful not to step on anyone, I got down off the bench and made my way around the floor, dropping to my knees for a better angle here, climbing back up on a bench for a better angle there. Suddenly every angle was perfect. Patiently, not hurrying things, I shot image after image until that roll of 1000 film was out. I had not the slightest doubt that I'd succeeded, though I'd never used a roll of 1000 ASA-speed film before.

Later, after the film had been processed and printed, I learned what I had sensed at that moment in the longhouse: Not one frame was blurry or out of focus, and virtually every composition was as I'd envisioned it. Even the hard-eyed photo editors at the magazine, usually my harshest critics, announced, "Zingers! A whole roll of zingers!"

Actually, they were wrong, as usual. These weren't zingers at all, just good, honest, unstaged pictures that were meant to be taken. Just as some poems come to a poet, so those pictures inside the Mohawk longhouse came to me that evening after so many failures. Unplanned. Unexpected. Spontaneous. Unpretentious. Perfect—or as perfect as this photographer is ever likely to get. The photograph was later published in our Iroquois article and my book *Wisdom's Daughter.*

After finishing my picture-taking there in the longhouse, I put away the camera and for once just enjoyed watching a scene, not trying to capture it on film. Yet I have to confess that when I just watch, I'm only an onlooker. But when I step out of a scene, put my eye behind a lens, and try to photograph that scene, then—and only then, it seems—am I truly *in* it. It's paradoxical, I know. I have to get outside of an event to be inside it. I guess that's the curse and the blessing of being a photographer. Without the curse there wouldn't be any blessing.

Chapter 16

WITH the spirit-claw retrieved from Fred and Aren Kline, I now had to find my old Chumash friend Joe Parra in order to return it and complete the circle. From Santa Fe we dropped back down to Albuquerque, reconnected with I-40, and headed west, California bound.

"Maybe we can have a couple more of Jess Bluebird's Holy Smokes along here somewhere," I suggested to Steve. "Maybe another little ceremony'll give us a little extra help finding Joe."

"Harvey," Steve chided me, "you'll get addicted to those things again."

"Jess said they couldn't hurt us," I insisted.

"Well," Steve said, shaking his head with a tolerant smile, "I guess if that's what you want, let's find us a place."

"Go on," I said. "Take the next turnoff. Pick a road, any road. Let's drive awhile and find a place to have our little ceremony. Make it somewhere near the road. My sciatica's killing me. It really gets bad when I sit here in the car like this all day. My whole right leg's aching, from my hip joint to my toes. It would be good to get out and just walk around—but not too far!"

I scanned the desert and mountains around us. We had just crossed the border from Arizona into California. We were somewhere west of Needles, south of the Mohave, just a couple of hours from Barstow. A small road sign read PROVIDENCE MOUNTAINS.

"Providence—that's 'good luck'!" I said.

"Hell," Steve muttered, "I'll turn off right at this next exit. We'll find us the perfect place."

We took the turnoff and went down a narrow paved road that seemed to head nowhere at all, right into haze and mountains, right into the Dreamtime. We were about an hour from sunset, and the landscape had taken on a ruddy color. It seemed almost translucent, glowing from within.

"Maybe we should climb one of those hills," I suggested. "Have ourselves a makeshift ceremony up there on top. A little communion with the gods."

"Hell, there's a thousand hills out there," Steve said. "Which one? How'll we choose?"

"You pick it," I told him. "I trust your instincts. You're the navigator, Steve. You've never led us wrong yet."

We tooled along the arrow-straight road for ten minutes or so, casing the topography for potential sites. Low hills swelled out of the undulating desert on every side. One seemed pretty much the same as the next.

"No sense driving very far," Steve said. "They all look about the same."

"Pick one of the lower ones," I suggested, "I'm not up to any heavy-duty climbing."

We spotted a low stony hillock off to the left, just fifty yards or so from the road. It was maybe fifty or sixty feet high and appeared to have a flattish top.

"How about that one?" Steve asked me. "Think you could make it up to the top with your sciatica?"

"You bet. Let's do it before the sun sets."

We pulled over, grabbed our camera bags, and headed up the rocky scree toward the hilltop. Halfway up the slope I had to sit down on a rock and pick half a dozen inch-long thorns out of my shoes. Steve hiked ahead of me to the top.

"Hey, Harvey," he called down. "Come on up here. You've got to see this!"

"Got one of these thorns right through my shoe," I shouted, limping up the incline. "Just a minute."

I made it to the top, and I couldn't believe it. There was a man-made circle of rough rocks on top of the hillock, a low fortress—or even a kind of medicine wheel, like those I'd once seen in Wyoming's Bighorn Mountains. It was about ten feet in diameter and two feet high. The ground inside the circle looked swept clean. There wasn't a footprint.

"It's some kind of holy place," Steve said.

"But whose?" I wondered.

"Guess it's ours for now," Steve said. "Perfect place for a ceremony."

A minute before he was grumbling, now he was ecstatic. And so was I.

"Imagine," I said, "here we go out in the middle of nowhere and pick a hill for a ceremony at random—and damned if there isn't a little ceremonial temple of some kind waiting for us on top. It's weird. Fred Kline would love this place."

"You think it's Indian?" Steve asked.

"I don't know. I can't tell if it's two months old or two centuries. How would you tell? Looks like someone's been keeping it up, that's for sure. Hell, it's been swept clean."

"Maybe just by the wind," Steve said.

"What did Fred call his construction? The Temple of the Hills? I know," I suggested, "let's call it the Temple of the Wind!"

"Doesn't seem like much of a temple to me," Steve said. "It just looks like a pile of rocks in a circle. Besides, *I* discovered this place, so *I* get to name it."

I shrugged. "Okay. Go ahead. Name it!"

"I'm thinking," Steve said, "I'm thinking."

On a sudden impulse he grabbed a hefty grapefruit-sized rock off the top of the low wall, fell on his knees in the center of the circle, and set the rock down gently but solidly on the ground.

"There. That's for Lee Lyons," he announced, his voice thick with emotion. "It's a remembrance rock. We'll call this place Remembrance Rock. It'll be a memorial to all the Wisdomkeepers we've met who have passed on."

I nodded, enthusiastic. It was the perfect idea. We were actually in agreement for once. I grabbed another rock off the wall, held it up, contemplated it in my hand for a moment, then set it down on top of Steve's.

"And that's for Irv Powless, Senior," I declared, recalling the great Iroquois Wisdomkeeper.

Steve picked up a third rock and set it firmly on top of the other two. "And that's for Vernon Cooper!" he said loudly, recalling the wonderful old Lumbee medicine man.

I set down a fourth rock. "That's for Mat King!"

Steve set down a fifth. "And that's for Corbett Sundown!"

I set down a sixth. "And that's for Frank Fools Crow!"

Steve set down a seventh. "And there's one for Buffalo Jim!"

We could have gone on. There were dozens of others we might have added.

"That's enough," I said. "Let those stand for all those who have passed on."

I saw that Steve had picked one more rock off the wall, holding it uncertainly in his hand. He looked at me with a pained look in his eyes.

"Since we're honoring people who have died . . . I was going to set one down for my Dad," he said, "but he was no Wisdomkeeper."

"He was as wise as he knew how to be," I said. "Wise as any of us. Probably wiser. Go on. Add a rock for your Dad, Steve."

He held it in his hand, a rough piece of sandstone.

"It's rough like my Dad," he said, "hard like my Dad. It has a crack in it. It's fragile, just like my Dad."

"Remember," I said, "how Mat King said, 'The rocks are alive. They talk to us, and we talk to them.'"

Steve held the eighth rock up and squeezed it gently, as you'd squeeze someone's hand.

"Dad," he said, his voice cracking. "I've been feeling you real near these past few days on this journey of ours, nearer than you ever were in life. And so . . . this rock's just for you!"

He set it lightly on top of the pile of rocks, then lurched away.

"That's enough ceremonies for a while," he announced.

While he reassembled his emotions, I sat on the low rock wall plucking dozens of thorns out of my shoes and socks and trousers.

"Devilish little things, these thorns," I groaned. "They don't kill you, but they keep you alert! Like Eddie Benton-Banai told us, 'Pay attention!' These bloody thorns sure make you pay attention!"

Steve checked himself. He plucked a lone thorn from his trouser cuff and flicked it away. He didn't seem to have any others, though I was like a pincushion.

Steve looked over at me, smiling now and shaking his head.

"Harvey, how did you get into so many thorns? I didn't get but one."

"I guess these thorns are my sign for this little ceremony of ours. *Pay attention!* they're telling me."

"Well, it's about time you did!" Steve barked.

"Shouldn't we smoke some of the Holy Smokes?" I asked him, holding up a couple of Jess's cigarettes.

"We don't have to smoke them," Steve said. "Just put them up on the pile of rocks there. Leave them for the spirits. Maybe the spirits would like a Holy Smoke."

I tucked two Holy Smokes among the rocks on the pile. We headed back down the hill, leaving the assemblage of eight rocks and two Holy Smokes for whoever followed us to ponder.

Turning back onto I-40, we headed right into the sunset.

"Finding that medicine wheel or whatever it was, we could never have planned that," I said. "It was like it was waiting for us! Hills everywhere, and we pick the one with the stone circle on top! We could probably never find that hill again if we tried!"

"I know exactly where it's at," Steve insisted.

I believed him.

A red ball sun hit the tops of the mountains and started sliding behind, swallowing the enormous landscape in shadow. We drove on.

❊

At a roadside motel I spent hours making phone calls in search of Joe Parra. First I tried calling Juanita Centeno, the wonderful Chumash elder who had introduced me to Joe that summer in 1982. It had been several years since we had spoken, and the telephone number I had for her was out of service. After a dozen or so unsuccessful calls, I finally reached a man she had known in Lompoc.

"But . . . but . . . I'm sorry," he told me. "Juanita died two years ago."

My heart dropped. I asked him if he knew Joe Parra's number. He didn't, though he'd met Joe years before.

"Maybe he's gone back to his family in Oxnard. That's south of Santa Barbara. I don't know. I'm not even sure the family lives there anymore."

"Do you know his father's name?"

"Nope. Sorry."

I called Oxnard information. No Joe Parra was listed. There were a dozen or so Parras in Oxnard, I was told, dozens more in the nearby Ventura and Santa Barbara areas. I called several of those in Oxnard, but no luck. None had heard of a Juanita Centeno or a Joe Parra.

"Well," I told Steve, "I guess we'll just have to go to Oxnard and see if we can find him . . . or at least find the family. We'll call every Parra in California if we have to. Maybe someone will know where he is."

"And if you can't find him, what then?" Steve asked. "What'll you do with the claw?"

I could hear the doubt in his voice.

"We'll figure that out when we get there," I said. "Maybe we'll find a Chumash elder and give him the remains of the claw for a proper burial or whatever it is they do with such things. Or maybe we'll just go out on the beach and have a little ceremony of our own. Bury the claw in the sand ourselves, I suppose."

"It doesn't seem right somehow," Steve said. "Sounds sort of anti-climactic, don't you think? We drive across the entire continent to return the claw and then just dump it in the sand somewhere?"

"Well, maybe we'll find Joe after all," I said. "Let's not give up yet."

We drove on to Oxnard, to another motel, and I began calling every Parra in the Oxnard phone book. Halfway down the list of fifteen names I reached the number of a Miguel and Anna Parra. A young woman's voice answered. When I asked to speak to Joe Parra, she sounded definitely suspicious. "Mmmmm," she responded to my unlikely explanation about trying to return an owl's claw power stick that Joe had given me back in 1982. "Mmmmm, well, I don't know. Maybe leave your number. I don't know."

"You mean you know him?" I asked hopefully.

"Mmmmm. Could be. Probably not the same Joe Parra."

She would say no more. I told her we'd be in Oxnard for the next day or so. I left our motel number. She didn't sound promising.

I tried the last seven Parras in the phone book. No luck.

"How's it going?" Steve asked.

I shook my head. "But I see in the phone book here that there's a Chumash council of some kind in Ventura. Maybe we can find an elder there we can give the claw to."

"It'll work out," Steve said.

"I suppose," I said doubtfully. "Maybe that one gal I talked to will get a message to him, and he'll call back—if it's the right Joe Parra."

Steve nodded. "Harvey, if we're supposed to see him, we'll see him."

Looking ahead to the return of his eagle feather, Steve tried calling both Leon and Roben White. Leon was out of town, according to his wife, Thelma, and there was only an answering machine at Roben's. Steve asked Thelma to have Leon call us at the motel, and he left the same message on Roben's machine.

"What if we can't reach Leon or Joe or Roben?" I grumbled.

"If we're supposed to reach them, we will," Steve counseled, stubbornly optimistic. "Whatever happens, happens. No expectations, remember? Just possibilities. If we look at it that way, there's no way we can fail."

We waited for the phone to ring. A day passed. We made more calls, left more messages. We sat around the motel room, grousing at each other, swilling diet Cokes and potato chips and candy bars. Two days went by. The phone remained silent. It was as if we'd dropped right off the wind and landed suddenly and hard back in the ordinary world. We were just two aimless travelers killing time in a bleak motel room, watching afternoon soaps, falling asleep to old black-and-white movies on cable, hiding out from the universe.

After two days and nights of this, Steve finally announced: "Harvey, if Joe doesn't call by tomorrow morning, we'll have to head up the coast. Maybe we can find some Chumash elders in Ventura and leave the claw with them. We need to get up to San Francisco to meet Leon. We can't stay here forever."

He was right. No expectations. Just possibilities. If one possibility doesn't materialize, that only makes room for some other possibility. If you hew to that philosophy while following the path, the only impossibility is failure itself. Every seeming failure can be, must be, transcended and transmuted. What appears momentarily to be a failure should be seen instead as a gift, an opening to undreamed of new possibilities. The notion of failure is always a fiction, a false self-judgment, self-deceit. On the path of the Wisdomkeepers, there is no failure; there's only the closing of one possibility and the opening of infinite others.

We slept late, got up, lazed around the room. Still no calls. It was a quarter to ten.

"We have to give this room up by eleven or pay another day," Steve said. "We can't wait here forever wondering if Joe's going to call or not. Harvey, I'm taking a shower. Why don't you go out and get us some coffee. If he hasn't called by eleven, we'll take off."

Dutifully I went out and got two Styrofoam cups of coffee at the hot plate in the front office. I brought them back to the room. Steve was still in the shower. And then I noticed that the red light on the phone was blinking!

"Hey, Steve!" I shouted through the bathroom door. "Are you alive in there? Couldn't you answer the phone?"

He came out, dripping, wrapped in a towel.

"I was in the shower. Didn't hear it!"

I rang the front desk. "You have a message someone called?"

"Two calls," the woman at the front desk announced. "Both came at once."

"Did they leave messages?"

"Well, yes." She sounded flustered. "Let me see. The second call was from a Mr. Roben White. He says to tell you he's expecting you whenever you get there. Give him a call just before you arrive."

"And the first call?"

"Uh, well, the first call . . . That was from a Mr. Joe Parra."

"Did he leave a message?"

"Yes . . . but . . . He was giving me his telephone number . . . but right then the other gentleman called. I only managed to write down the first three digits of his number. I'm sorry."

Oh, Lord. It was as if the feather and the claw had both called at once, and we'd botched the message!

We rented the room for another day. We waited. Waited some more. No call. No doubt Joe was expecting our call, but maybe he would call back. We waited all day. At last we slept, then woke up and waited some more. Still no call from Joe. It approached 11 A.M. once more. I made one final call back to the number of Miguel and Anna Parra. The same young woman answered. I explained that Joe had called but that the woman at the desk had missed his number.

"Can't you give us his phone number?" I asked.

"Uhhh, I'm sorry. I left your message for him. He's out of town. I'm not allowed to give out his number. You'll have to wait and see if he calls again."

"*If* he calls! Can't you get a message back to him?"

"I'll try. But I don't know . . ."

This was getting ridiculous.

"Would it be all right if my partner and I stopped by your house? Maybe we could leave the claw with you."

"Uhhh, well . . . I suppose. Are you sure you have the right Joe Parra?"

We checked out of the motel and drove to the Parra address. We knocked on the door of a small house on a quiet side street. The door opened a crack, and a suspicious eye peered out at us.

"Yes?"

"We're the fellows with the claw," I announced, realizing even as I spoke how weird and unlikely it must have sounded. How many people would open their door to two complete strangers claiming to have a claw?

Thankfully, these were Indians, and after a pause the door opened. An elderly woman stood there, wiping her hands on an apron. A younger woman stood behind her. I could hear a baby crying.

The older woman looked us up and down. She smiled cautiously.

"I'm Joe's mother," she said. "This is his sister Melissa behind me here. And you—you're that fellow from *National Geographic,* right?"

"Uhhh, well, I *used* to be from *National Geographic,* but no longer. And this is my colleague Steve Wall. We're hoping to see Joe. You see, we have this claw . . ."

I was about to launch into my long-winded explanation when she waved her hand for me to stop.

"I know all about that claw, young man! I was there when Joe gave it to you, don't you remember? It was my sixty-fifth birthday party up in Lompoc. You came there with my cousin Juanita Centeno. You were writing an article for your magazine. That's when Joe gave you that owl's claw stick! And you promised to send us pictures! Remember? You took all those pictures. And you never sent us any!"

Uh-oh. White man's broken promises. I remembered the pictures only vaguely. They were probably still sitting in a drawer at home.

"I . . . I'm sorry. I completely forgot."

She sniffed. "Well, I hope you'll remember to send them now! We'd love to see them. We all wondered what ever happened to you! Joe liked you so much. He wanted you to have that owl's claw stick! He made it himself. It's a sacred thing. You took it. You promised to send pictures. And then you never called us again!"

All I could do was stammer and apologize.

"Well," she said, her cautious smile returning, "Joe's out of town right now. But come on in. Come on in! You boys want some coffee? What's all this Melissa tells me about your wanting to return the claw?"

We had hardly sat down on the couch in the parlor than the phone rang. Melissa answered. "It's Joe!" she called out to us. "He says he called your motel, but you never called back. I told him you were here. He wants to talk to you!"

Steve and I locked glances. I rushed to the phone.

"Joe!"

"Harvey!"

It turned out he was a two-hour drive away, about to be released for the weekend from a rehabilitation center where he was doing soft time—mostly attending classes—after a driving-under-the-influence conviction. That was why Melissa hadn't given me his telephone number when I'd called. You don't hand out such information to strangers over the phone.

Joe told me the next train back to Oxnard wasn't until the next morning.

"But we'll drive right out and pick you up," I insisted, and we did.

We reached the gates of the rehabilitation center a couple of hours later, and there was Joe Parra, standing there waiting for us, a canvas bag on the ground beside him. He looked hardly older than when I'd met him in 1982, a darkly handsome man with mystic, penetrating eyes. He smiled wide, waving at us, and immediately wrapped me in a bear hug as if we'd last seen each other the week before.

"I knew something good was going to happen today!" he exclaimed. "This morning a hummingbird flew right into the window of the building where I'm staying! I kept watching it fly around and around. The custodian started to chase him out, and I told him, 'Don't hurt it! Don't touch him! Leave him alone! He's a soul catcher. He catches souls and takes them back to the Great Spirit!' Then the others all got worried he was coming to take one of *their* souls! And I told them, 'Don't worry! He's carrying a soul to the other world, and his path just leads through here. He'll get out on his own, and he'll take it where it's going.' Finally he flew back out the window. I knew that was a good omen. He was trying to tell me something, give me a message. That's why he flew in there. I knew something good was about to happen. I told everybody, 'Today's gonna be a good day!' I'd called your motel yesterday and left a message. I was waiting for you to call back, and you didn't. Then I called home, and you guys were there! I was amazed. And now . . . *you're here!* So the hummingbird was right!"

As we drove back to Oxnard, I tried explaining to Joe why we were there, how we'd come to return the claw, how it had been eaten by Aren Kline's cat, how Two Trees had predicted we would each receive signs.

Most people would have been put off completely by such an unlikely story, I suppose. But not Joe Parra. Not an Indian.

Joe nodded warmly, smiling. He understood. He was instantly in sync with us.

Steve asked, "Joe, what ever made you give that claw to Harvey in the first place?"

"Because . . ." Joe said, hesitating, "because I saw someone who believed."

Steve snorted. "Harvey? Believe? Hell, Harvey's from Chicago. He doesn't believe in *anything!*"

"Oh, yes, he does," Joe said. "Maybe he doesn't know it, but he *does!* He came to my mother's birthday party that day with our cousin Juanita. He listened to us. He respected us. I could see he really enjoyed being with us. I remember he had another appointment that same day, but he canceled it to stay with us. He seemed to really care. You know, I watch people. I study them. I could see he was a person who shared, who didn't keep everything for himself. I had a good feeling about him. I sensed something special. And, I don't know, it just came over me. When I get a feeling like that, I act on it. That feeling is always right! And I remembered I had that owl's claw stick out in the car. I wanted to share something with him, something that would watch over him, something to keep the bad things away from him, something to guide him."

I winced with embarrassment at his words. "But I had no idea at the time of its significance. I tried to refuse it, but you wouldn't let me. You said if I refused it, it would be like a slap in the face. And then, like a damn fool, I actually forgot it at Fred Kline's!"

"And then the claw became the Seminole's sorcerer's cane!" Steve put in.

Joe nodded. "That's how it happens. These things go where they want to go. They do their work, and then they go on. I made that claw maybe fifteen years ago. The idea just came to me one day. It was like I was *instructed* to make it. It's not an old-style power stick. Those are made out of elderberry, and this one's just bamboo. I made it out of whatever was at hand—a scrap of rabbit fur, some feathers. I got the claw itself from a guy at the zoo who was going to throw it away. I just put them all together, and there it was! I'd made a sacred thing without even knowing how! You could feel its power right off. My son, Joe Junior, used it in his first ceremonial dance. And now after all these years it's come back to us. It wanted to be here. Even though the claw itself is gone, it's still here. It can't be destroyed by cats or anything else!"

"It's become a spirit-claw," I heard myself saying.

I had to suppress a tingle on the back of my neck.

Joe continued: "The power of the owl is observing. He's the *observer.* He watches over you and guides you."

"Two Trees told us he was a symbol of death," Steve recalled.

"Sometimes," Joe said. "But he's also the symbol of life. It all depends."

"Depends on what?" I asked.

"The owl's a foreteller," Joe explained. "He foretells death, that's true, but he also foretells life. So it depends on where your soul's at. We see owls all the time, but that doesn't mean we're going to die anytime soon. He's a good omen. He'll come when you're born. He'll come to guide you many times in your life. Then he'll come when you're about to die. He doesn't *cause* your death. He just announces it."

This jogged my memory.

"Juanita told me how she used to tend a flock of sheep as a little girl—right out there among the dunes where Vandenberg Air Force Base is today—and she said at night when she was taking the sheep back to her village, her way would be lighted by the owls' glowing eyes. She said they guided her home the same way an airport's landing lights guide an airplane to the ground at night."

"So, you see," Joe said, "the owl's a helper, a guide."

"Then how come Two Trees was afraid to touch it?" Steve asked. "He warned us that claw could be dangerous."

Joe shook his head. "Only when it's in the wrong hands. When it's in the right hands, it does only good. No way that claw could do Harvey any harm."

Admittedly, I found this comforting.

"Maybe," Steve said, "it was Two Trees who had the wrong hands. That's why he wouldn't touch it!"

"Anyway," I pointed out, "the claw itself—the physical claw, I mean—has gone on its way. But at least the three feathers are left."

"Those are hawk feathers," Joe explained. "They represent the three winds."

"Three winds?" I asked.

"Yes. For most people there are four winds, of course, coming from the four directions, you know? But we Chumash people say there are only three winds. That's because, living right on the coast up against the sea, we have the high cliff behind us. It cuts off the east wind. We're the People of the Three Winds. We have a saying, 'The fourth wind is always back home . . . in our hearts.'"

Joe was talking a natural poetry here. Pure metaphor. His voice was gentle, sincere, poignant, utterly without affectation. He was just saying what he knew in his heart—the loveliest poetry of all.

❊

When we reached Oxnard, Joe's mother was at the door to greet us.

"So," she said, smiling. "You've brought me back my wayward son!"

She took us inside. I presented Joe with the claw's remnants, still wrapped in the newspaper Aren Kline had given us.

"So the claw's come home at last!" I announced.

"Or what's left of it," Steve added somberly.

Joe unrolled the newspaper. He winced for a moment at the sight of the clawless claw and its three badly frayed hawk's feathers. Then he smiled.

"Yeah! It's back! Looks like it's had a really hard time. Harvey, I'll have to make you another one!"

"Oh, please, no!" I pleaded, laughing. "That would mean a whole new journey! Why don't we just have a little ceremony out on the beach? Do you want to bury it out there in the sand . . . or what?" I asked Joe.

He shook his head. "No, not bury it. We'll want to say some prayers over it, maybe. Then, I don't know. I think I'll just keep it awhile. I'll probably cremate it. It's a holy thing. It'll let me know what it wants me to do with it. That'll be private, just between me and the claw."

We drove out to the beach with Joe's family and had our ceremony, a very simple affair, just a few briefly worded prayers by Mrs. Parra, Joe, and me, and then a round of thank-you's. It was over quickly. I'd completed my obligation to the claw. I breathed deep. I don't know what I expected to happen. It all seemed fitting yet somehow anticlimactic. I gazed out at the ocean. I squinted my eyes, longing to see a dolphin, perhaps a rainbow, even an owl or a hummingbird—a confirmatory sign of some kind. But the sky was empty, the horizon bare, the ocean calm, flat, and ordinary-looking. No signs. It was just as well, I suppose.

"Hey, Harvey," Joe called out as Steve and I got back in the van to head up the coast after the ceremony. "I have something for you before you leave, a little gift. Something I made as part of my therapy at the rehab center. Not much, really, but I want you to have it."

He presented me with a small roughly woven basket no larger than a sparrow's nest, about four inches in diameter, two inches deep. It couldn't have been more ordinary or, to me at that moment, more precious. It was perfect.

I told him: "So now this little basket has exchanged itself for the claw, just as the claw exchanged itself for the Seminole sorcerer's cane and then became the claw again! I guess it's as much a sign as any of the others!"

"A sign of our friendship!" Joe said, his hand on my shoulder.

"I'll keep it on the shelf above my desk at home," I promised him. "It'll be a reminder to me of all that's happened. Something ordinary, something *extraordinarily* ordinary!"

That holy little basket sits above my desk as I write these words.

Chapter 17

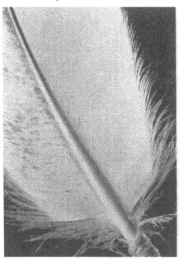

NEXT, the return of the feather. Harvey had found a certain emotional closure by returning the remnants of the owl's claw to Joe Parra. "That was really beautiful out on the beach back there," he enthused. "That ceremony, returning the claw to Joe after all these years, the spirit-claw—that's real *poetry!*" But the matter of returning Bob White's eagle feather was somewhat more problematical. Chief Shenandoah was due to meet us with the feather in San Francisco a week hence. I'd been trying to reach him for days, but his wife, Thelma, told me he was away on Confederacy business. Had he found the feather? Thelma didn't know. On our way up the coast from Oxnard, I stopped at a roadside telephone booth and called again.

This time, thankfully, Leon himself answered.

"Leon, it's Steve Wall. So you finally got home!"

"Well, yeah" came his familiar voice. "Steve! Good to hear your voice! Thelma said you'd called. I've been away on business. Where *are* you guys?"

"Leon, we're in California. We're waiting for *you!* What would you think of coming out here right away? We got out here a few days earlier than we'd figured. We'd like to change the reservation on that ticket we sent you. When's the soonest you can fly out?"

There was a long pause. I could hear him muffling the mouthpiece with his hand and shouting something to someone. Now his voice came through again.

"Well, Steve. Thelma says—darnedest thing—we've lost that ticket somehow. Can't find it. Looked everywhere around the house. I know I had it, but I put it somewhere and . . ."

Oh, no.

"Uhhh, Leon, did you ever find the eagle feather?" My heart was sinking to my shoe tops.

"Well, Steve . . . Not yet, I'm afraid. Been looking everywhere, but . . . I'm sure I have it around here somewhere. I'll keep looking."

"You mean you can't find the ticket *or* the feather?"

"I . . . uhhh . . . I'm afraid so. Darnedest thing!"

Oh, Lord. I'd had a feeling this was going to happen.

"Listen, Steve," Leon went on, "I've been thinking about this trip. Maybe I'm not supposed to go out there to California with that feather. Maybe that's why I can't find it. And maybe that's why the ticket is missing, too. It's like they don't wanna be found! I think you guys should go on without me."

"But, Leon . . . We came all the way out here to meet you!"

I could hear the shrillness in my voice. I gave myself a shake. What was the matter with me? I'd been trapped by my own expectations! What happens, happens—right?

"Leon, you're right," I finally agreed. "I think that feather doesn't *want* to come out here! That's why you can't find it. That's why the ticket got lost. Harvey and I can still drive up to see Roben White. We'll explain what happened. He'll understand. At least we can pay him a visit."

"It'll work out, you'll see," Leon said. "You don't need me for this. You can do it on your own. You guys go on. The feather's not supposed to be out there, and neither am I! Anyway, you guys come on up and see me here at Onondaga when you get back. You can tell me how it worked out."

"We'll do that, Leon."

Somehow I was suddenly feeling *good* about this strange twist of circumstance. I knew I should be feeling disappointed, but if there are no expectations, just possibilities, then there are no disappointments, right? You simply go on to the next possibility. It's impossible to fail!

"Leon's not coming," I announced to Harvey when I got back to the van. "He never found the feather. And, besides, he even lost the ticket."

Harvey grimaced. "So what next?" he asked.

"We'll drive up to see Roben anyway," I said. "Pay him a visit of respect, explain that the feather has been lost."

"Hey," Harvey said, "didn't I just give the spirit-claw back to Joe Parra? Why can't you give the spirit-feather back to Roben White?"

"I already figured that's what I'd do," I told him.

We headed on up the coast.

❊

My mind harked back to the first time I'd driven up here along this same spectacular coastal highway in 1982. I was heading up to the Smith River on the California-Oregon border to photograph a chapter in Geographic's *Wild and Scenic Rivers* book. Just south of the Oregon border I stopped at the Pelican Beach Motel, a pleasantly rustic place that turned out to be run by Bob White, the Cheyenne-Lakota man with the wild white hair who bestowed the feather on me that memorable night. Moved as I was, I could hardly have imagined the significance it would take on for me. Nor could I have dreamed I'd be coming back up here nearly fifteen years later to return that feather—now transformed into a spirit-feather!—to Bob's son Roben.

I remembered Roben as a devilishly handsome and high-spirited young fellow who guided me around on the Smith River. We had struck a chord with each other but had lost touch after I left. It was only when I had called him a few months back, while Harvey and I were first planning this journey, that I learned from Roben of Bob's death from a cerebral aneurism back in 1985. Compounding the trauma, one of Roben's brothers had committed suicide two weeks later. Then his mother was diagnosed with cancer. Roben had been shaken to the roots of his being. I'd called to tell him about returning the feather, but that suddenly seemed almost silly.

Still, when I mentioned the feather, Roben became excited. "Oh, yeah!" he said. "Please *do* bring it! I know my Dad would want you to! And I'd love to see you again, Steve! You've got to see the motel! I've completely refurbished it. It's all I've worked at these past few years. It's like a monument to my Dad, you know? It's like he's been after me to fix it up, keep it going. I can feel his spirit hovering around here all the time. I know he'd really be happy to see that feather again!"

I'd told Roben how Iroquois Chief Leon Shenandoah would be bringing the feather up with us. Now I'd have to explain to him that Leon wasn't coming and that there was no feather, only a spirit-feather. Who knew? Maybe that eagle feather had to be in spirit-feather form for Bob to take it back in the spirit world. Anyway, that's how we chose to look at it. You make your own meanings, after all.

It was nearly 1 A.M. when we drove up to the Pelican Beach Motel. And there was Roben White himself, my old buddy, standing at the front door, a big smile on his movie-handsome face. It had been twelve years since I'd seen him. With his curly blond hair, he looked more like a member of the Norwegian ski team than an Indian— but, once again, how's an Indian supposed to look?

We went inside, met Roben's charming wife, Sherri, and talked a blue streak over steaks and coffee until nearly 3 A.M. Roben understood instantly about the spirit-feather.

"To be honest, Steve, I'm actually relieved you don't have the real feather," he confessed. "It's got my Dad's power in it. I'm not sure I could handle it right now. He's still hovering around here, you know? Some nights we hear him walking around the motel, going from room to room. Sherri even thinks she saw him one night!"

His wife smiled uneasily. "Yeah, it was real scary. I heard this noise in the motel office, and I went in there. A painting had fallen right off the wall! I saw this shadow, and it had two yellow eyes looking right at me. Then it just melted away. I actually screamed!"

Sherri showed the sleepy-eyed Harvey to his room, leaving Roben and me alone.

"Oh, those were wild days, Roben!" I laughed, recalling our youthful misadventures. "Man!"

"Oh, baby!" He nodded with a big smile.

Smile or no, there was a palpable sadness in his eyes. I knew he'd been having some really hard times in recent years. We went out on the front porch, which looks out on the ocean, and while a fantastic display of heat lightning played in the night sky, he recited at length the dark tale of his father's death, his brother's suicide, and his mother's ongoing bout with cancer.

"It's just been one thing after the other," he said. "It's like there's been some kind of curse on us. The hardest thing was when my

brother killed himself. That's been nearly ten years, and I still can't accept it. God! Sometimes it seems I'm filled entirely with blackness! I get suicidal myself. I just keep busy working on the motel here. My Dad loved this place. It's like he doesn't want to leave it, like he's hanging around watching me as I fix it up. Damn, I'd really love to sell the place, but it's like he won't let me."

I confessed my own struggles with depression, how a relative of ours had killed himself a few years ago and how that had devastated the family, how I'd found myself under the table in my study one night with that pistol shoved up under my chin.

"I can really connect with what you're saying, Roben," I told him. "I know that pain. I've lived it. But that darkness is somehow necessary. It's like you've got to get past the shadow to reach the light. If you can just get past it, there's a new life out there."

"You know," Roben said, "I think it's the ones who die who have it easy. It's those of us who stay behind who have to live out the pain. A few months back, when things were really going dark inside me, I put all that pain into a painting. Just splashed a bunch of leftover house paints on a piece of plywood. And there it was staring back at me—my own depression! It's the same painting that fell off the wall when Sherri saw my Dad's ghost. I keep it out in the garage now. I'll show you in the morning."

"Well," I said, "maybe the spirit-feather we've brought will bring some kind of closure for you. I know bringing it back's a kind of closure for me. I think your Dad would be pleased I've brought it back."

Roben looked around almost as if expecting Bob to walk right up and sit down beside us there on the porch.

"Oh, yeah," he said, "I *know* he's happy you've brought it back!"

"Maybe tomorrow morning," I suggested, "we can find ourselves a grove of redwoods nearby here somewhere. Have us a little ceremony. Formally return the spirit-feather to you . . . and pay our respects to your Dad, too."

"I'd like that." Roben nodded. "And so would *he!*"

❧

I sat out on the porch alone for a while after Roben and the others had gone to bed, watching the play of distant lightning in the sky over the Pacific. A storm was gathering out there, moving slowly toward land. Above the muffled distant thunder I could hear the breakers crashing on the invisible shore, maybe a hundred yards away. Their rhythm flowed right into me, right through me. Lord, this was beautiful. I could see what drew Bob White out here.

I'd never seen anything quite like this particular storm; it wasn't so much a storm as a panoramic celestial display. Spidery thin long-legged streaks of lightning were crawling out from under a low lid of clouds, not striking downward but scuttling horizontally this way and that across the sky, casting a pulsating blue light over everything. Some low houses across the road off to the left flickered like an old-time silent movie. The surf was writhing, breaking incandescent on the dark shore. The wind kicked up fitfully with a high eerie moan, then died down, then kicked up again. There was no rain. And yet the air was alive, electric, expectant. There was hardly any thunder, only that distant rumble. Silent lightning. I thought of waking Harvey to see it, then thought better of it. Let him sleep. He'd just ruin it with his wisecracks and Chicagoese. This one was *my* storm.

It was moving straight at me. Gripping the arms of my redwood deck chair like some celestial navigator, I just relaxed, feeling the spanking breeze in my beard and hair, and let the storm happen. It was an amazing spectacle. The lightning looked unreal, like something you'd expect to see in a mad scientist's laboratory. Great leaping blue-white snaps of charged energy bristled in jagged arcs across the sky, then exploded into a dozen shattered pieces, each a near replica of the original. There was something clawlike about them—gaunt-fingered, clutching, twitching. Almost as if some invisible presence were stretching its fingers into our dimension, reaching right toward me. I leaned back in the deck chair. This porch was my Stone Canoe, and I was riding right into the lightning! I felt a wild exhilaration. It was like that storm was happening *inside* me!

Here and there, amid the exploding pyrotechnics, I could see patches of open sky among the fast-moving clouds, seemingly brief glimpses of some other dimension. And for one fleeting instant I could actually see stars shining up there! I remembered a similar moment of near revelation a few years back while I was down in Costa Rica working on my book *Shadowcatchers*. I was riding in the back of an open truck down a steep and twisting road on the nine-thousand-foot Cerro de la Muerte, the Mountain of Death. It was night, rainy, and densely foggy, and we were *flying*, let me tell you! The truck was bouncing and careening at madcap speed down a series of terrifying hairpin curves, every one of them marked with white wooden crosses set up by grieving families to mark the spot where their loved ones had plunged over the edge into the void. I prayed as hard as I ever have in my life: "Lord, don't let them put up one of those crosses for me!" It was a silly thought, I know, because no one in Costa Rica would have grieved the loss of this nameless gringo intruder. And there's no way that B.J. would have gone down there to put one up! I felt sure my time had come when, looking upward, I caught sight of a single star shining down from a crack in the fog and clouds. It was like—I don't know. That single star was a kind of star of Bethlehem for me! I took it as a sign that there *was* a conscious, caring presence up there and that I was being watched over by a loving eye. I suddenly knew I'd be okay.

Seeing those stars briefly glinting so peacefully now in that small patch of open sky above the Pelican Motel gave me that same sense. Yes, there *is* a presence. Everything will be all right. Just take it all in, I told myself, become a part of it.

I finally headed back to our motel room and flung myself, exhausted, onto the bed. Harvey was long asleep. I felt drained. I buried my face in the pillows. I didn't bother to take off my clothes. Heat lightning still flashing in my mind, I fell asleep—slowly falling, drifting like a dead leaf to the bottom of a deep pond.

Now I'm in a dark room. It's this same motel room. Have I woken up? I glance over at Harvey. He's still asleep in his bed. But I sense something malevolent in the room, behind the half-open door leading to the bathroom. My heart goes cold with fear. I get out of bed and stand in the darkness. I can hear Harvey softly snoring, but there's another sound—someone, something else breathing. I try walking toward the open door, but my legs will hardly move. I feel my way along the wall with my hands. Oh, I know: This is a dream. It can only be a dream. I reach out to give the door a push. My fingers are shaking.

And I feel a hand suddenly clutch my back, right under my left shoulder blade. Another hand and arm wrap around my head and neck, and yank me into the shadows behind the door! I'm being pulled down, smothered, engulfed by some huge dark figure. I can't breathe. I yell out, but the scream catches in my throat. All that comes out is a desperate moaning, as if I'd been punched in the stomach. *Uhhhh-h! Uhhhh-h! Uhhhh-h!* It's the same sound I used to make as a child when my Dad would whup me. He'd never let me cry out loud. If I did, he'd just whup me all the harder. So I'd just let out those deep involuntary moans. *Uhhhh-h! Uhhhh-h! Uhhhh-h!*

I was being shaken. A voice was shouting: "Hey, Steve! Wake up! Wake up, damn it! You're groaning something awful!"

Thank God, it was Harvey! I sat upright, abruptly awake. I realized

I had Harvey's wrist in my hand. I was clutching it as if he had a knife in it!

"Let go, will you?" he cried. "You'll break my wrist!"

He wrenched his arm away.

"Oh, Harvey!" I blurted out, my body shaking spastically. "Oh, Lord."

I snapped on the bedlight. I was still in my clothes, barefoot, sitting upright in bed. I looked toward the bathroom door. It was still half-open.

"Go look behind that door!" I told Harvey.

"Go look yourself! You're scaring the *bejeezus* out of me!"

I crawled off the bed and hesitantly pulled open the bathroom door and took a quick reassuring peek behind it. Nothing, of course. Just the empty bathroom. I reeled backward into my bed. My knees were literally shaking, knocking with fear. Harvey touched my shoulder again, and I almost jumped through the ceiling!

"Oh, *my!* Oh, man, that seemed so *real*," I said. "I mean—I knew it was a dream, but it seemed so real! I couldn't get away. You heard me scream?"

"It wasn't a scream," Harvey said. "It was more like a groan. You were going *uhhhh-h, uhhhh-h!* over and over again. You were writhing in the bed. Woke me out of a dead sleep!"

I described the dream to him. Harvey stared at me hard throughout the recitation.

"And the man who was strangling you behind the bathroom door in your dream. Who was that—*me?*"

"No, damn it. It wasn't you. I saw you lying here in your bed. Besides, I think I know who it was."

"Two Trees?"

"No."

"Your father?"

"No, absolutely not. I've got the sense it was, well, it was Bob White! He was big as a grizzly like Bob. He was powerful like Bob."

"But why in hell would Bob White want to strangle you?"

A shudder went through my body.

"Damned if I know, but that's how it seemed. When you shook me, I thought it was him! I grabbed his wrist."

"*My* wrist, damn you! You nearly broke it."

Harvey twitched his nose.

"I once read," he said, ". . . I think it was in Jung, that all these characters in our dreams are just aspects of ourself, subconscious splinters of our own personalities."

"Oh, man. Please, Harvey, don't psychoanalyze me right now! That was Bob White, I tell you—not some part of myself. Man, look at me. I'm still shaking!"

Harvey half-smiled. "Maybe . . . maybe Bob's mad that you didn't bring the feather back."

"Well, maybe, I don't know. But Bob would understand about the feather. Hell, he'd think the spirit-feather was more than enough. He'd be delighted I've come to bring it back to him. Bob wouldn't want to do me any harm."

"Then, why . . ."

"Who knows? He's been haunting Roben and Sherri, hasn't he? Why would he be scaring *them*? It's as if he's stranded in this world and can't get away. His soul's stuck here in this damned motel!"

I doubt I slept more than an hour or two all night. In the morning we walked over to the motel cafe. Roben was there behind the counter, frying up some eggs.

"Did you guys catch that lightning storm?" he asked. "Man, I've never seen anything like it!"

I told Roben about the dream. I didn't mention my sense that the figure in the dream had been his father, Bob White, but I could see his eyes widen.

"Uhhh," Roben said. "Just don't tell Sherri about that!"

Just then Sherri came in the room, as if on cue.

"Don't tell me about *what*?" she asked cheerily, coming up to us with three cups and a pot of coffee.

"Oh," Roben said, "nothing."

"Steve here had a bad dream last night, that's all," Harvey chirped in stupidly.

"Oh, about what?" Sherri asked.

I tried to explain, "Just . . . It was like some dark figure came to me in the room last night. He tried—I mean I *dreamed* he tried—to strangle me."

I managed a weak smile, almost scoffing now at myself.

Sherri's eyes went wide. She almost dropped the coffeepot. She was suddenly shaking visibly.

"It's Roben's Dad!" she said, her voice a cracked whisper. "He's here. I know he's here. I've seen him, too. He's the one who knocked the painting off the wall!"

Roben winced.

"That painting!" he said. "Man! There's something about it! A couple of women stayed at the motel a while back. I think they'd been nipping a few. Nice ladies, really. They went back in the office there and started looking at the painting. Couldn't pull themselves away. They started getting excited. They said the painting was haunted. One of them screamed that the painting was trying to *get* her! It was *demonic,* she cried. Darned if they didn't check right out of the motel!"

"I've got to see that painting!" I insisted.

"I've been hiding it in the garage," Roben said. "Sherri hates it. She won't let me keep it on the wall."

He went out and came back carrying a piece of plywood. He set it on the ground in front of him.

"Well," he said, "here it is! That's the whole story, right there. That's what's been *inside* me!"

I was stunned. Two yellow eyes were leering at me out of a ghastly face. There was some terrible recognition in them. Was that Bob White? Was that *myself?* I shuddered.

"I had to get it outside of me," Roben said, "or I swear I would have killed myself."

The face glared at me. Those yellow eyes were jumping out at me.

"That's the face of depression if ever there was," I said, shaken. "Hell, I recognize it! I *know* that face! That's *everybody's* depression!"

"I call it the 'Motel from Hell'!" Roben said, smiling wanly.

"God, I wish we could get rid of it!" Sherri shuddered.

I had a sudden thought.

"You want to sell it?" I asked Roben.

I couldn't believe I was saying it!

"Sell it?" he said. "You're kidding!"

"No, I mean it. How much do you want? Name your price!"

"Hell, Steve, if you want it, it's yours! Consider it a gift!"

Sherri clapped her hands.

"You mean you'll actually take it away?" she asked.

"Let's put it right in the van!" I announced. "Let's say we're exchanging it for the spirit-feather! It'll be a way of releasing your Dad, Roben. You've got to let him go!"

I could see Harvey grimacing, but Sherri's face was alight with gratitude. She was ecstatic, absolutely delighted.

"Are you *sure*, Steve?" Roben asked.

"Yeah, I'm sure! I'll take it out of your life! Hell, Roben, that's a powerful work of art! I'll hang it in my study. I've been through it all myself. It can't hurt me anymore."

"I'll help you into the van with it," Roben said, smiling wide with relief. "Man! That demon's out of here! I've been released! He ain't *never* coming back!"

We barely managed to wedge the painting into the back of the van, facedown.

"Wait'll B.J. sees it!" I said.

"Oh, yeah," Harvey said. "Just wait!"

❄

We had our little ceremony of returning Bob White's spirit-feather to Roben the next morning out in a nearby redwood grove. It was as if we had walked into an outdoor cathedral. The beams of sunlight filtered through the towering trees as if passing through stained glass.

"Can't build any fires out here," Roben said.

"Let's just have some of Jess Bluebird's Holy Smokes," Harvey suggested. "Just be sure to put out the butts and take them with us."

We lit up three of Jess's Holy Smokes, watching the thin wisps of white smoke curl skyward, caught in the stained-glass sunbeams.

Roben cleared his throat.

"I'm not up to saying any prayers," he said. "Smoking these Holy Smokes will have to be prayer enough. But I do want to say thanks to you two guys. It means a lot to me, your coming back here, Steve, after all these years. Who'd ever have thought we'd be out here all these years later having a ceremony of all things! Hell, since my Dad died, I never thought I'd get involved in any ceremony again."

We fell into a contemplative silence for a minute or two. Then suddenly we heard a loud whirring and whooshing and flapping sound. Something, a blurred form, exploded out of the lower branches of the redwood we were standing under and flew directly over our heads.

"What's that?" Harvey asked, peering upward with a startled look on his face. "Sounds just like that condor that night with the Maestro in Peru!"

"No, not a condor. It's an owl!" Roben exclaimed. "It's a big old brown owl! Must have been sitting right there above our heads!"

"It's my *owl!*" Harvey exulted. "He's come to join our ceremony!"

The moving shadow swooped not ten feet above our heads, then glided away across the clearing into the far stand of redwoods, threading beams of stained-glass sunlight.

We stood there, watching after it—three tiny human presences among the gigantic presences of the redwoods.

"If that's a sign, I'll take it," Harvey said softly.

"Yeah," I said, "but how come *your* sign comes to *my* ceremony?"

"Isn't that the way it's gone from the beginning?"

"I guess so," I acknowledged. "It's like that owl's come and grabbed Bob's feather in its claw."

"Everything's come together," Harvey said.

We felt confirmed.

We finished off Jess Bluebird's Holy Smokes.

"No litter!" Harvey barked. "Here, give me the butts."

He gathered the three partially smoked Holy Smokes, carefully stubbed them out, and returned them to the pack Jess had given us.

"I'll keep them for souvenirs!" he announced.

We said our good-byes to Roben.

"And thanks again for that spirit-feather, you guys," he said.

He threw his arms around me and gave me a brotherly bear hug. The same for Harvey. The three of us stood there at the foot of the immense redwoods, hugging one another like madmen in the stained-glass light of that outdoor cathedral.

"Don't wait twelve years for the next visit," Roben said.

"I won't," I promised.

"Tha-a-a-nk you-o-o," he called out after us as we pulled away in the van, headed for home.

"We're heading home!" I announced triumphantly to Harvey. "Do you realize we've gone more than five thousand miles in thirteen days?"

"And both the feather and the claw have been returned," he said.

"We did it!" I yelled out. "We *did* it! The circle is complete."

And it was.

I leaned back in my seat, gripped the steering wheel, and—I couldn't help it—gave the horn three loud honks. They echoed in the silence of the redwoods around us.

"What's the matter?" Harvey asked.

"Nothing," I said. "I just feel like honking. Maybe the spirits are listening."

Harvey smiled and nodded. "Well, give them three honks for me, too!"

I honked three more times. Then I shifted the Stone Canoe into drive, and we headed on home.

Chapter 18

WE learned recently of Two Trees' death in April 1995. A friend sent us a copy of his obituary in the Charlotte *Observer.* He was always rooted in that other reality anyway; unless he's gotten himself stranded on this side, it'll be but a short journey for him to get over there. I can't say we were shocked by his passing. Saddened, yes, but— terrible as it is to say—there was almost a sense of relief, as if something had been lifted from us. We had talked of going to see him, but time and again had put it off. Probably just as well. Steve is convinced that Two Trees cast some spells on him years ago, that Two Trees was really a sorcerer. I don't know. Maybe.

For us, Two Trees had been the Gatekeeper, not the Guide. And I'm forever grateful to him for showing us the entranceway to Great Turtle Island. He pointed the way and led us to the path of the Wisdomkeepers. We would never have found it without him. He, too, was a runner between worlds. Whatever his imperfections, I believe he meant well. And whatever mysteries he took with him will forever remain just that—mysteries. So be it. He'd want it that way. In any case, for the record, let me say here, from both Steve and me: Two Trees, *thank you!*

❀

We drove up to Onondaga to see Leon shortly after our journey out west. We debriefed Leon on the return of the feather and the claw. He nodded with satisfaction at our report.

"I told you you didn't need me *or* the feather," he told us. "You needed to do it all yourselves, not relying on anybody. Nobody else can travel the path for you. You have to walk it by yourself."

It felt good sitting there around the kitchen table of Leon's little yellow clapboard house at the center of Great Turtle Island, the center of the universe, exchanging yarns with the Tadodaho.

Thelma gave each of us a motherly hug before we left.

"You boys want one more cup of coffee?" she asked.

"No, we'll be heading on, Thelma. It's a long drive back."

Just as we were about to leave, I noticed that Steve looked distracted. He'd wandered over to the china cabinet and was staring up at the large stuffed brown eagle with Leon's befeathered and antlered ceremonial headgear, the *gastoweh,* beneath its outstretched right wing.

"Leon," Steve asked, "is this where you keep your feathers, up here with the *gastoweh?*"

"Yup," Leon murmured.

"You mind if I look up here?" Steve asked. "I just have a feeling . . ."

"Go ahead," Leon said.

Steve got up on his tiptoes and reached on top of the cabinet. He gently lifted the *gastoweh* and looked underneath. He pulled out a white envelope and a piece of folded cardboard.

"Leon!" he all but yelped. "This envelope—it has my writing on it! Leon, it's the ticket we sent you. It's in here!"

Leon looked up, shaking his head. "I'll be darned! So *that's* where it was. But, Steve, I looked up there! So did Thelma! That's the first place we looked, and it wasn't *there!*"

"Well, it's here *now.* And you know, Leon, this ticket is still good! It hasn't been a year yet. You can use it to go anywhere you want."

Leon shrugged. "Ain't going nowhere right now. But that's good to know."

"And what's this cardboard?" Steve asked, holding out the folded piece of cardboard.

"That's my feathers for ceremonies," Leon said.

I sensed what was coming, although I could see that the folded cardboard was not the old balsa-backed one Bob White had given Steve with the feather. Still . . .

Steve pulled off the rubber band and opened the cardboard folder.

We all stared at the contents. Three feathers—two short red feathers . . .

"Oh, those are my red hawk's-tail feathers," Leon murmured.

And the third feather was an eagle's feather, of course.

Steve held it up in the air.

"Leon! It's my feather! It's Bob White's feather!"

Steve looked at me, his lips trembling, triumph in his eyes. He held up the feather in his fingers.

"Harvey, look at that! There it is!"

He stroked it lovingly. The feather looked a bit the worse for wear, but those markings—the dark spot, the white sunburst, the leather-bound quill with the thong handle. It was definitely Bob White's eagle feather!

Steve sat down at the dining room table, the feather in his hand.

"Somehow," he said, "I don't know how, but that stuffed eagle up there on top of the cabinet was, well, calling out to me. 'Look here,' it called. 'Look *here* under the *gastoweh*.'"

Leon shook his head. He smiled wide.

"So the feather's back!" he said.

We gazed at it in wonder.

Steve handed the feather to Leon.

"Here, Leon. This is yours."

"No," Leon said. "You take it, Steve."

I could see Steve hesitate.

"*No-o-o!*" I hissed at him. "Don't take it, Steve. *Don't!* It'll start everything all over again!"

Steve pulled back his hand. I could see how badly he wanted that feather, but, thankfully, he resisted.

"No," he said finally, "you keep it, Leon. I'm through with it. I don't need it anymore. It's done its work. Maybe someone else needs it. Let it go where it wants."

Leon gave him a big smile. He put the feather back in the cardboard holder and folded it shut.

"It's over," I announced. "The spirit-journey is over!"

Leon grinned at me. "Yup, it's over . . . till it starts again!"

Chapter 19

A large crowd had already gathered at the longhouse by the time Harvey and I arrived at Onondaga a few months later. Shadowy figures huddled together in the night, their outlines dimly highlighted by low-watt bulbs on the mudhouse porch. Seneca and Tuscarora chiefs sipped coffee and spoke in near whispers. Clan mothers moved slowly from one building to the next. Children played while under the watchful eyes of their mothers. No one walked about alone.

Harvey and I stuck close together like everyone else. We had been warned at Lee Lyons's wake many years earlier by his brother Oren. "Never go out alone after someone dies," he had said. "There are spirits in the night."

Later I spoke with Leon about what Oren had said. When I brought up the subject, Leon remained very still. His eyes were shut, and I wondered if he had heard me. Maybe he was asleep. I waited after repeating what I had said, then hesitated a little longer. It was good that I had because he had heard and was pondering his response.

"The way it tells us in our instructions," he began, "people who passed away can help us and harm us. That's why we never go out into the night alone. We don't know which way the spirits will go. I've seen them at times. Saw them out in Kentucky when those grave robbers dug up all those graves. The spirits were there and seeing what was happening to their bones."

"Even after hundreds of years?" I asked.

"Umm huh. The spirits got stirred up. I had to burn tobacco to tell them, to reach them. Tobacco is to send a message to the Creator. It's the tobacco that makes the message reach the Creator— like an antenna—so I can reach the spirits to talk to them. But I had to burn tobacco to open the path to the spirits. It was to calm them. The spirits were concerned. They knew their bones were down there. They were very much alive, like a human being, but they were into another world, the spiritual world. I had to do ceremonies so the bad luck wouldn't go to the people around there. When you dig up graves and expose the bones to the air, it's bad luck—very bad."

"And you could see them?"

"I knew they were around. It's just like I could see them. They were standing right next to me."

Leon had become quiet again, pulling hard on his old pipe. Then he said, "I'll tell you an example." He looked out through the windshield to the road in front of us—and beyond. He was seeing the scene all over again. "Vince Johnson was at my mother's wake. We always have a wake for the dead." Leon stopped, and I was sure he was back at his mother's side. Taking a deep breath and capping the emotional wave with a sigh, he went on: "Well, during the wake at night, Vince said, 'I'll stay,' when everyone was going to go and eat. So while he was there alone walking around, he looked out through the window at night. Couldn't see anything. Well, what do the lights do on the window at night? They reflect back what's in-side. When he looked out the window, he saw that reflection. There were people sitting there. They were all sitting there, the women with the shawls over their heads. They were having a wake. They were there. All the people had left, but he saw those people in the reflection.

"When he looked back from the window, looked around, there was nobody there. He was sure then that there were dead people who came back."

Putting his pipe back in his mouth, Leon drew hard. Soon smoke was billowing, filling the car. I strained to hear what he'd say next. I didn't have to wait long. His words came out muffled, barely understandable. I leaned closer to hear better.

"When the body's dead," he said, "well, the spirit's right there. We never leave the body alone, not even at the hospital or the funeral home. And that's why our speakers at the wake say to the spirit, 'We're trying to do everything to your liking.'

"We try to appease them. When we fill the plates with food, we set one aside—that's for the dead. Put it on the coffin. That's what we did for Lee—for him to eat with us. You feed them so they won't harm you. Then we give all their things away on the tenth day after we plant them—put them in the ground. We give everything away so the spirit won't be back for them. But you keep back one thing that's kept by the family, something they valued, so the family can look at it to remind them of the one who passed away."

Now Leon spoke even more softly: "They're watching. They hear you. They watch you and listen to everything you say. That's why there's no such thing as good-bye in our language. They've gone on into the spiritual world. We say they've gone on ahead. When you die, you go on ahead."

Taking my eyes off the road and looking straight at him, I asked, "What's it like in your teaching to be with the Creator?"

Leon's response was quicker than usual: "He's sent His message on down so each of us can follow his instructions. That will lead us back to Him."

"But, Leon, once you get back, what's it like?" I asked him.

"There's no suffering. No sickness. Strawberries and all those things are growing there. Just like here on the ground. It's a paradise."

"Is the Creator like a person?" I asked.

"Yeah! You have to earn it if you want to go up there and see what He looks like, though. We're all visitors here. We'll all go back to Mother Earth, but our spirit . . . The Creator has given instructions how to get back to where He is. He wants us to get back, but the evil says No. It's working pretty hard to control us, so we won't get back to the Creator. The evil is always working against good. If you're weak, it has you. You can be strong by listening to the Creator's instructions. You just have to use common sense.

"When there's a wake, you're never supposed to go out into the night alone. There are spirits. All the spirits are there. There's both good and bad spirits there at the same time. Good spirits are protectors. The others are trying to hurt you. The bad spirits never make it up there. They never made it to the Creator. That's why they're always hungry. They come back every day, late in the afternoon. And they leave early in the morning. That's why I say there's no such thing as no witness. There's always a witness around. They're witnessing things. When you think you're alone doing things, that nobody sees you, well . . . the spirits do!"

❊

Now, with spirits on my mind, I made my way toward the old white plank building that had been the longhouse before the new log one was built and was now the site of Leon's wake. I remembered sadly what Leon had said during our last visit here. Placing the eagle feather back in the cardboard holder, I had proclaimed, "It's over. The spirit-journey is over."

Leon had grinned at me. "Yup," he chuckled knowingly, "it's over . . . till it starts again." He always chose what he said very carefully. Although he never admitted it publicly, I knew he could see things. He could see our journey better than Harvey and I could, but he never let on how much he could see. On one occasion he had told us that everyone has a path whether he can see it or not. He was cagey. He let you know about the path, but then he'd leave it up to you to find it yourself. That was the wise man's way.

Now, as I stumbled along over the darkened courtyard, I looked out of habit, expecting to see him show up any minute. Unless he was sick and unable to lift himself out of bed, he was at every happening at the longhouse since being installed as Tadodaho in 1969. And by holding title to that highest of positions in the Six Nations Confederacy, it was his duty to call all the meetings and preside over every occasion. He was always there. I knew, however, that on this night it would be different.

After stopping to talk with one friend after another, friends Harvey and I had made early on in our travels to the Wisdomkeepers beginning in 1982, we were approached by one of the Onandaga chiefs and invited inside to view the body and pay respects to the family. Harvey looked at me, a questioning look on his face, as if to say, "Are you ready, or do you want to hold off a bit longer?" We've always had a way of communicating. Sometimes we don't have to say a word. But in this case he was taking no chances of miscommunicating. It was clear he was waiting for me before proceeding. I was grateful. Viewing the body was going to be an ordeal for me. I would much prefer to remember a person's life when it was being lived and the good times we had together. Instead, by standing over the coffin, more times than not one's last memory of the deceased will be that of the body lifeless, waxy-looking. That recollection can be haunting, yet I knew that by that last act one can bring closure. So I drew a deep breath and said, "Okay. Let's do it."

After climbing the last step before entering the old but stately one-room building—a structure that must have been built about the time Leon was born, some eighty-one years earlier—I braced myself against the door frame that held layer after layer of thick white paint. Taking a minute before going over the threshold, I thought, "This must have been the place of Leon's earliest memories." He'd grown up in the longhouse, sat at the feet of the elders of his time. He once told me, "Everything I learned, I learned in the longhouse. Learned from the elders, learned what they learned of the message from the Creator. And then practiced it. That was real education, not what we call education today. The education we teach, it reforms you for the benefit of yourself and your people so that you can go back to where the Creator is. And that's what He wants—for all His people to get back. There's no beginning, no end. When you figure that out, there'll be your Friend who is looking for you.

"Life's a circle, which means there's no beginning, no end. You just go back to the beginning. There is a center. You could go over there, go way around and come back, and you'd be at your center. That means that the center is everywhere. Common sense! You're the center. Doesn't that make sense?" He laughed, knowing he had made a riddle for me to try to figure out.

After pondering what he said, I asked, "Leon, knowledge and wisdom are two different things. You can have knowledge, but you're not necessarily wise."

Leon's eyes twinkled. "I guess so."

"What makes one wise?"

"Wise is not having to ask why," he said.

Gaining courage, I started across the old worn wooden floor. With my every step there was a creaking as if the boards would give way, but I knew better. They had withstood much more than my frame would stress them. What's more, if they could talk, they would tell a tale of many dances that carried scores of people over decades around in circles and wore the shiny permanent grooves now adding character in their inward slope from the edges of the room to its middle. About halfway into the room I was struck by the light. Several bare bulbs hung from the high ceiling, yet the room was ablaze with a brilliant whiteness that stopped me dead in my tracks. It was too bright, I thought, much more than those mere lights could illuminate. This brightness was not coming from one single source. It was everywhere. Even the corners were as even in light as the center. Pausing, I caught myself blinking, believing that it was just my eyes and the adjustment they needed from having come from the darkness on the other side of the door. Glancing about, I noticed Thelma, Leon's wife, and several clan mothers watching. One of the clan mothers waved me in. Inching closer to the open casket, I became convinced that it was not my eyes; they had plenty of time to compensate for the difference in light levels. No, something else was going on. Of course it could just be in my mind.

Shaking hands with those closest to the coffin, I turned and looked down at the tiny figure laid out before me. From somewhere behind me I heard, "He looks so good . . . considering what he's been through . . ." The voice trailed off. Immediately I wanted to counter, "Ain't no dead body I ever saw looked good to me," but I didn't. Probably a thousand others would have agreed with me, but at that moment I stood alone with that thought and many others rushing around in my mind. A part of me said deep within my soul: "He's not dead. He's alive!" But my head knew better. Not concerned that others were waiting behind me to pay their customary last respects, I stood firm, taking all the time I needed to commune with Leon. I just couldn't believe he was gone from this reality into the greater one.

"I will miss you, old friend. You've been closer than a brother to me. And you have been my teacher, my mentor, my friend." My words, heard only in the spirit world, spilled from my heart like a waterfall. I couldn't stop them as my heart pounded harder and harder. "Oh, how I loved our travels together. Yes, I remember that wild flight to South Dakota when Dennis Banks surrendered. And that time in England when the Iroquois Nationals, the Confederacy's lacrosse team, played Team England—and how proud you were! How proud we *all* were! And how many car trips we made! We went everywhere. Covered all the territory of the Confederacy. Then there were all those plane rides in and out of New York.

"It's true, Leon. I've been blessed just knowing you. You've been like a father to me and, in some respects, more. More than anything you trusted me and took me in as a member of your family."

His body there in the casket looked more like a doll than a person. He seemed so much smaller than I had remembered him in life. With the full length of the coffin open, his entire body was stretched out for all to see his full form. I thought: "So little, but what a giant of a human being!"

His head was adorned with his feathered *gastoweh,* its deer antlers rising above the side of the coffin and reaching heavenward. His shirt and pants were buckskin. Around his neck was a beaded necklace, and on his pillow a string of wampum beads signifying his appointed office. On his feet were his prized moccasins.

On one of our road trips I had asked Leon a question about people with special gifts. He told me: "There are gifts from the Creator. All those gifts were so they could help people."

"But what's the most important of all?" I asked.

He was emphatic and to the point: "Helping the people is the most important. The way I was made, according to my Mother, I had a special duty. My Indian name, Ah-be-gay-he-ha-tay, means 'unfinished business.' I was given that name when I was a baby. Then I was burned by hot boiling water. I don't know how old I was. My Mother never told me, just that I was creeping—maybe three or four. That same day my Mother was told by a psychic that when I grew up I would have a high position, the highest in the Confederacy. Nobody thought I would live because of how bad I had been scalded. But my Mother got a healer, and they used ceremonies that treated me. My name must have meant something because I didn't die. I had unfinished business. I was to help people. I guess that was why I was made a leader by my people."

Knowing how serious burns can be, I asked, "Do you still have the scars?"

Leon answered with his infamous dry wit: "I don't know about scars. I can't look at my back and see. The Creator didn't give me that to make my head turn around." We laughed, and then both of us fell silent for a while.

From his faded flannel shirt pocket he had pulled out his old black pipe, its stem nearly worn through from his biting down on it so hard. Next the package of tobacco. He loaded it slowly, sucked on it to clear the passageway, and fired it up. Smoke rose rapidly. Then propping his arm on the armrest, pipe in hand, he said, "When I was younger and saw a kid who wanted to get back to his house but was afraid of the night, I'd take him home. The other guys wouldn't do it. His fear was fun to them. And they said I was chickenhearted because I was helping other people. My heart—" He stopped. The wait for him to continue seemed like an eternity, but I was not about to interrupt his focus.

"My heart—" he started again, with a shorter pause. "My heart . . . I couldn't go without helping them. Guys said it was easy to pick up my heart." He stopped again and looked right at me, then continued: "I pay attention to little kids. They called it chickenhearted. Some call it tenderhearted. My heart . . . I couldn't stand to see a kid suffer. I had their feelings . . . felt sorry for the kids. A kid wanted to go home but was afraid because of the dark. So I went out of my way and helped them. I've been that way all my life. It's the way I am."

❅

Breaking my train of thought, of conversations in the past, and bringing me back to the reality of the wake, my eyes fell on Leon's hands. Those gentle hands were so very twisted. My eyes filled with tears, and I wanted to cry out, to just let the mourning flow, but I fought back. I couldn't show myself, I thought, because the last time I couldn't contain myself I had created a scene. It was at my father's funeral. I had done so well in maintaining my composure in making the final arrangements, standing by my mother, and being strong for my children's sake. But when I stood over the casket and saw my father's hands, I lost it. Actually it had not been his hands, it had been one of his index fingers—the one just two joints long, the last one having been lost in an accident at the cabinet shop where he worked. By taking his attention away from the saw blade for just one second, part of his finger had been cut through. He had grabbed the severed part and was rushed to the emergency room. Doctors tried to reattach it, but had to remove it because of infection. For the rest of his life he had one finger shorter than the others, yet it had still been useful. As a joke he would shove the short finger up one nos-

tril, and passersby would flip out thinking he had the entire end of that very big finger up his small nose.

So when I saw that finger, it made his death even more real to me. I cried, but it was more than cry. Everything, every part of my being, came rushing up and out. First there were little sobs, then they became louder and louder, until I was bawling so loud and so hard that the room shook. Others began crying. It was contagious. And now I didn't want a repeat performance here in the longhouse. I had to work to keep my emotions in check.

Staring at his hands, the hot tears came rushing to my eyes. Several times over the course of our long friendship Leon and I had discussed his hands. Every time he would hold them out as if seeing them himself for the first time.

"Do your hands hurt, Leon?" I asked.

"No."

"Were they always shaped like that?"

"Umm huh. From a child," he added. "Some think I have arthritis. Lots of women think I have that. They rub my hands," he said, looking up at me to see my reaction. Then he went on: "One used to rub my hands and say, 'Oh, that must hurt.' I said, 'Yeah, don't stop rubbing'!" And the two of us laughed so hard and so long we both started coughing.

As I held my gaze on his hands, the reality of his death hit home—hard. Chief Leon Shenandoah, Tadodaho of the Six Nations Iroquois Confederacy, was dead. For some reason his dying had never been in the realm of possibility to me. I hadn't been too concerned when Harvey called the previous Sunday evening to inform me that Leon was very sick again and had been taken to the hospital in Syracuse. Since I had known him, it was as if something from another world would attack him from time to time. First he had been thrown from a horse while visiting a friend in Colorado. Next he had to have a series of operations on his eyes to help him regain his sight. Good thing he did, because he continued to drive his old car around the rez and up and down Interstate 81. Once he was stopped by the highway patrol on his way to the airport. He'd been clocked going almost ninety miles an hour in a forty-five zone. He had talked his way out of the ticket by claiming, of all things, that he couldn't see and that the old car couldn't possibly go that fast, nor would he drive at that speed even if the car could. The officer—no doubt utterly mystified—let him go with a warning. And Leon never stopped talking about it.

Then he had come down with pneumonia on a visit to Santa Fe. That put him back in the hospital once again. Some time later he had another bout of pneumonia, this time threatening to derail his trip to address world leaders at the Rio Earth Summit in Brazil. He went anyway. On his return from that trip he fell over some luggage in the Syracuse airport, hitting his head and creating a problem for which he had to have brain surgery. He always bounced back from all his ordeals. Many times when I called, he appeared so weak that he seemed hardly able to talk, but he had fortitude and an eternally youthful spirit, and believed he would recover. And he always did. In my heart I believed he would this time as well. I told Harvey as much.

"Leon's strong as an ox," I said. "He'll make it out of this. He always has and always will." I believed what I was saying. "Leon will live forever. He'll plant us before he goes. There's no one like him, no one I've ever seen before or probably will ever see again."

After hanging up the phone with Harvey, I mentally went over all the ups and downs I knew that Leon had gone through. While sitting under the shade of a huge tree during a visit to the Six Nations Reserve in Ontario, I'd asked him if anyone had ever tried to work bad medicine on him. At first he didn't want to talk about it. Neither of us said anything more about it or anything else for a long while. We just sat and enjoyed the breeze. Breaking the silence he finally whispered, "I don't know anything about that."

But he didn't stop there. He went on: "People who work bad medicine do it on their own. Those who do it, do it to make money. Some who go to those people do it to get back at somebody they think has hurt them, or they're jealous. So they use the dead people, the bad spirits, the ones who never made it to the Creator. See, there are two levels in the spiritual world. Ones who went to the Creator and ones who didn't make it. The ones who didn't make it, they're in the part where they're hungry. That's why they're willing to do the evil."

Sitting with his head drooping, he said, "I don't know how they do it 'cause what I have said is that I'm not interested. I'm only studying medicine that's good and helps people. I stay away from the other. I don't touch it. So I guess I'll never find out about it."

❀

The day we learned of his death, I'd gotten up very early, something very unusual for me since I stay up to the wee hours writing, thinking, or just messing around. Those hours are mine. I'm more alive at that time. My most creative thoughts, when I have them, come while my family is safe at home and almost always asleep. And the world seems to be asleep as well. So when someone talks about getting up with the sun, that's a fairy tale to me. Yet that Monday I somehow woke up early.

After walking into my office, something stopped me. Looking at the cabinet to my right, I had a strange urge. A thought out of the blue came into my mind: "Where are the posters of the 'We're Still Here' video you had Leon sign?"

Opening the door of the tall bookcase, I questioned myself: "What am I doing? Why do I need to find them?" Just as I started moving things around to look at the back of the shelf where I had left them, a cool breeze caught the nape of my neck. Startled, I turned around, feeling that someone behind me was breathing down my neck. No one was there, but I immediately thought of Leon and said aloud, shocking myself in doing so, "Leon, you're making your rounds." I stopped in stunned disbelief that those words had flowed from my mouth with such certainty. I knew from somewhere deep within my soul that this time Leon was worse than I wanted to admit. What he once told me about dying came to mind.

"When you die," he instructed me, "your spirit starts its journey to the Creator. First it has to go back and visit everyone you knew in your life. You have ten days to do it. That's the time from dying to when there's the giveaway and the spirit is released to go into the spiritual world." He'd laughed then, and added, "I guess I'll have some traveling to do because I've traveled a lot, met a lot of people. Getting to all of them in ten days, that'll be a job!"

Leon had loved this world and all the people and creatures in it. He wanted to experience it all. While doing a photographic coverage of the Mohawk ironworkers in New York City, I asked Leon if he wanted to come along. I didn't have to ask twice. Almost as fast as I could turn around, his little gym bag was packed and he was ready. Once in New York I made arrangements to photograph the ironworkers in action. The building going up was in Brooklyn, and the Mohawks were working at the thirty-eighth-floor level. I had been very apprehensive about the heights. Not Leon. He was right by my side. He had worked for a short time in his youth as an ironworker. That was way back when he had to catch the red-hot bolts with a metal scoop while hanging from a steel beam that was to be bolted to another one floating on cables. Getting back on those beams delighted him.

His excitement carried over into everything he did. It was as if everything was new to him. He had an eternal innocence. He could always find something to captivate him. When he ate, for instance, he savored every bite and took his time, making sure that he not only sampled everything on the table but finished every bite on his plate. And he would try new foods, dishes containing things he could not even recognize or, for that matter, pronounce.

There were few things he liked more than hot peppers, the hotter the better. He never came across a hot pepper he couldn't eat. Once when he visited B.J. and me in North Carolina, we took him to a

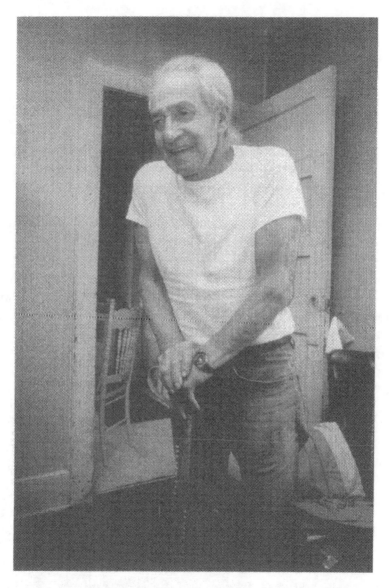

Thai restaurant. The variety of dishes we ordered intrigued him, but when hot sauces in little jars arranged on a silver treelike condiment tray were placed on the table in front of him, his eyes lit up. We warned him that the jars contained peppers with varying degrees of intensity—in other words, hot, hotter, hottest, and hotter still. All he asked was "Which one is the hottest?" He would hear nothing of working his way up to the hottest. The hottest is where he wanted to start, and there was no talking him out of it. Within minutes his face turned red, water filled his eyes, and sweat started rolling down his face. My wife and I looked at each other, and, as if on cue, we both spoke at the same time. "Leon? Maybe you should go slow on the peppers. We don't want you to set yourself on fire or die from those peppers burning you up. The people at Onondaga will never forgive us."

Leon just murmured, "These are hot," and kept on eating. When B.J. and I had finished dinner, Leon was still, ever so slowly, eating away, but the jars of peppers had been scraped clean. He seemed to be in heaven.

Another time, back at home, B.J. went to the cupboard and produced a jar of cayennes she had "put up" or canned for me. They're my favorites, but one jar would last me about a year. Immediately Leon was ready to dig in. By the time he was to return home, a matter of a few days, that jar had been emptied. B.J. surprised him with another jar as a going-away gift. I remember wondering if he made it home with an unopened jar. I doubted he would.

A year ago Harvey, my son Chris, and I paid Leon a visit at Onondaga. My wife, B.J., had me carry along a gift for him—a jar of cayennes. As soon as I presented it to him, he cradled it as if it were some valuable prize. Gently putting it down on the eating table, he slowly walked past us into the kitchen. A few seconds later he returned with a napkin and a fork. Seating himself he cupped his hand over the lid and twisted hard. The ring unscrewed with ease. Next he took the fork and popped the lip. A swishing sound erupted, and the aroma of the hot peppers and savory vinegar soon filled the room. Leon's mouth was watering as he speared three or four of the fiery pods and meticulously lined them up on the napkin. One by one he ate them. Then he repeated the ceremony. While we watched he ate ten or twelve with no bread or water. That familiar red face reemerged, and the watery eyes and the sweat. And, yes, his famous contented smile. It was as if he had been presented the most precious gift anyone could have given.

Of all the people I have ever known, he is the only one who I believe lived totally in the *now*. It's true he could talk about the past or look to the future, but the past wasn't filled with regrets, nor was the future viewed with expectation. Foremost for Leon was the *now*. Shakespeare wrote in *Hamlet*, "To be or not to be, that is the question." There was never a question for the Tadodaho. It was only "to be." Always!

The posters! I was back in my office trying to disentangle insistent memories and asking myself, "What am I doing? This is madness!" Still, I made sure the posters were there and then sat down at my desk. As soon as I did, the phone rang. Jumping nearly out of my seat, I debated a ring or two as to whether I was going to answer it or let the answering machine do it for me. Back and forth I flip-flopped until just before the fourth ring when the machine would take over. I picked it up and said, "H-e-l-l-o?"

It could not be good news, I argued between the hello and the sound of the voice on the other end. No one ever calls me until about midmorning. So something was up, and I feared what might be coming.

"Steve." It was Harvey. There was a telltale cracking in his voice, but he went on before I could say a word. "Leon's gone. He's dead. Died just a little while ago."

And all I could say was "I'll call you later. We'll talk, 'cause I don't know what to say right now."

Later in the day I called Harvey back. Our conversation centered on Leon, of course. We told each other stories about him. Sometimes our memories were very similar; other times he remembered something I didn't or I mentioned an event or happening he had not been part of. We were both in shock and mourning. After an hour or more of talk, we planned for our trip to attend his wake.

❋

Talking about the wake and attending it are two different things. Being here is like being frozen in time, in a dream state. I see Leon's body before me, close enough to touch, but in my mind I'm traveling with him, talking with him, laughing with him. I asked him during a trip, "Why is it that Indians laugh so much?" It was no trivial question. During the years working with Native Americans I found that laughter was one of the constants in every community and every home. There was so much laughter that I wanted to understand it.

Leon didn't hesitate in answering: "We're told in our instructions there must be laughter. Even when we have something very sincere or we're dealing with a heavy problem, someone will joke, and then everybody will start laughing. It's in there. It's what the Creator instructed."

There was nothing I could think of to joke about as I stood next to him. If he were able, he would have come up with something, and it would have been funny.

"Oh, Tadodaho," I whispered. As I did, it came home to me that the Six Nations would be without a Tadodaho until a new one could be installed. Leon and I had discussed just that possibility years ago. I had asked him, "Where would the chiefs turn today for another Tadodaho if, God forbid, there was a need to appoint a new one?"

Leon looked at me. We had become so close I could almost hear his thoughts. Surely he must have been thinking that I was rushing things. For me it seemed a logical question. He took my probing in stride. "Some are learning," he said, "but I don't know how much."

"If you had to choose a new Tadodaho," I asked, "who would you choose?"

Sitting back, puffing on his pipe, Leon continued, "I would pick a man who I thought knew the most, but I would also consider his conduct and whether he's honest and would be truthful with his people. He couldn't do things he shouldn't be doing.

"You go to the longhouse to learn how to conduct yourself. You have to learn your language, the meaning of things. I sometimes wonder . . . I do a lot of thinking. Actually it's not my worry, but yet it is. You would have to get somebody to guide the people and work for the people because it will affect my family and my relatives—all the way to the seventh generation coming up behind me."

"Are you talking about what's going to happen in the future?" I asked.

"I've said hard times are coming. That's why we do our ceremonies all the time. If we don't do them, the Creator will take everything away from us. We have to show our appreciation. We have to keep giving thanks. There's no end to our thanks."

I asked him, "What is it that keeps you going when so few listen to what the Indians are saying?"

Leon's voice dropped to a whisper. "We're trying to keep the world going on a little longer. Everything around us is trying to destroy us by getting us to forget our language and forget our way of life. That's why we're fighting over land for the benefit of the people."

Suddenly there was a hint of fire in his eyes. "A long time ago they tried to get us to get an education and make us forget what land means to us. They've tried everything to make us forget who we are, but we will never forget what the land means. It tells us in the instructions to live off the land. That's like a mother nursing the baby. We're doing the same thing when we live off the land. We understand what that means. We're not going to look for any more mansions. We're going to look for land that will turn out crops.

"I'll tell you a story." He paused. "There was this one man who sold lots around Buffalo, New York. We were told that he never reached the Creator's place when he died. His punishment for selling the land the way he did was to dig up dirt here and carry it over there and dig up dirt there and carry it here—in the spirit world. He was an Indian. He sold the land. That was his punishment for selling the land, and he's still got another punishment coming when the end of the world goes into fire. He's going into it!"

The end of the world! I thought about it and wondered aloud to Leon: "What's going to happen then—at the end of the world?"

"Nature will take care of it. Someday . . . someday the people will be shown that they have no power at all, and nature will show them. You can't control nature. You have to live with it. That's where harmony comes from." He stopped for a moment. After thinking he said, "But yet I have found when it's almost time for the world to come to an end, He's going to send His helpers down here to pick up seeds. The helpers will pick up seeds. You've got to have seeds to plant again."

"Helpers?" I asked. "Who are the helpers?"

"We call them the Four Protectors. Like angels, they've been here already. They never died. They're always up there with the Creator. Then the Creator sent them down here as our protectors. They're right now watching over me. They do that for only certain ones who ask for it.

"Some people don't know about the Four Protectors. But they're here now. You communicate with them with the sacred tobacco. Lots of people ask me to burn tobacco when they go to the hospital. A lot of Indians have lost their way, but they still kind of believe in our way. And when someone goes to the hospital, right away they come for tobacco. Then what happens next depends on the Peacemaker.

"You communicate by burning the sacred tobacco. We burn it to ask that the world continue on, but we know that the world will be going through hard changes. I've seen things. My spirit travels when I sleep. I've been shown how it's going to be, how people won't be ready when the world starts to change, how they'll all be running and screaming. And then just nothing—nothing at all. That's what I was shown. I had an awful feeling when I finally woke up. I was left with just the grief."

"Tell me, Leon, what did it feel like?" I asked.

"It feels like an emptiness. It almost feels like there's nothing. It's like one minute you're right at the edge of a cliff, and then you go down and that's it. Or else it's the end of your life. When I woke up, oh, I was glad it was just a dream. There were my kids, my family. I was glad to wake up."

"How can we be ready?" I asked.

"What did I tell you! Live off the earth. Plant your own food and save the seeds so you can plant it over.

"The world will change. In the meantime it tells us in the instructions that we are all visitors here. We're only visiting this earth. We're all going to come and go continuously. We're not here forever. So we have to make the best of it while we're here visiting."

I had stood there over Leon's open coffin for a long time—several eternities, it seemed to me. I was holding up a line of mourners. Just as I started to walk around the ominous box, I noticed something I had missed. To his right, nearly out of sight, rested his lacrosse stick—the one he would be using in that eternal game going on in the spirit world. He had always been close to the spirit world; he had always been able to see into it. But it was a power he didn't acknowledge having. He didn't seek it. He wanted no powers for himself. When someone was needed for prophecy or psychic seeing, Leon always consulted others. He often spoke with the greatest respect of those who could speak to the spirits.

One woman he consulted, a woman I had met personally, aided the Syracuse police, through him, in closing the books on a number of murders. I came to appreciate such individuals and to accept the idea that there could be something to the concept of the spiritual world. During visits over the years with other Native American Elders, I had witnessed many "coincidences" that convinced me there is a spiritual world—a realm most of us do not see with our earthly eyes. Cecilia Mitchell, the renowned Mohawk medicine woman, said, "Just because you don't see it doesn't mean it doesn't exist. You can't see electricity. Does that mean it doesn't exist?" Leon saw that world and helped me understand it just a little better.

A cozy warmth seemed to envelop me. As I took one last look at him, I wanted to think that the sensation was Leon's spirit comforting me. Walking away, I looked back and saw what had been right in front of me all along: the eagle feather! It was on his left side. How could I have missed it? I peered more closely. It was the one I had given him—the same one Bob White had given me. The realization struck me like a bolt of lightning. I felt dizzy. Harvey had seen it before me and had tried to get my attention, had tried to get me to see it. For him the meaning had been obvious. The feather—the spirit-feather, at least—was going into the spiritual world, as Leon would call it. It was going with him. Traveling together. Forever.

"Oh, my God, Harvey," I muttered. "The journey's not over! It's not ever going to be over!"

After a cup of coffee or two, short conversations with a few old friends, and farewells to Leon's family and clan mother, Harvey and I returned home that night. We chose not to be there the next morning for Leon's "planting," as he would have called it. We decided, rightly or wrongly, that we would forgo that memory. I know Leon understands why we didn't go. Going to a funeral is for closure—but we just don't want closure so far as Leon's concerned. He's still traveling with us in the Stone Canoe.

❀

Since that day I've thought about the many, many things Leon taught me. Coming from a different background and culture, I'd found it difficult to understand all the things he had tried to convey. Slowly a light came on. The path into his way of life began to emerge. I've jotted some of the finer points down so that my memory won't fail me.

More than once Leon said, "Learn to listen."

"Speak softly and use good mind."

"There is no force spirituality."

"It *is* the force!"

"The Creator is sending the message of what is right."

"Good is the thing to follow. Always choose good. The Creator is telling you to do good things. It's harder to do good than bad."

"Everything depends on one another."

"You can be strong by listening to the Creator's instructions. If your mind is strong on positive things, then you will not follow the instructions of the bad mind."

"You can see the spiritual world more if you use common sense. You just have to use common sense."

"Live off the land. That's where you get your nourishment. All the plants are working with Mother Earth. They're working, keeping the balance."

"We are the Creator's children. Our duty is to give thanks to the Creator for all the things He has left for us to survive, for human beings to survive. There is no reason to ask. He has given us everything for us to enjoy. That's why we have to thank Him for what He left here, the land to survive by planting, all kinds of medicine, berries, water, and especially air. To show our appreciation to the Creator we have ceremony."

"Wisdom is what you've learned from spirituality."

"You prove who you are by the way you act."

One of the last things I remember Leon saying was "I can only tell you what I know. Beyond that you'll have to ask the Creator."

With his passing into the spiritual world, he has left me no choice. So to the Creator I say thank you for allowing my path and Leon's to cross and intertwine. I'm grateful to have been given the rare privilege of traveling at the side of such an extraordinary human being. For me *he* was the Fourth Landing—though he'd chew me out good if he heard such talk.

And to you, Leon, thank you. Knowing you has not only enriched my life but has changed my way of thinking, my way of being. You got my attention when you said, "You have to listen when I tell you things." I learned that lesson. I listened. Believe me when I say, "You did good." Though I can never live up to your example—who could?—I'm still guided along the path by the light that was—and is—your living presence. You showed me that following the path of the Wisdomkeepers, having a good laugh, and eating hot peppers are all part of the same essential act—the act of being truly human.

I remember that you told me there is no word for good-bye in your language. That's good. I won't have to say good-bye, not here or ever.

Like you say, there's no reason for good-bye. You've just gone ahead.

Chapter 20

MINE are the only footsteps in the snow as I make my pilgrimage up the slopes of Bear Butte this icy March morning. The air glints clear and crisp and sparkling. A classic Dakota ground blizzard blew through here last night, moaning and raging from nightfall to dawn like some demented beast. Hardly any new snow fell, but every flake of old snow, every loose little speck of ice not cold-welded to the ground and prairie grass had been yanked aloft by the sixty-mile-an-hour  wind and whipped into a howling frenzy of opaque whiteness. Through the frosted double glass of my motel window I had caught occasional glimpses of winking stars and shards of moonlight through flying breaks in the swirling whiteout—comforting signs of the calm that precedes and follows every storm, every life.

When I awoke just after 6 A.M., all was utterly still outside, the first steely blue light of a perfectly clear day creeping out from the still-dark horizons of a mother-of-pearl sky. Skipping breakfast, my Dakota Winnebago friend Scott Barta and I scraped the ice coating off his car and headed up to Bear Butte State Park, laying down new tracks off the main road for the last couple of miles up to the visitors' center and parking in an otherwise empty parking lot beside a sign that said CLOSED FOR THE SEASON. Scott immediately got out and said, "See you back here in a couple of hours," and was gone. Good. Like him, I wanted—needed—to be alone.

Booting my way through ankle-deep crunching ice up to the little plaza in front of the padlocked visitor center building, I paid my respects to the bronze statue of Lakota high ceremonial chief Frank Fools Crow (1890–1989), who prayed an eagle out of the sky before our eyes that day at Wounded Knee in 1983 and then directed us to Mat King. Here were two of the greatest gifts ever given to me by one person in my life, and I never gave more than a perfunctory thanks to this wonderful man. We hope our appreciations of him in *Wisdomkeepers* and these pages serve as a kind of thanks from these two unlikely *wasichu*, Steve Wall and Harvey Arden. We know people like Frank Fools Crow and Mat King worked without thanks much of the time. They didn't do what they did for thanks, not even from Indian people. And certainly not from us, from whom they doubtless expected none.

I remember Mat once saying to Steve and me, looking us hard and fierce in the eye: "You white men took everything and gave us back nothing, but worst of all"—and he leaned forward, peering into our very souls—". . . worst of all, you never thanked us! You never even bothered to say thank you!"

When Mat talked about "white men"—*wasichu*—he wasn't talking about some abstract generic white men; he was talking about *us,* these two very same *wasichu* in front of him.

"*You* killed the eagles," he would fume, and you could almost see the blue smoke pouring out his ears. "*You* slaughtered the buffalo. *You* murdered my people and stole the land. But God gave us this land. *You can't have it!*"

And then, seeing our stricken eyes, he would abruptly smile and chuckle. "'Course I know you boys are trying to change that." He wasn't trying to chase us, just chasten us. And we were chastened. And then he said, "'Course you can't change that. You can only change yourselves."

He told us the meaning of the Lakota word for the white man, *wasichu*. He said, "It means 'the one who steals the fat.' The first white man we Lakota people ever saw stumbled into one of our camps one winter's night. He didn't talk to nobody. He just sneaked up to the store of food, grabbed all the fat, and ran off with it. You know, in those days, in winter, it was the fat that kept you alive. If you didn't have fat, you died. So that white man, he just took all the fat. Not only did he steal it, but he refused to share it at all. He never even asked. He took it all for himself. That's why he's *wasichu*. Maybe if he changes his ways, we'll change his name."

God knows I never learned about being a white man until I tried to learn what it was like to be a red man. Scott Barta has insisted to me: "Harvey, I don't think of you as *wasichu*. You're not *wasichu* to me." I hope he always feels the same. I'm going to keep working at it.

That, in fact, is why I'm here on Bear Butte this late winter day—to maintain an old friendship, to fulfill an old obligation, to say hello to and have a little talk with an old friend—Mat King. I didn't have to explain to Scott why I wanted to come up here. He understood. Each of us has been many times to the mountain—called Bear Butte by the white man, Mato Paha (Bear Mountain) by the Lakota, and Noavasse (The Good Mountain) by the Northern Cheyenne. To the latter two it's one of the holy of holies of the sacred Black Hills. To the former—the *wasichu*—it's the chief attraction of Bear Butte State Park: $2 admission, please. The United States has offered the Lakota people hundreds of millions of dollars for having admittedly violated the Fort Laramie treaties of 1851 and 1868 and unilaterally usurping ownership of the Black Hills—acknowledged by our own high courts to have been stolen from the Lakota people in 1877, barely a year after Custer's well-earned demise, in "the most ripe and rank case of dishonorable dealing in our history." Mat and Frank had insisted: "The Black Hills are not for sale!" They—and the Lakota people to this day—have refused the monies, now totaling around $400 million, which continue earning interest in the U.S. Treasury.

Scott had heard me say at a lecture at the University of South Dakota in Vermillion how Frank and Mat had worked all their lives for the return of the Black Hills and had died without having gotten so much back as a pebble. Scott came up to me afterward. "Harvey, you've got it wrong," he told me, shaking his head. "There's no way the white man can give the Black Hills *back*. We've never given them up! They're ours right now!"

Now I stand in front of Fools Crow's statue—a bronze bust surmounting a small rock pylon—and I'm moved as always by the little colored-felt prayer ties, dried flowers, clumps of sage and sweetgrass, tobacco tins, packs of cigarettes, and individual cigarettes that visitors have reverently tucked into every nook and crevice of the statue, all rimed with ice this day. I could wish a similar statue of Mat King stood across the little plaza from Frank. I've been hoping to raise the funds to have one sculptured and installed. I know the two old boys would like that—looking across at each other, no doubt with an unseen nod and wink. It would be another way of saying thanks, and I'm working on it.

In my hand I carry Mat's book *Noble Red Man,* published in 1994, five years after his passing on to the Great Reality. I've been wanting to present it to him somehow, and it seemed Bear Butte, where Mat always went to "talk to God," would be the perfect place, even on an icy winter's day or perhaps especially on such a day. Bear Butte, of course, is the "hill" Mat referred to when he said, "When we want wisdom, we go up on the hill." This imposing 4,422-foot monolith of granite and sandstone stands out in lonely splendor from the northeastern Black Hills. I have walked the trail up to the top in summer and wandered the long and narrow ridge where the wind-stunted jackpines are covered with hundreds of little colored-felt prayer ties, each containing a pinch of sacred tobacco, each the physical embodiment of a prayer by one of the many Indian vision questers who frequent these heights "crying for a vision," as they say.

I won't be climbing to the top this icy winter morning. What's more, there's no need to do so. Every part of this mountain is holy, and all along the trail to the top and around the sides of the mountain the vision questers have left their prayer ties and red and black prayer flags affixed to the branches of nearly every tree. Today all is deep-frozen; the weather-bleached colored-felt ties and flags and the tree branches are themselves encased in an armor of icy white that has covered and congealed to everything, including the crunching snow beneath my feet. Each blade of grass, each boulder and pebble has its own diamond-bright suit of rime. The very air sparkles and tinkles.

I head up the trail to find a likely place for my little ceremony. This is no vision quest. I don't have to fast four days and four nights, as Mat did and the vision questers do to this day. I'm not supposed to steal or even imitate his ceremonies. Those are his and his people's, not mine. I may occasionally share in them, when invited, but I will never appropriate them as my own. Just skipping breakfast this morning is enough of a token of reverence—and remembering how holy a place Mat held this to be. Here his granduncle Crazy Horse had come to pray, as had all the great Lakota leaders—Sitting Bull, Red Cloud, Bigfoot, and the others. Their spirits hover here. I remember Mat saying that sometimes he came up here during rainstorms and could hear Crazy Horse actually talking in the sky. He wasn't speaking figuratively. His eyes had sparkled as he spoke to me of that memory, and I'll always remember his words about Crazy Horse: "His voice was thunder. His tongue was lightning."

The path leads past a side trail marked with a wooden sign reading:

INDIANS PRAYING
DO NOT PASS BEYOND THIS POINT

I've followed that path with Lakota friends on past visits in the summer. In the little meadow beyond that knoll, you'll find the sweat lodges where the vision questers purify themselves before ascending the holy mountain Mato Paha. Mat King's daughter Lavon told me how, since Mat's death, she comes up here to talk to him. She says she's seen him up there, walking the heights, shielding his eyes with his hand as he looked across at her. "He won't speak," she says. "He just looks at me with a real stern look on his face. I think he's mad because these hills still aren't ours to use for ceremony." When, back in 1981, government authorities had routinely refused permits for Indians to hold their ceremonies here, Mat had helped lead a takeover of a piece of Black Hills land that they called Yellow Thunder Camp—after Wesley Yellow Thunder, a Lakota man who had been brutalized and murdered in a nearby town. Mat himself went down to the state office and signed the official papers—which were rejected, of course—applying for the special-use permit to use this piece of land for religious purposes. He signed the application "Noble Red Man," one of his Indian names, taken from his grandfather who had been murdered by Seventh Cavalry rogue killers after Custer's "massacre." With elders like Mat and Frank on hand, and support from even the less traditional Lakota people, Yellow Thunder Camp held on for four years—avoiding the national notoriety of Wounded Knee and finally fading away without bloodshed. A new generation today continues fighting the same battle with the same slogan: "The Black Hills are not for sale!" I, for one, believe it. To me this is Lakota territory. That's what our own courts have said. It's also what Mathew King said, and I never knew Mat King to lie.

I leave the trail and strike off on a path of my own across a tilting snow meadow and sit down beside an ice-crusted jackpine that could be out of an old Japanese painting, so pleasingly placed is it on a small knoll looking directly up at one of the soaring rough rock walls of the mountain. I'm glad not to hear the crunching of my own footsteps for a while. For a few minutes I just contemplate the wonderful living silence that seems to surround me, all blue and frozen. Now I take Mat's book in one hand and stand up. No louder than if he were before me, I tell him: "Hey, Mat. Here's your book. We got it done. I hope you like it."

I speak aloud. I don't know if I close my eyes or open them. I do my best to commune with Mat. I'm not really good at these things. Mat could pray at the smallest pretext, but I'm uneasy here on foreign territory both geographically and spiritually. Yet this day, at least, I won't let my disbelief get in the way of higher possibilities. Yes, I talk with Mat. I hold up his book high with my right hand, and I speak to him—not so much with words, though I mumble a few, but with my presence, the living presence he taught me about.

"Everyone is sacred," he told us. "You guys are sacred, and me, I'm sacred, too. Every time you blink your eyes or I blink my eyes, God blinks His eyes. God sees through your eyes and mine. We're sacred, each and every one of us."

Mat's words, like Leon's, aren't just words. If you listen to them, if you really hear them, they become acts. They're not words you believe; they're words you do. The word becomes act. Words like these can inhabit you, change you, transform you.

I gaze up at the mountain, holy Bear Butte, a great prow of stone plowing like some great canoe through waves of time. I scan the sparkling blue sky. I admit it: I look for an eagle or maybe a hawk. Even a rabbit in the brush would do. Some sign. Some vision. A tiny little miracle. But none comes.

I am not disappointed. Simply being open to the miracle is enough. You don't need the miracle itself. This day, each and every day, is a miracle, Mat taught us.

❉

Steve and I have been among the lucky ones of this world to know the likes of Leon Shenandoah and Mat King and all the others. Their words have the power of acts. You'll find few better examples of the word-become-act than Mat King's "Life is not an entertainment. Life is a holy task." Or Leon Shenandoah's "I'm working for the Creation. I refuse to take part in its destruction."

We went out looking for wisdom, Steve and I, and, to the best of our abilities and sensibilities, we found it. But what is wisdom? Lumbee medicine man Vernon Cooper taught us "Knowledge is of the past. Wisdom is of the future."

Wisdom, we've learned, is something you do, an action you take in this world, an effort on behalf of something immeasurably more important than yourself: other people, the Us instead of the Me. Without the Us, the Me becomes a devil.

Mat King spoke often of the devil in each of us, certainly a time-honored metaphor. But he spoke much more often of the goodness in all of us and how that goodness is the very gateway to our own highest possibilities. These days when people speak of angels, it seems to me they're speaking of that same goodness within us all, a living manifestation of that goodness.

"You can feel it inside yourself," Mat said. "You know when you feel good inside." Then he chuckled that wheezing chuckle of his and went on: "Look for that goodness deep inside yourself. And then when you find it, take that goodness and put it out into the world!"

Mat thrust out his hand as he spoke, as if putting that goodness out into the world. Yes, the word becomes act.

Here, indeed, is one of the Original Instructions he spoke of—instructions for every human being.

Although his soul was informed by dreams and visions, Mat King interacted with the real world. Wounded Knee and Yellow Thunder, these were not imaginary. They happened. They were actions in the real world, spiritual actions. The world to Mat King was a spiritual place requiring a spiritual life from each one of us. "Materialism without spirituality," he taught, "is the curse of this world. Being spiritual—that's what makes us *human!*" And he'd nod his head and wink, a mystic gleam in his eye. "God wants a spiritual life from each of us, *without exception!* Yes, from every one of us. Even you!"

The Stone Canoe has become a special metaphor for us on this spirit-journey. To the Iroquois we extend our apologies for borrowing it in these pages for our personal uses. And yet it teaches so much with its poetic vision of the Peacemaker and the Stone Canoe that took him wherever he was supposed to go. We all need such a Stone Canoe, which has become for me the symbol, the metaphor, for going with my best intentions, for going with the part of me that Mat King called "goodness." Going with that goodness is riding in the Stone Canoe. The two are one and the same.

I sit back down, with Mat's book resting closed in my lap, and do my best to pray, to commune, to be here, wholly present, in this holy unstoppable Now. This is an act of mind and soul that I'm still learning about after a lifetime's study. You have to be careful with such matters. They're not for everyone. The path of the Wisdomkeepers, I reiterate, isn't easy or materially rewarding or even conducive to spiritual comfort. It's a hard path, bumpy, irregular, enormously elusive. If you keep walking straight, you'll very likely walk right off it. That's how signs help—if you care to see them—because signs mark curves and disjunctures and spokes in the path. A crow on a fence post *does* have a meaning if you ascribe one to it. There *are* angels if you find yourself moved by an angel.

Yes, I know, I know—it's all metaphor, the play of metaphor in the poem of the world, as Fred Kline might say.

I get up, brush the ice off my Levis, and turn to head back down the path. I take Mat's book, which I've decided I'll leave at the visitors' center, propped up on Frank Fools Crow's statue among the other offerings. Whoever finds it will be the one who needs it. The icy snow crust creaks and squeaks beneath my boots as I turn to follow my own footsteps back down across the tilting snow meadow to the trail.

As I pivot around there's a strange sound, an almost metallic rustling off to my right, just a few feet behind me. My heart leaps. An animal? Scott? I spin around just in time to see the ice-crusted jack-pine whose Japanese contours I'd admired abruptly divesting itself of its freight of snow and ice, like an armored knight shucking off his glinting armor. All that glistening, diamond-sparkling ice rime, several inches thick, fell in an instant, seemingly in a single piece, off the upper branches of the tree with an almost metallic *whoosh,* something like the sound of silver foil crumpling at your ear but magnified a dozen times. The ice fell off the sloping branches as if the tree had shrugged or been suddenly shaken, but there was no wind, only a light breeze. The ice wrapped itself around the base of the tree like a silvery wreath, shining prismatically.

Well, that's enough of a sign, enough of a miracle for me. If I want to see that as Mat King answering me, giving me a friendly nod, I'll do so without apology or embarrassment. That was unquestionably Mat King. I could almost hear his high-pitched wheezing laugh in that silvery rustle of falling ice. He reached out from the Great Reality and touched that tree with his little finger. Yes, he did. It was a sign, a definite sign—yes, even a wonder, if only a very small and private one. Not a glimpse of the otherworld, that Great Reality, but a visionary glimpse of *this* world, our ordinary world. And I'll gladly settle for that.

Feeling somehow absolutely right about things, and without the slightest idea where life will lead me next, I head back down the mountainside, following my own footsteps.

That's where the path always is. Right there beneath your feet.

We ourselves are the path.

Three

Living the Path

*

Chapter 21

THIS journey won't end. Our ongoing travels have taken us in recent years from South America and Central America to Aboriginal Australia—and who knows where next? There's an old Aboriginal saying, "A friend always leaves a trail." We've done our best to leave a trail, a record of what we've seen and heard on the path of the Wisdomkeepers. Their words, in a sense, are tracks on that trail, showing the way to those of us who care to follow.

In the pages ahead, "Living the Path," we present a compendium of the Wisdomkeepers' words, nuggets of instruction and insight as they spoke them to us. Many we've reiterated from the text; a number of others we've reshaped here from our earlier work. From each Wisdomkeeper we learned something, pieces of an ever-evolving whole. Each taught us by the content of their acts as well as the content of their words. As we've come to realize, words become acts, and acts, too, have a way of being transmuted back into words.

In addition to the Wisdomkeepers' own shining words, we add here and there with a certain trepidation some rephrasings of our own, trying to put the unspoken into words, hoping to share what it is we've learned or think we've learned on the path of the Wisdomkeepers. Where we have fallen short or erred outright, or omitted something essential or beyond our understanding, we ask forbearance. Pieces of the message are surely missing or distorted, and in any case the message for you may be different from the message for us. But we feel certain you'll find echoed herein some of the "Original Instructions for being human" that apply to everyone, along with other life-enhancing insights of the Wisdomkeepers. We make no claims to setting forth a fully conceived and overarching system of belief in these pages, only a series of suggestions for *a way of being in the world*. There are no commands here, only choices. Life itself is a choice we've all made. We hope there's wisdom and poetry and insights enough in these pages to assist other journeyers not only to find and to follow the path but—like the Wisdomkeepers themselves—to *live* the path.

❀

There is a Path . . .

And there are

Original Instructions

For following that Path.

❀

THE PATH

Everything's laid out for you. Your path is straight ahead of you. Sometimes it's invisible, but it's there. You may not know where it's going, but still you've got to follow that path. It's the path to the Creator. That's the only path worth following.

LEON SHENANDOAH, IROQUOIS

Everyone got to find the right path. You can't see it so it's hard to find. No one can show you. Each person's got to find the path by himself.

CHARLIE KNIGHT, UTE

No point in walking anyone else's path. That'll only get you nowhere.

FRANK DAVIS, PAWNEE

There's a special path we follow. We call it a song line or a story line. The songs and stories tell us where to move along that line, that path. Those are the only safe places to go. They're paths for travelers and for messengers, too. They're tracks the Wandjina, our Creator, made for us to follow.

DAVID MOWARJARLIE, NGARINYIN, AUSTRALIAN ABORIGINAL

You're going one of two ways. You're either on the spiritual path or you're on the material path. It's your choice, and your choice only, which of the two you follow.

LEANDIS, MEXICO

❋

The Path

Is

Under Your Feet.

The Gate

Is

Where You Are.

❋

ORIGINAL INSTRUCTIONS

You don't have to explain why you're here. I know why you're here. White man forgot his Original Instructions. That's why you're here. We Indians have never forgotten our Instructions.

Our Instructions are very simple: to respect the Earth and to respect each other, to respect ourselves, to respect life itself. That's our first commandment. That's the first line of our Gospel.

MATHEW KING, LAKOTA

In the beginning were the Instructions. The Instructions were to love and respect one another.

VICKIE DOWNEY, TEWA-TUSUQUE PUEBLO

Instructions come just when you've lost hope and you don't know which way to go. That's when you find out what your Instructions are and which path to take.

LORRAINE CANOE, MOHAWK

It's our duty to survive as a people. That's part of God's Instructions to us. To survive!

MATHEW KING, LAKOTA

You can't live someone else's Instructions.
You've got to live your own.
Some of God's Instructions are for all of us. They're the Original Instructions on being human. They're for everyone, even you guys.

MATHEW KING, LAKOTA

God gives His Instructions to every creature, according to His plan for the world. He gave His Instructions to all the things of nature. The birch tree and the pine tree, they still follow their instructions and do their duty in God's world. The flowers, even the littlest flower, they bloom and they pass away according to His Instructions. The birds, even the smallest bird, they live and they fly and they sing according to His Instructions.

Should human beings be any different?

MATHEW KING, LAKOTA

The Material Life

is not worth living.

It's the spiritual life

that makes us human.

MATHEW KING, LAKOTA

ON BEING HUMAN

Everyone's got a purpose.

LEON SHENANDOAH, IROQUOIS

I'm just a man, that's who I am. Just a man. That's my job.

TOBY WHITE, AUSTRALIAN ABORIGINAL

God gave us three powers—material, spiritual, supernatural.

We need them all. Material power is the goodness of this Earth. Spiritual power is the goodness of human beings. Supernatural power is the goodness of God.

The three powers are separate. They're not connected.

It's the job of human beings to make that connection.

Being spiritual—doing good—that's what makes us human.

MATHEW KING, LAKOTA

✿

The Greatest Strength

Is

Gentleness.

LEON SHENANDOAH, IROQUOIS

✿

GOODNESS

Goodness is the natural state of this world. The world is good! Even when it seems evil, it's good. There's only goodness in God. And that same goodness is in us all. You can feel it inside yourself. You know when you feel good inside. Love the goodness in yourself.

Then, put that goodness into the world.

That's everybody's Instructions!

MATHEW KING, LAKOTA

✻

Life is Not an Entertainment.

Life is a Holy Task.

✻

You don't have to be perfect

to do holy work.

You don't even have to be holy.

✻

SIGNS

You never go on a spirit-journey without a sign that it's time to begin.

TWO TREES, CHEROKEE

You don't just get an eagle feather by accident. There's always a reason.

LEILA FISHER, HOH

The spirits did that. They turned the feather around in Jess's hatband. They gave us a sign. Just a little sign but still a sign. A tiny little miracle so we'd know they heard our prayers.

MARY BLUEBIRD, SHAWNEE-DELAWARE

On my hand the fourth finger's the longest. See? That's my marking. That's the sign I'm a spiritual leader. So I was born to it.

The Stone Canoe was the Peacemaker's sign. It showed everyone he was really sent by the Creator.

LEON SHENANDOAH, IROQUOIS

❋

There's nothing

more Natural

than

the Miraculous.

❋

ATTENTION

There's only one price I ask you to pay. And, I'm sorry, it's a very high price. I ask you to pay the price of attention! If you're willing to pay that price, you may just learn something.

EDDIE BENTON-BANAI, OJIBWAY

Damn you! Pay attention!

TWO TREES, CHEROKEE

You guys better listen. You got a lot to learn.

MATHEW KING, LAKOTA

When you're talking, you can't listen.
Learn to listen.
Hear with your heart.

LEANDIS, MEXICO

❋

Ask me Questions

from your Heart,

and I'll give you Answers

from my Heart.

BUFFALO JIM, SEMINOLE

❋

MYSTERY

I want you to learn some mysteries. I want you to come
study with me.

AMONYEETA WOLF SEQUOIAH, CHEROKEE

There are no mysteries. There's only common sense.

OREN LYONS, IROQUOIS

You can call Wakan Tanka by any name you like. In English I
call Him God or the Great Spirit.
He's the Great Mystery, the Great Mysterious. That's what
Wakan Tanka really means—the Great Mysterious.
You can't define Him. He's not actually a "He" or a "She," a

"Him" or a "Her." We have to use those kinds of words because you can't just say "It." God's never an "It."

So call Wakan Tanka whatever you like.

Just be sure to call Him.

He wants to talk to you.

MATHEW KING, LAKOTA

What's important is beyond understanding—that's the first thing you must understand.

Everything's a mystery. Once it stops being a mystery, it stops being true.

DAVID MOWARJARLIE, NGARINYIN, AUSTRALIAN ABORIGINAL

❈

The Dreamtime is Now!

REG BIRCH, BUNABA, AUSTRALIAN ABORIGINAL

❈

EARTHKEEPERS

We are Earthkeepers.

LEANDIS, MEXICO

We are the guardians of Grandmother Earth.

MATHEW KING, LAKOTA

We want our land back. Not money. Just the land. The land, the ground, the sand, you know? That's all we want. Just to go

back and live there, to sit down on the ground and be there, do-
ing whatever we like—listen to the wind, listen to the rain, lis-
ten to the stars.

All these things, the plants and the trees, the mountains and
hills and stars and the clouds, we represent them. You see these
trees? We represent them. Yes, and the reeds, too, in the waters,
and the frogs and the tadpoles and the fish, even the crickets,
all kinds of things. We represent them! We represent everything
that God gave us . . . or, we say, that Wandjina gave us, you
know?

DAISY UTEMORRAH, WORRORA, AUSTRALIAN ABORIGINAL

Man's job is not to exploit but to oversee, to be a steward of
the earth. Man has responsibility, not power.

OREN LYONS, IROQUOIS

W E

We are all related.

LAKOTA PROVERB

We're all one family,
All together,
We human beings.
All one big mob!

TED CARLTON, MIRIWOONG, AUSTRALIAN ABORIGINAL

We're all connected. We're one with all things. The weak-
nesses we see in others are our own. That's a reflection.

LEANDIS, MEXICO

We are all one people throughout the whole world.

TOMAS AGUILAR, CABECAR, COSTA RICA

I'm a dreamer, and I'll tell you my dream. Someday Red Man and White Man will sit down with all the races of humankind, and we'll solve our problems together. We'll all follow God's Law. We'll even pray together. You'll do it your way and we'll do it our way, but we'll all do it together.

MATHEW KING, LAKOTA

Everyone is a human being. There is nothing that separates me from them. We are one another.

MARY LEITKA, HOH

❈

Be open to Causes other than your own.

The Other is yourself.

❈

THE SEVENTH GENERATION

Think not forever of yourselves, O Chiefs,
nor of your own generation.
Think of continuing generations of our families,
think of our grandchildren
and of those yet unborn,
whose faces are coming from beneath the ground.

THE PEACEMAKER, FOUNDER OF THE IROQUOIS CONFEDERACY,

CIRCA A.D. 1000

In our way, with every decision we make, we always keep in mind the Seventh Generation to come. It's our job to see that the people coming ahead, the generations still unborn, have a world no worse than ours—and hopefully better. When we walk upon Mother Earth, we always plant our feet carefully because we know the faces of our future generations are looking up at us from beneath the ground. We never forget them.

OREN LYONS, IROQUOIS

Think about it. You yourself are a Seventh Generation!

LEON SHENANDOAH, IROQUOIS

❊

Truth isn't something you think.

It's something you feel.

Wisdom isn't something you believe.

It's something you do.

❊

WISDOM

You're not supposed to preserve wisdom. You're supposed to live it.

CORBETT SUNDOWN, IROQUOIS

Knowledge is of the past. Wisdom is of the future.

VERNON COOPER, LUMBEE

Wisdom comes only when you stop looking for it.

LEILA FISHER, HOH

Wisdom is like bread. If you find the right ingredients to make the dough, it'll rise for you and give you life.

FRANK DAVIS, PAWNEE

When we want wisdom we go up on the hill and talk to God.

MATHEW KING, LAKOTA

❀

Look for the Poetry

And You'll Find the Wisdom.

❀

WORLD'S END: SEVEN PROPHECIES

I can see what's coming. I prophesy what's going to happen. You're going to fall and fall hard. You're going to be crying and wailing. You'll realize you can't get away with destroying God's world. Don't think you can get away with it. God's going to wipe the wickedness from the earth. You can see His signs. Out on the West Coast, Mount St. Helena's volcano—that's a sign. And there's going to be earthquakes. Maybe half of California and half of Washington and Oregon will go into the water. The same in the East and in the South. You're going to have volcanoes and earthquakes and hurricanes.

MATHEW KING, LAKOTA

Our Prophecies speak of the Gourd of Ashes that the White Man will throw back and forth, and there will be a fire in the sky that no one can put out. If you don't stop what you're doing, Nature will intervene. Other forces far beyond your control will come into play. The last stages are here now. All these earthquakes and volcanoes and fires and hurricanes—these are the final signs, the final warnings. These are the last stages. It's all happening now. We pray and meditate and ask the Great Spirit to keep the world together a while longer. But it's coming. The Purifiers are coming!

THOMAS BANYACYA, HOPI

You will see many tears in this country. Then a great wind will come, a wind that will make a hurricane seem like a whisper. It will cleanse the earth and return it to its original state. That will be the punishment for what we've done to the Creation.

LEON SHENANDOAH, IROQUOIS

The earth is like an animal. When an animal is sick, it wiggles and twitches. Just before it dies it shakes even harder, shakes all over. That's what we call the earthquake and the volcano and the hurricane. You'll see, it's already starting to happen. The world is wiggling and twitching and shaking just before it dies.

BUFFALO JIM, SEMINOLE

We see what's happening. There's a lot of water coming. A lot of wind. A lot of eruptions. Floods and hurricanes and volcanoes and earthquakes. We think of these as our punishments for what human beings are doing to our Mother the Earth. But she's not really trying to punish us. She's sick, and all these things we call natural disasters—that's how she heals herself.

VICKIE DOWNEY, TEWA-TUSUQUE PUEBLO

I see the end of things. It's coming! God'll wipe all this wicked world away like you wipe a dirty window with a rag. Only God's gonna use the tornado for a rag. He's gonna use the hurricane for a rag. He's gonna use the earthquake for a rag. He's gonna wipe away all the wicked world. Only the sky be left. Just clear blue sky . . . like a clean window.

JESS BLUEBIRD, CHEROKEE

This is a dangerous age, the most dangerous in human history. We can't keep ruining the earth and poisoning it and think we can get away with it. Certain destruction is going to hit one of these days. We're on the verge of a change such as has never been before. God is going to intervene.

VERNON COOPER, LUMBEE

✻

I'm working for the Creation.

I refuse to take part

in its destruction.

LEON SHENANDOAH, IROQUOIS

✻

To change the world, we have to change ourselves.
You must become the change you want to see in the world.

REG BIRCH, BUNABA, AUSTRALIAN ABORIGINAL

AT THE EDGE

There are no breakthroughs without hard work and sacrifice. Discoveries come only from the edge.

LEANDIS, MEXICO

Be careful what you get into. It's never what you think. So be careful.

MASANEA, KICKAPOO, MEXICO

Do not go around the edges or else you'll fall.
No good that place or else you slip.

DAISY UTEMORRAH, WORRORA, AUSTRALIAN ABORIGINAL

Don't look down as you cross the Rainbow Bridge.
If you do, you'll fall!

JOE PARRA, CHUMASH

✳

Pick a Road,

Any Road,

and Follow it.

✳

To the Rest of your Life.

No Expectations.

Just Possibilities.

✳

When ya leavin'?

CHARLIE KNIGHT, UTE

✳